Listening Again to the Text

New Testament Studies in Honor of George Lyons

Listening Again to the Text

New Testament Studies in Honor of George Lyons

Richard P. Thompson, editor

Claremont Studies in New Testament and Christian Origins 5

Listening Again to the Text
New Testament Studies in Honor of George Lyons
©2020 Claremont Press
1235 N. College Ave.
Claremont, CA 91711

ISBN 978-1-946230-44-7 (print)
    978-1-946230-45-4 (ebook)

Library of Congress Cataloging-in-Publication Data

Listening Again to the Text: New Testament Studies in Honor of George Lyons / Richard P. Thompson
    xv + 247 pp. 22 x 15 cm. –(Claremont Studies in New
    Testament and Christian Origins 5)
    Includes bibliographic references and indices.
    ISBN   978-1-946230-44-7 (print)
            978-1-946230-45-4 (ebook)

    Bible. New Testament Criticism, interpretation, etc.

    BS 2555.52 T466 2020

Cover Image: *Sacra Famiglia* (Holy Family) by Luca Signorelli (c. 1485-90) in the Vatican Museum, Rome.

Contents

George Lyons: Professor, Scholar, Churchman   vii
    Richard P. Thompson

A Tribute to George Lyons   xi
    Tat-siong Benny Liew and Pamela K. Liew

PART I
LISTENING AGAIN TO THE GOSPELS

"Can Salt Really Lose Its Saltiness?"   3
    Reading and Listening to Matthew 5:13 Again
    Richard P. Thompson

Hearing Voices: Identity and Mission in Mark   25
    Kent E. Brower

"Little Daughters" and Big Scriptural Allusions   45
    Reading Three of Mark's Stories Featuring
    Women with Care
    Kara J. Lyons-Pardue

PART II
LISTENING AGAIN INTRACANONICALLY

Gospel Themes as "Glue" for Pauline Ecclesiological   73
Images
    Andy Johnson

Loving Neighbor, Loving One Another, and   95
Loving Enemies
    Three New Testament Ethics of Love
    Thomas E. Phillips

Part III
Listening Again to the Letters

Love Empowered Knowledge   117
   How the Way of the Cross Determines Behavior in
   1 Corinthians 8
   David A. Ackerman

Translating λόγος as DNA in First Peter 1:22-25   133
   Troy W. Martin

Part IV
Listening Again to the Apocalypse

The Remedy for Vengeance: Blood in the Apocalypse   153
   Carol J. Rotz

Divine Judgment and the Missio Dei *in the Book*   171
of Revelation
   Dean Flemming

List of Contributors   193

Bibliography   197

Index of Modern Authors   211

Index of Biblical Texts   219

Index of Ancient Sources   245

George Lyons: Professor, Scholar, Churchman

Richard P. Thompson

When George Lyons matriculated as an undergraduate student at Olivet Nazarene College (now University) in the village of Bourbonnais, Illinois (about an hour south of Chicago), little did he know what was in his future. His vocational plans were to become a professor of chemistry, so there was no dream of the biblical professor and scholar he would become. Yet required general education courses in Bible and theology as well as participation and later leadership in student groups like the ONC "Prayer Band" led this fledgling chemistry student to recognize a different passion and divine calling that would order his life: to pursue biblical studies and to serve as a professor and biblical scholar of the church. In other words, his call or passion was to lead and teach others about the Bible as the church's sacred Scriptures in deeper and faithful ways than they had done before.

But that was a different era in the Church of the Nazarene. Few in the denomination pursued or possessed the highest academic credentials in biblical studies in order to serve and enable the church in the ways George imagined. Yet this was the largely uncharted path on which he embarked, first by switching his major and graduating with an undergraduate degree in biblical literature from Olivet in 1970, then earning the Master of Divinity degree from Nazarene Theological Seminary in 1973, and finally being accepted into the Ph.D. program at Emory University, which granted him the Ph.D. in New Testament in 1982. Dr. Lyons' dissertation, *Pauline Autobiography: Toward a New Understanding,* was soon published in the prestigious Society of Biblical Literature Dissertation Series (1985), which continues to be cited in scholarly circles for his groundbreaking work in rethinking and reinterpreting the apostle Paul's self-descriptions in his letters of Galatians and 1 Thessalonians.[1]

Dr. Lyons completed thirty-six years of teaching in two institutions of higher education within the Church of the Nazarene. His teaching ministry began in 1977, when he joined the faculty of the Division of Religion and Philosophy at his alma mater, Olivet Nazarene College (now University), where he spent fourteen distinguished years teaching mostly New Testament and Greek, achieving the rank of Full Professor and leading the Master of Arts program in Religion. In 1991, Dr. Lyons accepted the invitation to join the religion faculty of Northwest Nazarene College (now University), where he continued to serve with distinction by embodying what it truly means to receive the rank of Full Professor. In addition to serving on various faculty committees, he also served as the Chair of the University Faculty (2008-10). Within the School of Theology and Christian Ministries, Dr. Lyons was influential in beginning online graduate programs, as he piloted its first online course offering (2002). His passion for teaching translated well into the online context, as he received several awards from online graduate students for his excellence in teaching (despite also earning the reputation for having grueling course requirements!). What should not be overlooked is that Dr. Lyons gave of himself in teaching and mentoring others during sabbaticals, summers, and whenever else he had opportunity in numerous Nazarene institutions around the world, because the passion that drove him to follow his divine calling continued to motivate him throughout his career. As a result of Dr. Lyons' modeling of his love for Scripture and his commitment to serious scholarship, today among Dr. Lyons' former students are countless pastors, some district superintendents, and numerous religion faculty serving in both Nazarene and other Christian institutions of higher education.

Dr. Lyons has also served the church globally, the Wesleyan-Holiness tradition within which the Church of the Nazarene finds herself, and his denomination. In addition to the publication of his significant dissertation work, his earlier monographs include *A*

---

[1] George Lyons, *Pauline Autobiography: Toward a New Understanding*, SBLDS 73 (Atlanta: Scholars, 1985).

Dictionary of the Bible and Christian Doctrine in Everyday English (co-edited with Al Truesdale and J. Wesley Eby),[1] *Holiness in Everyday Life*,[2] *More Holiness in Everyday Life*,[3] and *Listening for God through Revelation*[4] — all works that focus on the church more broadly. He has several articles that appear in the *Wesleyan Theological Journal*, having served as President of the Wesleyan Theological Society (1993-94). He is a frequent contributor to denominational Sunday school curricula and devotional materials used in thousands of local churches across the world. In the last decade, he has given exemplary leadership as New Testament Editor of the New Beacon Bible Commentary, part of the Centennial Project of Beacon Hill Press of Kansas City (now The Foundry Publishing). His own contribution in addition to William Greathouse's analysis of Paul's letter to the Romans led to the release of their two-volume commentary on Paul's letter to the Romans within that series in 2008,[5] as well as Dr. Lyons' own commentaries on Galatians[6] and Ephesians[7] released later within that same series.[8]

---

[1] J. Wesley Eby, George Lyons, and Al Truesdale, eds., *A Dictionary of the Bible and Christian Doctrine in Everyday Life* (Kansas City, MO: Beacon Hill, 1986).

[2] George Lyons, *Holiness in Everyday Life* (Kansas City, MO: Beacon Hill, 1992).

[3] George Lyons, *More Holiness in Everyday Life* (Kansas City, MO: Beacon Hill, 1997).

[4] George Lyons, *Listening for God through Revelation* (Indianapolis: Wesleyan Publishing, 2006).

[5] William Greathouse with George Lyons, *Romans: A Commentary in the Wesleyan Tradition*, 2 vols., NBBC (Kansas City, MO: Beacon Hill, 2008).

[6] George Lyons, *Galatians: A Commentary in the Wesleyan Tradition*, NBBC (Kansas City, MO: Beacon Bible Commentary, 2012).

[7] George Lyons, "Ephesians," in *Ephesians, Colossians, Philemon: A Commentary in the Wesleyan Tradition*, NBBC (Kansas City, MO: Beacon Hill, 2019).

[8] In addition to the commentaries already mention, see his contribution to the forthcoming commentary on the Gospel of John within the New Beacon Bible Commentary series.

In addition to his publication, Dr. Lyons has given himself to the church in many other ways. In the 1990s, he conceptualized and developed the online Wesley Center for Applied Theology[1] that provides Wesleyan-Holiness resources for pastors and church leaders. His pioneering work sought to digitize rare Wesleyan and Holiness resources that were once unavailable to most pastors. Because of that work, the online Wesley Center is the world's largest website for Wesleyan-Holiness resources. In addition to these theological resources, Dr. Lyons also was among the first to digitize and make available online non-canonical materials for reading and research. Dr. Lyons also taught a Sunday school class at College Church of the Nazarene in Nampa for twenty-two years, serving as a pastor to this group of senior adults and conducting many of their funerals. Thus, he has demonstrated himself to be a person of the church who is committed to God and the mission of the Church of the Nazarene through a life devoted to the elevation of biblical teaching for church leaders, pastors, and laity alike.

Dr. Lyons is married to Terre, who has distinguished herself as a mathematics teacher and an adjunct professor of mathematics at Northwest Nazarene University. They have two children who are NNU alumni: Kara (married to Charlie Lyons-Pardue), who serves as a professor of New Testament at Point Loma Nazarene University in San Diego, California (and a contributor to this collection); and Nathanael (married to NNU alumna Laura Hansen), who is a registered nurse in Portland, Oregon.

The contributors of this collection are pleased to dedicate this book to Dr. George Lyons, a faithful servant of Christ, a passionate professor, a diligent scholar, and an exemplary churchman and minister of the gospel of Jesus Christ. His legacy through his work and students gives evidence of his love and faithfulness for God and the church.

---

[1] See the online Wesley Center for Applied Theology at Northwest Nazarene University: http://wesley.nnu.edu.

A Tribute to George Lyons

Tat-siong Benny Liew and Pamela K. Liew

George Lyons is an oxymoron, and we are probably not the only ones who think so. When we both thought about the possibility of a tribute for Dr. Lyons, we decided to collaborate on the project, which is only fitting since Dr. Lyons played a role in our relationship as a couple, back when we were his students at Olivet Nazarene University. But this may be getting ahead of ourselves. As we began to reminisce about our experiences with Dr. Lyons, a theme seems to have emerged. See for yourself.

Back when we were students, the buzz on campus was that Dr. Lyons was a young radical, maybe even a bit of a heretic in the eyes of those who bristled at the way he poked at our personal piety, pushing us to consider the possibility that a life of faith might involve more than just a soul-soothing one-on-one relationship with God and a ticket to paradise. He introduced his classes to books like *Rich Christians in an Age of Hunger*[1] and *The Mustard Seed Conspiracy*,[2] and he unflinchingly fielded our often-defensive reactions with patience and kindness, never pretending that he had hard and fast answers to the difficult questions he was prodding us to ask. *A humble maverick....*

Departing from what was standard in many of our other classes, Dr. Lyons didn't try to teach his students *what* to think about the Bible. Rather, he taught us that *we had to* think about the Bible. With this confident approach, he transmitted the idea that the Bible is important enough to require serious and thoughtful engagement. Rather than discouraging us from asking questions of the text, Dr. Lyons taught us that the Bible matters enough to be wrestled with. *A searching guide....*

---

[1] Ronald J. Sider, *Rich Christians in an Age of Hunger: A Biblical Study* (Downers Grove, IL: IVP, 1977).

[2] Tom Sine, *The Mustard Seed Conspiracy: You Can Make a Difference in Tomorrow's Troubled World* (Waco, TX: Word, 1981).

Whether they knew it or not, we were watching for signs that our professors were more than just knowledgeable and articulate. Dr. Lyons showed up. We can still picture him with his little girl (now a New Testament scholar in her own right) walking in the community Hunger-Walks. Someone once told us that Dr. Lyons and his wife Terre had committed to a price-matching scheme wherein they would give away an equal amount of money for every item they purchased for themselves. We don't know if the doubling of expense was a short-term or long-term project, but it certainly fits the theme. *An austere philanthropist....*

Pam recalls a conversation with Dr. Lyons after he heard her sing with her trio in the university chapel. He led off with a compliment, but then proceeded to ask about the lyrics of one of the more upbeat gospel-type songs that spoke of being free from worry over problems in this world, because it was all just a prelude to the life to come for those who were about to be caught up "in the twinkling of an eye." What stuck with her was the way he went about it. He noted that it didn't seem to line up with what he had come to know of her views and commitments, and so he asked her if she was concerned that she might be perpetuating a theology she didn't actually embrace. She took away two lessons from this brief encounter. First, speech in any form has implications and comes with a responsibility. Second, there is tremendous power in a charitable correction that indicates faith in your intentions while also imparting a beneficial check. *A compassionate challenger....*

We also remember a conversation that Dr. Lyons clearly didn't want to have with us. Dr. Lyons had gotten wind of a concerted effort by some of his colleagues at the university to persuade us that our relationship may be a "hindrance to future ministry." You see, Dr. Lyons' faculty colleagues were concerned that our interracial relationship might not be viewed favorably by some church members (one should remember the conservative Midwestern context of the 1980s). As the one person in the religion department who actually knew both of us, he was so offended by this suggestion that he found himself compelled to counter with an emphatically opposing opinion, which he did, clearly uncomfortable to be volunteering unsolicited advice on such a personal issue. We are not suggesting that he had the last word on the matter, but we both remember how much his reluctant contribution to this unfortunate conversation actually meant to us. *An un-intrusive intruder....*

On a lighter note, Benny remembers the outrage of the Christmas "give-away" question in Dr. Lyons' Greek class, as he was the only one in the class who couldn't come up with the name of "the reindeer with the red nose" and ended up losing precious points in these daily quizzes! *A benevolent thief....*

Dr. Lyons was the kind of teacher who inspired total investment in his classes. We all wanted to be his best student, and we all knew that his demanding evaluation was going to require our very best efforts to do well. At the same time, he was always approachable, and he never made his students feel incapable, even if we struggled at times to meet his high standard. Benny still remembers when Dr. Lyons assigned him the grade of an A minus for a course—Benny's first "less-than-perfect" grade at that point in his academic history in the USA—for an independent reading course in Greek, no less! Benny pleaded that Dr. Lyons give him a chance to do something for extra credit to move the grade up to an A. In response, Dr. Lyons said with his customarily wry smile that it would actually be good for Benny to be freed from an obsession with perfectionism, and extolled the virtue of studying for the pursuit of knowledge rather than the pursuit of a perfect GPA. As you can imagine, the wisdom of that pitch was not appreciated then, as a student, as much as it is now, as a teacher, but looking back on it there is some irony in the fact that the teacher who inspired our best efforts deliberately discouraged an obsession with perfection. *A Nazarene non-perfectionist....*

I think we've supported our thesis, and we hope that it is clear that it is a statement of deep respect, warm admiration, and abiding gratitude. We feel so fortunate to have been impacted by the teaching and example of such a wonderful person. George Lyons is an oxymoron, and we can't imagine a more Christ-like metaphor.

Listening Again to the Gospels

"Can Salt Really Lose Its Saltiness?"

Reading and Listening to Matthew 5:13 Again[1]

Richard P. Thompson

Introduction

The verse, after all, is a familiar one. Certainly one would have little difficulty and few questions in working with the Greek text, offering a translation, and coming to some basic exegetical conclusions with such a familiar passage. And so, when the students of my undergraduate course in New Testament Greek exegesis and I came to Matt 5:13, we admittedly anticipated to find what would confirm the translation that was familiar to us and consistently rendered in English: "You are the salt of the earth; but if salt has lost its taste, how can its saltiness be restored? It is no longer good for anything, but is thrown out and trampled under foot" (NRSV). But as we worked more closely and carefully with the Greek text, several questions began to emerge: Does the subjunctive μωρανθῇ really connote the idea of tastelessness or lost taste? What is the significance of the passive voice of this subjunctive, particularly since English translations usually translate this verb as an active voice? Do both the intensive construction, "having been thrown out to be trampled" (βληθὲν ἔξω καταπατεῖσθαι), which also

---

[1] I offer this essay in honor of Professor George Lyons, who was my first Greek professor and later asked me to serve as a Greek tutor while I was an undergraduate student at Olivet Nazarene College (now University). Little did he or I know that this request and experience of working with struggling Greek students was the first of many steps that led to my pursuit of an academic calling/career in biblical studies. Little did we know back then that I would follow him as a professor of New Testament and Greek at Olivet Nazarene University and later serve with him as colleagues at Northwest Nazarene University. I count it a privilege to call him my teacher, colleague, friend, and fellow worshiper in Christ.

includes two verbal forms in the passive voice, and the persecution language of the preceding verses (Matt 5:10-12) offer a context that suggests a different or stronger reading than one of salt merely losing its taste?

This essay is a product of the research and study that were provoked by those initial efforts. Its purpose is to offer a reading of Matt 5:13 that accounts for the grammar and syntax of the Greek text and for both its literary and historical contexts. Thus, what will be offered here is an alternative reading of this passage that interprets the "losing of taste" as something that would happen to the disciples particularly in a context of opposition or persecution, when these disciples are functioning as Jesus identified them: as "the salt of the earth." Thus, for the purposes of this essay, the following three parts will be included: (1) a general examination of the interpretation of Matt 5:13 in recent scholarship, (2) a study of this verse with reference to its synoptic parallels (Mark 9:50; Luke 14:34-35), and (3) an interpretation of this verse in light of its literary and historical contexts.

Matthew 5:13 in Recent Scholarship

Scholars have reflected a common understanding of the "salt of the earth" metaphor as one of two declarative maxims that describe the mission of the disciples.[1] Hans Dieter Betz stresses that the evidence from the synoptic tradition indicates that this saying using the salt image or metaphor was already understood as signifying discipleship, prior to its use here in the Sermon on the Mount.[2] Within the context of Matthew 5:13-16, Betz contends that what is described is "what the community addressed is, what they

---

[1] Donald A. Hagner, *Matthew*, 2 vols., WBC (Dallas, TX: Word, 1993), 1:98 stresses that these maxims, Ὑμεῖς ἐστε τὸ ἅλας τῆς γῆς (Matt 5:13) and Ὑμεῖς ἐστε τὸ φῶς τοῦ κόσμου (5:14) are parallel in form. See also M. Eugene Boring, "The Gospel of Matthew: Introduction, Commentary, and Reflections," in *NIB*, 8:181; Frederick D. Bruner, *Matthew, A Commentary* (Dallas, TX: Word, 1990), 159-60.

[2] Hans Dieter Betz, *A Commentary on the Sermon on the Mount*, Hermeneia (Minneapolis: Fortress, 1995), 157.

should be, and what they ought to do."[1] Thus, Jesus addresses the disciples and both emphatically and metaphorically affirms their mission as salt and light, because empirical Israel had failed in its mission to the nations.[2] As Donald Hagner states,

> The disciples—the blessed recipients of the kingdom—are thus of vital importance for the accomplishment of God's purpose in the world. They constitute the salt... without which the earth cannot survive.[3]

Given the metaphorical use of salt in describing the disciples, one finds numerous options as to what the salt imagery could mean in this saying and context. One general explanation often given for the relationship between salt and the mission of the disciples is the use of salt in everyday life.[4] In the ancient world, salt was used as a preservative and as a basic ingredient for life itself. Pliny stated, "[T]here is nothing more useful than salt and sunshine" (Nat. 31.102). Diogenes Laertius suggested that salt "should be brought to table to remind us of what is right; for salt preserves whatever it finds, and it arises from the purest sources, sun and sea" (8.1.35). Another explanation for the relationship between salt and the mission of the disciples is the use of salt in covenants (see Num 18:19; 2 Chr 13:5) and as a sign of friendship, loyalty, or peace (see Ezra 4:14).[5] Aristotle asserted regarding the

---

[1] Betz, *A Commentary on the Sermon on the Mount*, 155.

[2] William D. Davies and Dale C. Allison, *A Critical and Exegetical Commentary on the Gospel according to Saint Matthew*, 3 vols., ICC (Edinburgh: T&T Clark, 1988), 1:471-72; Boring, "The Gospel of Matthew," 8:182; and Eduard Schweizer, *The Good News according to Matthew*, trans. David E. Green (Atlanta: John Knox, 1975), 102.

[3] Hagner, *Matthew*, 1:102.

[4] Those who offer this explanation include, e.g., Davies and Allison, *A Critical and Exegetical Commentary on the Gospel according to Saint Matthew*, 1:472; and Bruner, *Matthew, A Commentary*, 159-60.

[5] Those who offer this explanation include, for example, Davies and Allison, *A Critical and Exegetical Commentary on the Gospel according to Saint Matthew*, 1:472; David E. Garland, *Reading Matthew: A Literary and Theological Commentary on the First Gospel* (New York: Crossroad, 1993), 60; and Friedrick Hauck, "ἅλας," *TDNT* 1:228.

intimacy of friendship: "[A]s the saying goes, you cannot get to know a man till you have consumed the proverbial amount of salt in his company" (Eth. nic. 8.3.8; LCL). A third explanation is the religious use of salt, either to be added to sacrifices or for purification.¹ Leviticus 2:13 states, "You shall not omit from your grain offerings the salt of the covenant with your God; with all your offerings you shall offer salt" (NRSV).² A fourth explanation is the association of salt with wisdom. Wolfgang Nauck contends that the salt imagery, which he compares to statements with similar imagery in rabbinic literature, refers to wisdom in the disciple.³ Other commentators also note that, although this saying is unique in describing persons as salt, the rabbis often described Torah as salt.⁴ The association of the verb μωραίνειν (which has the predominant meaning of "to be foolish" or "to make foolish") with salt, then, maintains the saying's Semitic background, which would have emphasized the quality of things (such as being unsavory) but could also refer to human characteristics (such as being foolish).⁵

---

¹ Those who offer this explanation include, e.g., Davies and Allison, *A Critical and Exegetical Commentary on the Gospel according to Saint Matthew*, 1:472; Schweizer, *The Good News according to Matthew*, 101; and Daniel Patte, *The Gospel According to Matthew: A Structural Commentary on Matthew's Faith* (Philadelphia: Fortress, 1987), 70. Cf. Hauck, "ἅλας," *TDNT* 1:228 who states, "In the NT its [salt's] cultic significance is lost."

² LXX: καὶ πᾶν δῶρον θυσίας ὑμῶν ἁλὶ ἁλισθήσεται, οὐ διαπαύσετε ἅλα διαθήκης κυρίου ἀπὸ θυσιασμάτων ὑμῶν, ἐπὶ παντὸς δώρου ὑμῶν προσοίσετε κυρίῳ τῷ θεῷ ὑμῶν ἅλας. See also Ezek 43:24 (NRSV): "You shall present them before the Lord, and the priests shall throw salt on them and offer them up as a burnt offering to the Lord" (LXX: καὶ προσοίσετε ἐναντίον κυρίου, καὶ ἐπιρρίψουσιν οἱ ἱερεῖς ἐπ' αὐτὰ ἅλα καὶ ἀνοίσουσιν αὐτὰ ὁλοκαυτώματα τῷ κυρίῳ.).

³ Wolfgang Nauck, "Salt as a Metaphor in Instructions for Discipleship," *ST* 6 (1952): 165–78. Cf. David Hill, *The Gospel of Matthew*, NCB (Grand Rapids: Eerdmans, 1972), 115. See also David L. Turner, *Matthew*, BECNT (Grand Rapids: Baker Academic, 2008), 154, who notes that in the Mishnah, salt was associated with wisdom (*m. Soṭah* 9.15).

⁴ See, e.g., Walter Grundmann,. *Das Evangelium nach Matthäus*, THKNT 1 (Berlin: Evangelische Verlagsanstalt, 1968), 137.

⁵ Nauck, "Salt as a Metaphor in Instructions for Discipleship," 175–76. Mark 9:50 does not reflect the Semitic background clearly, because ἄναλον γένηται

Nauck concludes that the wisdom implied here is "an active and practical wisdom, a knowledge that is worked out in acts."[1] Although one finds commentators who lean toward one or two of these explanations, others recognize the multiple layers of meaning for the salt imagery in Matthew's context and thereby suggest that one not limit an interpretation to only one option or explanation.[2]

Although a general scholarly consensus exists for the image of salt in terms of discipleship and mission, one discovers differences in the interpretation of what is meant by salt losing its taste or saltiness (ἐὰν δὲ τὸ ἅλας μωρανθῇ, ἐν τίνι ἁλισθήσεται; Matt 5:13). Since salt itself simply cannot lose its saltiness or taste, given the chemical stability of the salt compound, discussions have attempted to interpret the meaning of this idea or image as a proverbial expression. Two explanations arise from these discussions. One explanation is that the suggestion of salt actually losing its saltiness or taste is preposterous—an impossibility that reflects also the impossibility of being a disciple while having lost one's mission as a disciple.[3] Thus, the complete imagery functions as a "hypothetical hyperbole"[4] that states what is an "impossible possibility":[5] "This cannot happen, if one is truly a disciple." The verb μωραίνειν, therefore, connotes the foolishness reflected in a

---

does not include the nuance of foolishness. Cf. Matthew Black, *An Aramaic Approach to the Gospels and Acts*, 3rd ed. (Oxford: Clarendon, 1967), 166–67, who sees this as a faulty translation of the Aramaic; and Joachim Jeremias, *The Parables of Jesus*, trans. S. H. Hooke, rev. ed. (New York: Charles Scribner's Sons, 1963), 168.

[1] Nauck, "Salt as a Metaphor in Instructions for Discipleship," 176.

[2] See, e.g., Davies and Allison, *A Critical and Exegetical Commentary on the Gospel according to Saint Matthew*, 1:473; Boring, "The Gospel of Matthew," 8:181; and Robert H. Gundry, *Matthew* (Grand Rapids: Eerdmans, 1982), 120–21.

[3] See John Nolland, *The Gospel of Matthew: A Commentary on the Greek Text*, NIGTC (Grand Rapids: Eerdmans, 2005), 213.

[4] Davies and Allison, *A Critical and Exegetical Commentary on the Gospel according to Saint Matthew*, 1:473. Cf. Georg Bertram, "μωρός κτλ.," *TDNT* 4:838; and Schweizer, *The Good News according to Matthew*, 101–2.

[5] Ulrich Luz, *Matthew 1–7: A Continental Commentary*, trans. Wilhelm C. Linss (Minneapolis: Fortress, 1989), 250.

disciple who has lost one's identity and mission.[1] The second explanation is that, although salt itself cannot lose its taste or saltiness, it may become so tainted and mixed with impurities that its value and function are diminished, thereby rendering the salt useless.[2] Thus, the salt to which Jesus's statement alludes, which may have come from the Dead Sea but may also have been mixed with gypsum and other similar crystals, could have been mistaken as "pure" salt until someone tasted or used it (cf. Pliny, *Nat. Hist.* 31, 44).[3] Given the emphatic declaration to the disciples that they are the salt of the earth (note the emphatic ὑμεῖς, "you"; Matt 5:13), the hypothetical situation of that salt losing its saltiness is not a challenge to those disciples to become salty but a challenge to remain salty—to fulfill their function within society as Jesus's followers.[4] Although these discussions about what is meant by salt losing its taste or saltiness have different nuances, the general consensus is that this imagery focuses on the disciples' mission and function, which they may also lose. Clearly, these interpretations direct one's attention to the disciples as responsible for the loss of "taste," function, and mission.

The tendency to interpret the first half of Matt 5:13 as the failure of the disciples in their mission and function as disciples continues in the discussions regarding the last half of that verse. Since interpretations of Matthew's "salt of the earth" passage generally place upon the disciples the blame for the failure of discipleship, one should not be surprised to find this trend

---

[1] Hagner, *Matthew*, 1:99; Nauck, "Salt as a Metaphor in Instructions for Discipleship," 175–76; and Black, *An Aramaic Approach to the Gospels and Acts*, 166–67.

[2] Robert H. Mounce, *Matthew*, Good News Commentary (San Francisco: Harper and Row, 1985), 39 suggests that "explaining how salt can be adulterated… is unnecessary. It is the metaphor itself, not the image it employs, that is being extended."

[3] Hauck, "ἅλας," *TDNT* 1:229; Hagner, *Matthew*, 1:99; Jeremias, *The Parables of Jesus*, 169; and Daniel J. Harrington, *The Gospel of Matthew*, SP (Collegeville, MN: Liturgical, 1991), 80.

[4] Bruner, *Matthew, A Commentary*, 160. Cf. Patte, *The Gospel According to Matthew*, 69–70.

continue. Just as salt is useless if it cannot or does not fulfill its intended function (εἰς οὐδὲν ἰσχύει), so are those disciples who do not fulfill their divinely-given roles also useless. Most interpreters of the passage understand the salt imagery as a warning to these disciples. Eugene Boring states that

> the sentence might be translated, 'It is you [and not the others—Pharisees? the Jewish people?] who are the salt of the earth.' Yet there is no smugness, for the saying serves as a warning that if the disciples deny their mission, they (too) will be thrown out as useless.[1]

Robert Mounce states that "unless the disciples maintain their role as salt in the world they will become useless and will be rejected."[2] Frederick Bruner goes so far as to say that this verse "is meant to shake Christians up" and suggests what he calls "deserved persecution," which is not physical abuse but "often takes the form of simple contempt or complete disinterest."[3] And Betz asserts,

> If the disciples of Jesus fail in their mission, the people will throw them out like garbage.... [S]uch miserable failure is qualitatively different from persecution and other forms of harassment that are signs of strength ... but this passage does not consider this possibility.[4]

In such readings, the warning is about the disciples' failure in their mission, which will result in their rejection because of their uselessness. However, a minority voice in the discussion suggests that the persecution that many deny as a possible context for this saying may indeed contribute to the context and possible message for this saying. As Eduard Schweizer suggests,

> These allusions would hint [at] the foreignness of Jesus' disciples to the world, so that the disciples are seen not as

---

[1] Boring, "The Gospel of Matthew," 8:181. Cf. Alfred Plummer, *An Exegetical Commentary on the Gospel According to St. Matthew* (Grand Rapids: Baker, 1982), 72; and Hill, *The Gospel of Matthew*, 115.

[2] Mounce, *Matthew*, 40.

[3] Bruner, *Matthew, A Commentary*, 160.

[4] Betz, *A Commentary on the Sermon on the Mount*, 160.

gently influencing the world but as persevering even under persecution, or even if sacrificed completely.[1]

Nonetheless, one must note that Schweizer's comment goes against the stream of Matthean scholarship in dealing with this specific verse.

On the basis of this brief examination of recent scholarship on Matt 5:13, one may conclude that the initial questions offered for consideration are only marginally addressed. The common translation of the second part of the verse—"But if the salt loses its saltiness, how can it be made salty again?" (NRSV)—seems to be endorsed by most interpreters. A general consensus regarding the interpretation of the Matthean "salt of the earth" passage seems to exist, but these works delve little into issues of Greek syntax and literary context that this study raises. Thus, one must look elsewhere for answers to those initial questions.

A Study of Matthew 5:13 with Reference to the Synoptic Parallels

Given both the issues and questions that have been raised thus far, one is now compelled to examine the text of Matt 5:13 itself to discover whether translations and interpretations of this verse in terms of tastelessness and loss of mission adequately convey the nuances of the Greek text. Each section of the verse will be assessed, including attention to notable similarities and differences between it and its synoptic parallels, Mark 9:50 and Luke 14:34-35, as printed below.

> Matt 5:13 – Ὑμεῖς ἐστε τὸ ἅλας τῆς γῆς· ἐὰν δὲ τὸ ἅλας μωρανθῇ, ἐν τίνι ἁλισθήσεται; εἰς οὐδὲν ἰσχύει ἔτι εἰ μὴ βληθὲν ἔξω καταπατεῖσθαι ὑπὸ τῶν ἀνθρώπων. ("You are the salt of the earth; but if salt has lost its taste, how can its

---

[1] Schweizer, *The Good News according to Matthew*, 101. Cf. Davies and Allison, *A Critical and Exegetical Commentary on the Gospel according to Saint Matthew*, 1:472 who note the paradox that "the world is saved precisely by those it persecutes"; Garland, *Reading Matthew*, 60; and Plummer, *An Exegetical Commentary on the Gospel according to St. Matthew*, 72.

saltiness be restored? It is no longer good for anything, but is thrown out and trampled under foot." NRSV)

Mark 9:50 – Καλὸν τὸ ἅλας· ἐὰν δὲ τὸ ἅλας ἄναλον γένηται, ἐν τίνι αὐτὸ ἀρτύσετε; ἔχετε ἐν ἑαυτοῖς ἅλα καὶ εἰρηνεύετε ἐν ἀλλήλοις. ("Salt is good; but if salt has lost its saltiness, how can you season it? Have salt in yourselves, and be at peace with one another." NRSV)

Luke 14:34-35 – Καλὸν οὖν τὸ ἅλας· ἐὰν δὲ καὶ τὸ ἅλας μωρανθῇ, ἐν τίνι ἀρτυθήσεται; οὔτε εἰς γῆν οὔτε εἰς κοπρίαν εὔθετόν ἐστιν, ἔξω βάλλουσιν αὐτό. ὁ ἔχων ὦτα ἀκούειν ἀκουέτω. "Salt is good; but if salt has lost its taste, how can its saltiness be restored? It is fit neither for the soil nor for the manure pile; they throw it away. Let anyone with ears to hear listen!" NRSV)

Ὑμεῖς ἐστε τὸ ἅλας τῆς γῆς ("You are the salt of the earth"; NRSV)

Unlike the Markan and Lukan renderings, the Matthean version is directed to the disciples along with a second affirmation that only Matthew includes in the same context: "You are the light of the world" (Matt 5:14; NRSV). The second person plural address, Ὑμεῖς ἐστε, emphatically links the salt imagery to the disciples, who are the ones addressed by the second person plural verbs and pronouns in verses 11–12.[1] In addition, the use of the article with the predicate nominative ἅλας ("salt") suggests that this salt imagery or metaphor is to be perceived as identical with the subject[2] (literally, ὑμεῖς; the disciples) or as "that which alone merits the designation."[3] The clear inference here is that these disciples themselves, and not others, are those who are "the salt of the earth." Although the attempt to pinpoint precisely the specific nuance of the salt

---

[1] Cf. Davies and Allison, *A Critical and Exegetical Commentary on the Gospel according to Saint Matthew*, 1:472; and Ulrich Luz, *Matthew 1–7*, Hermeneia (Minneapolis: Fortress, 2007), 250.

[2] Herbert Weir Smyth, *Greek Grammar* (Cambridge: Harvard University, 1984), §1152.

[3] BDF §273 (1).

metaphor in this context is most difficult, such attempts may also be unnecessary, since images and metaphors typically lend themselves to multiple levels of interpretation. Since salt had various uses in Palestine and more generally the Greco-Roman world, it may be that the metaphor draws not only from salt's importance and usefulness in everyday life but also on the variety of its functionality.

An important question should be raised here regarding the genitive τῆς γῆς ("the earth") that modifies τὸ ἅλας: Is "the earth" to be understood as synonymous with "the world", since the genitive τοῦ κόσμου ("the world") modifies τὸ φῶς ("the light") in the second parallel affirmation or declarative maxim in verse 14? The parallel constructions seem to suggest that "earth" and "world" are used interchangeably in these two verses.[1] However, two points are worth noting here. First, the Matthean use of the noun γῆ typically refers to: (a) a land or region, (b) the earth in distinction to heaven (e.g., Matt 5:18; 6:19–20; 28:18), or (c) soil (e.g., 13:5, 8, 23; 25:18, 25).[2] Second, the reference to being trampled under persons' feet at the end of the verse implies more of an "earthiness" than what "world" implies. Betz notes that, in contrast to verse 12, which directs "the readers' eyes of imagination" to heaven, verse 13 "takes us back down to earth, indeed into the mud itself."[3] Betz further writes:

> The earth is the place where the community... lives. It is the place opposite to the sky, or "heaven"... This place is "among the people" (5:13, 16, 19; 6:1, 2, 5, 14–16, 18; 7:9, 12) and "in the world" (5:14).... Thus, "the salt of the earth" means that the faithful disciples must get involved with this earth and its life. They are to regard themselves as a most important ingredient of

---

[1] See, e.g., Boring, "The Gospel of Matthew," 8:181. Cf. Nolland, *The Gospel of Matthew*, 212–13.

[2] In parables, the term typically refers to "the ground" or soil.

[3] Betz, *A Commentary on the Sermon on the Mount*, 155 (emphasis added).

this life; to say it with the metaphor: they must be part of the dirt out of which this world is made.[1]

Therefore, one may tentatively suggest that, although the emphatic affirmations of verses 13 and 14 are parallel in construction, the "salt of the earth" image is literally more "down to earth."

ἐὰν δὲ τὸ ἅλας μωρανθῇ ("but if salt has lost its taste" NRSV)

Since the affirmation in the first part of verse 13 has already identified the disciples as salt, the repetition of the noun τὸ ἅλας ("the salt") clearly places these same disciples in this possible situation.[2] This association, however, is not the central question here. Rather, the questions focus on the subjunctive μωρανθῇ: What is the significance of the different verb when compared to the Markan account, and how is one to translate the verb μωραίνειν when linked with the noun τὸ ἅλας ("the salt") in Matt 5:13? And how does one render the passive voice of that subjunctive? Let's deal with both questions in order.

First, what is the significance of the different verb when compared to the Markan account, and how is one to translate the verb μωραίνειν when linked with the noun τὸ ἅλας ("the salt") in Matt 5:13? A comparison of the three synoptic parallels of this saying—Matt 5:13b, Mark 9:50b, and Luke 14:34b—indicates that the accounts in the Gospels of Matthew and Luke are basically identical (except for the addition of the conjunction καὶ in the Lukan version), but differ with Mark's account in the verbal construction:

Luke 14:34	ἐὰν δὲ καὶ τὸ ἅλας μωρανθῇ
Matt 5:13b	ἐὰν δὲ τὸ ἅλας μωρανθῇ
Mark 9:50b	ἐὰν δὲ τὸ ἅλας ἄναλον γένηται

---

[1] Ibid, 158 (emphasis added).
[2] The conditional clause with ἐάν and the aorist subjunctive suggests one of two scenarios: a general condition or truth, or something that is impending. See BDF §373; and Smyth, *Greek Grammar*, §§2297, 2335–39.

Thus, Matthew and Luke incorporate the subjunctive μωρανθῇ, whereas Mark includes the subjunctive construction ἄναλον γένηται. The scholarly trend has been to understand these two constructions as roughly synonymous, as seen most obviously in contemporary English translations. Since the Markan expression seems to refer to something (i.e., salt) becoming unsalty,[1] the Matthean and Lukan constructions have been understood in similar ways. But why, then, does the different verb appear in Matthew and Luke? If saltiness or taste is significant for these passages, it would seem as though the Markan expression states that clearly enough.[2] The verb μωραίνειν complicates the interpretation of the Matthean and Lukan texts, because both the verb and the adjective μωρός usually connote the idea of foolishness except, according to the lexicons and our English translations, in the two instances of Matt 5:13 and Luke 14:34.[3] Since no surviving Greek text includes a construction that combines the noun τὸ ἅλας ("the salt") with the verb μωραίνειν,[4] the only apparent bases for the conclusion that the verb connotes "becoming tasteless" or "losing its saltiness" are these: (a) the Markan passage, (b) the hypothesis of some unknown Semitic text or proverb behind the Greek text,[5] or (c) the use of the verb ἁλίζειν ("to salt") in the subsequent part of the sentence. Although the metaphor would suggest that any salt (disciple) that did not fulfill its function, including the seasoning of food (the

---

[1] The word ἄναλος is rare; only two references outside the NT are listed in LSJ, 112 (see Aristotle, *Prob.* 927a35; Galenus 10.401). Only two additional references were discovered in searching the *TLG* databases (Aeschylus, *Sept.* 814; Euripides, *Med.* 325). However, the word itself seems to have two parts that together suggest that it means "unsalty" or "without salt": ἀν-, which is a negation (see Smyth, *Greek Grammar*, §885 [1]); and ἅλας ("salt").

[2] Since neither Markan priority nor Matthean priority is the purpose of this paper, such issues will not be addressed here.

[3] See, e.g., LSJ, 1158; and BDAG, 663. See Nolland, *The Gospel of Matthew*, 213: "There is no documented use of the term in the sense clearly required here."

[4] This conclusion is based on a search of the *TLG* databases.

[5] See Black, *An Aramaic Approach to the Gospels and Acts*, 166–67; Jeremias, *The Parables of Jesus*, 168; and Nauck, "Salt as a Metaphor in Instructions for Discipleship," 165–78.

earth), would be "foolish" salt (disciple), such an interpretation seems to be founded more on the subsequent use of the verb ἀρτύειν ("to season") in Mark and Luke than on the Matthean passage itself. The association of "salt" with "foolishness" is unusual, to be sure, but the elimination of the "foolishness" connotations that the verb carries does not seem justified, based on the Matthean construction and the use of that verb in other contexts.[1]

Second, how does one render the passive voice of the subjunctive μωρανθῇ? Virtually everyone—including translators of this subjunctive and others who have analyzed and written about this verse—renders this verse like an active voice: "to become tasteless," "to lose its saltiness," even "to become foolish" or "to become dull."[2] After Georg Bertram identifies the subjunctive as a passive voice, he then states, as though it was an active voice, that it "means gradually to fade out, to disappear, and would make possible an explanation of the saying in terms of impure salt whose salt content wastes away."[3] The general consensus is that, even if one allows for the foolishness connotation in this passage, this foolishness is the responsibility of the disciple. In other words, the disciple becomes foolish when the disciple loses identity or mission. However, while the subject of the subjunctive μωρανθῇ is the noun τὸ ἅλας ("the salt"), which the opening of the verse identifies as the disciples, the passive voice suggests that the responsibility for "becoming foolish" may be opposite what has been assumed.

The contention here is that the passive voice of the subjunctive μωρανθῇ needs further consideration. It seems as though most translations and commentators interpret this subjunctive more like an active verb because they consider

---

[1] See Betz, *A Commentary on the Sermon on the Mount*, 159 who renders as "become dull" to "cover both the material and the figurative meaning"; and Bertram, "μωρός κτλ.," *TDNT* 4:837-39. Cf. Luz, *Matthew 1-7: A Continental Commentary*, 250, who renders the verb as "becoming dumb."

[2] Betz, *A Commentary on the Sermon on the Mount*, 159.

[3] Bertram, "μωρός κτλ.," *TDNT* 4:838.

μωραίνειν to be an intransitive verb, not a transitive one.[1] Although transitive verbs may have a direct object, the assumption is that intransitive verbs typically do not. Thus, the typical explanation of the difference between active and passive verbs—"The direct object of an active verb becomes the subject of the passive"[2]—would not seem to apply to intransitive verbs, especially when the verb is in the passive voice, since no direct object seemingly exists. Such a conclusion would also assume that a compatible subject for the hypothetical passive intransitive verb would also not exist. However, such an explanation or rule is something about which Greek knows nothing.[3] That is, Greek intransitive verbs often do appear in the passive voice, despite the fact that they have no direct object. Thus, rather than rendering such passive verbs in more active ways by using "to be ..." or "to become ..." to convey the verb's meaning, the passive voice may be interpreted and translated to direct the named action more toward the subject by the sense of "to allow oneself to be ..." or "to let oneself be...."[4] Even here, the subject of the sentence is the recipient of the action and not necessarily the responsible party for the described action.

If the passive voice functions to identify the action's recipient even in intransitive verbs, then one may tentatively offer for consideration a different reading of this part of verse 13 that accounts for the aorist passive subjunctive μωρανθῇ: although the disciples as "salt" could be those who merely become tasteless or foolish because of their own failures (of faith or mission), they could also be those who may have allowed themselves to become foolish or who may have been made out to be foolish, were seen to be foolish, or were treated as foolish by some unnamed persons or group. Such a reading places responsibility for the foolishness with other unnamed persons; all the while, the disciples are still the "salt

---

[1] See BDAG, 663.
[2] Smyth, *Greek Grammar*, §1743.
[3] Cf. A. T. Robertson, *A Grammar of the Greek New Testament in the Light of Historical Research* (Nashville: Broadman, 1934), 815; and BDF §312.
[4] See Smyth, *Greek Grammar*, §1736; and BDF §314.

of the earth," even though they may not be seen or treated like it by others.

A brief survey of the usage of the verb μωραίνειν elsewhere in the New Testament and in the Septuagint supports this initial reading of the passage. The verb appears in two other places in the New Testament (other than in Matt 5:13 and Luke 14:34–35) and five times in the Septuagint (2 Sam 24:10; Isa 19:11; 44:25; Jer 10:14; Sir 23:14). Only two occurrences use active forms of the verbs (Isa 44:25 LXX; 1 Cor 1:20); in both instances, God as the subject makes the counsel or advice (τὴν βουλήν) of the "diviners" (Isa 44:25) and "the wisdom of the world" (1 Cor 1:20) foolish.[1] In both instances, the verbs occur in a transitive sense, so that a direct object is provided (that could become the subject of those verbs if a passive form was employed in a sentence). And in both, the responsible party for making such persons or what they valued as foolish was not those persons themselves or something for which they were responsible but a different agent.

The remaining five occurrences use passive forms of μωραίνειν. In four instances, the passive voice leaves open the cause or "agent" behind the foolishness that comes upon the subject (2 Sam 24:10; Isa 19:11; Jer 10:14 LXX; Rom 1:22). Some are rather obvious. For instance, in 2 Sam 24:10, after counting the fighting men David responds contritely, "I have sinned greatly in what I have done. But now, O LORD, I pray you, take away the guilt of your servant; for I have done very foolishly" (NRSV) or "I became foolish (because of my sin) [ὅτι ἐμωράνθην σφόδρα; LXX]." In Rom 1:22, those who claimed to be wise "became fools [ἐμωράνθησαν]" (NRSV) due to their sinfulness (see Rom 1:18–21).[2] However, Sir 23:14 is most explicit: καὶ τῷ ἐθισμῷ σου μωρανθῇς ("you will be made foolish by your [bad] habits"; emphasis added). That is, this

---

[1] In the Isa 44:25 LXX passage, a derivative form of μωραίνειν appears: μωρεύειν.

[2] The LXX passages in Isa 19:11 and Jer 10:14 reflect a similar pattern: a description of becoming or being made foolish as a result of one's sinfulness or rebellion against God.

passage from Sirach explicitly indicates the cause or source of foolishness: "your [bad] habits" (τῷ ἐθισμῷ σου). Thus, one finds that the usage of passive forms of μωραίνειν consistently point to the cause or reason of that which makes a person or people foolish. Although these passive examples indicate that persons themselves may be responsible for what makes them foolish, the broader use of the verb μωραίνειν suggests that its passive voice refers to who or what causes the person to be foolish or to be perceived as foolish, and such causes should not be limited to themselves but should be considered with regard to other persons and circumstances, based on other contextual matters.

ἐν τίνι ἁλισθήσεται; ("how can its saltiness be restored?" NRSV)

By continuing the salt imagery, this question that follows the conditional clause emphasizes the predicament for the disciple who is treated as foolish. The Matthean version, unlike the Markan and Lukan versions, does not use the verb ἀρτύειν ("to season") to raise the question about restoring the taste of the salt, which further suggests that the loss of taste or saltiness is not the issue here. Rather, Matthew uses a third person singular passive form of the verb ἁλίζειν ("to salt")[1] — of which the subject is most likely the ἅλας ("salt") that was seen and treated as foolish[2] — to create the impossible picture of those who, on the one hand, are already "salt" yet rejected as such but who, on the other hand, are "being salted" by those who reject them. The issue here is not the impossibility of physical salt losing its qualities, of disciples losing their qualities as "salt of the earth," or even of salt or disciples being restored. Rather, the issue is the impossibility of those, who reject the disciples' "salt of the earth" mission as foolishness, simultaneously enabling those disciples to fulfill that same Christian mission.[3] The prepositional

---

[1] See Betz, *A Commentary on the Sermon on the Mount*, 159 who offers three options for translating the question, but two of which do not reflect the passive voice of the indicative ἁλισθήσεται.

[2] Cf. Hagner, *Matthew*, 1:99.

[3] See Grant R. Osborne, *Matthew*, ZECNT (Grand Rapids: Zondervan, 2010), 175: "Jesus' purpose was not scientific but ethical, making the point that his

phrase ἐν τινι preceding the verb raises the rhetorical question, "With what will this 'foolish' salt (i.e., disciples) be salted?" The implied answer is, quite bluntly, "Nothing!"

εἰς οὐδὲν ἰσχύει ἔτι εἰ μὴ βληθὲν ἔξω καταπατεῖσθαι ὑπὸ τῶν ἀνθρώπων.
("It is no longer good for anything, but is thrown out and trampled under foot" NRSV)

The final part of Matt 5:13 gives more fully the implied answer to the previous question. The implied subject of the indicative ἰσχύει is once again τὸ ἅλας ("the salt"), or, as the image suggests, the disciples. The emphatic position of the prepositional phrase εἰς οὐδέν highlights what is usually given as the translation here: "it is good for nothing."[1] The connotations of the verb ἰσχύειν, however, focus on "capacity" and "power" that, although similar to the verb δύναμαι, place "more emphasis on the actual power implied in ability or capacity, i.e., on the power which one possesses."[2] Betz rightly notes that such salt "has some power left but it leads to nothing, a meager result further described in the remainder of the sentence."[3] However, if one understands the foolishness as something that has been projected onto or toward the disciples as the "salt of the earth," as has been suggested here already, then this diminution of that salt's (i.e., the disciple's) functionality cannot be equated with the inability or powerlessness of that salt to function. Rather, the reason that the salt or disciples may seem to accomplish little is because of the response toward them.

The harsh results articulated at the end of this verse make it clear that salt perceived as "foolish" will be thrown outside (βληθὲν

---

disciples must never allow themselves to become useless in their mission. The verb μωρανθῇ means to 'become foolish' with the idea that such a disciple is a fool (cf. the 'foolish' [μωραί] virgins in 25:2–3, 8)."

[1] This specific prepositional phrase underscores a specific point of reference (BDAG, 291).

[2] Walter Grundmann, "ἰσχύω κτλ.," *TDNT* 3:397–402.

[3] Betz, *A Commentary on the Sermon on the Mount*, 159.

ἔξω)¹ and trampled under foot by fellow human beings (καταπατεῖσθαι ὑπὸ τῶν ἀνθρώπων). The passive infinitive καταπατεῖσθαι ("to be trampled under foot") has been interpreted as an infinitive either of purpose² or of result,³ although the latter seems more likely. However, since the prefix κατά may suggest hostile action against another, the infinitive may describe in negative, hostile terms what happens to the salt or disciple who is perceived as foolish.⁴ In other words, the imagery here appears to reflect a context of hostility or persecution.⁵ The depiction here is not of "miserable failure"⁶ or "deserved persecution"⁷ because of such failure. Although Betz is correct to argue that this kind of salt "is thus treated like dirt,"⁸ he interprets this as the disciples' failure or loss of mission rather than the hostile response to the disciples' mission. Yet Betz also notes that the metaphor of the disciples being the "salt of the earth" suggests that "they must be part of the dirt out of which this world is made."⁹ Could it be, then, that this one exception to the "able to achieve nothing" or "good for nothing" expression is the affirmation that these disciples still are the "salt of the earth" and that they are to be that salt, even if that means being

---

[1] Most scholars interpret the verb βάλλειν in an eschatological sense, but Betz (159 n 44) usefully notes that this is not the case here.

[2] BDF §390 (3).

[3] Hagner, *Matthew*, 1:99.

[4] See Heinrich Seesemann and Georg Bertram, "πατέω κτλ.," *TDNT* 5:941, 944.

[5] See Joachim Gnilka, *Das Matthäusevangelium*, 2 vols. HThKAT (Freiburg: Herder, 1986-88), 1:134, who sees such conflict not only here but throughout the preceding context (esp. Matt 5:9-12); and Nolland, *The Gospel of Matthew*, 211: "It is those who are persecuted for Jesus' sake who are identified as the salt and light, and to whom comes the challenge to sustain an active expression of this role despite all opposition." Cf. Schweizer, *The Good News according to Matthew*, 101; Luz, *Matthew 1-7: A Continental Commentary*, 247; and Plummer, *An Exegetical Commentary on the Gospel according to St. Matthew*, 72. See Contra Betz, *A Commentary on the Sermon on the Mount*, 160.

[6] Betz, *A Commentary on the Sermon on the Mount*, 160.

[7] Bruner, *Matthew, A Commentary*, 160.

[8] Betz, *A Commentary on the Sermon on the Mount*, 159.

[9] Ibid., 158.

treated poorly like dirt? Could it be that precisely at this dirt or earth level—where the disciples as perceived "foolish" salt are thrown—is precisely where they are to function as the "salt of the earth/dirt"?

An Interpretation of Matthew 5:13 in Light of its Literary and Historical Contexts

If these initial conclusions about Matt 5:13, based on the presented textual evidence, suggest its reading as an affirmation to disciples and their mission in the face of possible harsh treatment and opposition rather than as a warning to disciples against the loss of that mission, how does that reading "play out" in the literary and historical contexts within which one finds that passage? That is, what does one find, in the literary context or the historical context or both, that confirms or challenges this reading?

Literary Context

This reading or interpretation of Matt 5:13 is consistent with its immediate context in the Sermon on the Mount. Three reasons may be offered for this assertion. First, the ones to whom Jesus remarks are directed in verse 13 are the same ones addressed in verses 11-12 (or, more broadly, verses 3-12) and in verses 14-16. As has been already noted, the emphatic second person plural pronoun (Ὑμεῖς) links this verse to the addressees of verses 11 and 12, who are also addressed with second person plural pronouns and verbs. In addition, the addressees of verses 14-16 are addressed in the same way as those in verse 13, that is, with the emphatic Ὑμεῖς ἐστε. The identification of the addressees, however, simply means that all that is spoken is directed to the same group, which leads to the remaining two reasons.

Second, the theme of persecution or, at very least, the persecution language of Matt 5:10-12 provides the literary backdrop from which verse 13 may be interpreted. These verses describe the ones "persecuted for the sake of righteousness" (οἱ δεδιωγμένοι ἕνεκεν δικαιοσύνης; Matt 5:10) as those who are "blessed" (μακάριοι) and are treated like the prophets long ago.[1] Given this context, an interpretation of verse 13 as a warning against failure or the loss of Christian mission appears out of place. However, a reading of this passage as reflecting the same theme or language of persecution embraces the continuity of the larger literary unit and relates to the rhetoric of the passage.

Third, this reading of verse 13 complements the "light of the world" metaphor and the sayings of verses 14-16. To be sure, in comparison to the "light of the world" sayings, what is being offered here as an alternative reading of verse 13 may seem to be much more negative in its description of what may happen to the disciples. Schweizer cautiously suggests that readings about loss of mission "may distinguish the salt saying from the lamp saying, which places more emphasis on the active role played by the light."[2] Nonetheless, just as the disciples are called to function as light, which may lead them to dark places, they are called to function as salt, even in the midst of the "dirt" or "earth." These verses, then, complement one another by affirming the function of the disciples in the midst of their world. Although a reading of verse 13 in terms of warning may not be incongruous with verses 14-16 (that is, by contrasting the warning with the affirmation of verses 14-16), such a reading does not account for the larger context of affirmation in which one finds that verse (i.e., 5:10-16 or even 5:3-16).

Historical Context

Debates about the Sitz im Leben of the Matthean community certainly requires one to "tiptoe gently" when raising issues regarding historical context. The questions over the ethnic/religious configuration of the Matthean community and the relationship or

---

[1] Cf. R. T. France, *The Gospel of Matthew*, NICNT (Grand Rapids: Eerdmans, 2007), 171; Garland, *Reading Matthew*, 60; Gnilka, *Das Matthäusevangelium*, 1:134; Nolland, *The Gospel of Matthew*, 211; and Plummer, *An Exegetical Commentary on the Gospel according to St. Matthew*, 72.

[2] Schweizer, *The Good News according to Matthew*, 101.

connections between that community and Judaism cannot be solved or even adequately summarized here[1] However, a general consensus in contemporary readings of the Gospel of Matthew identifies the existence of crises, tension, and conflict between, on the one hand, the Matthean community and Judaism, and, on the other hand, the Matthean community and its non-Jewish neighbors. If one may assume, for the purposes of this essay, that this general description reflects, at least to some extent, the context in which the Matthean audience lived and to which this Gospel was written, then one may suggest that the alternative reading of Matt 5:13 proposed here not only accounts for the literary context in which the verse is found but also more adequately accounts for these historical context issues as well.

Conclusion

Current interpretations and translations of Matt 5:13 seem to read the peculiar sayings surrounding the Matthean "salt of the earth" metaphor through Markan lenses. That is to say, not only the conditional phrase, ἐὰν δὲ τὸ ἅλας μωρανθῇ ("But if salt has lost its taste;" Matt 5:13b NRSV), but the ending of that statement and the subsequent saying are all typically interpreted in ways that do not adequately consider the unusual association of the noun τὸ ἅλας ("the salt") and the verb μωραίνειν ("to make foolish") in the Gospel of Matthew. The alternative reading of Matt 5:13 offered here suggests that the "salt of the earth" metaphor and the sayings that accompany it, as applied to the disciples, are not warnings to

---

[1] See, e.g., Donald A. Hagner, "The *Sitz im Leben* of the Gospel of Matthew," in *Treasures New and Old: Recent Contributions to Matthean Studies*, ed. David R. Bauer and Mark Allan Powell, JBL Symposium Series (Atlanta: Scholars, 1996), 27-68; J. Andrew Overman, *Matthew's Gospel and Formative Judaism: The Social World of the Matthean Community* (Minneapolis: Fortress, 1990); Anthony J. Saldarini, "The Gospel of Matthew and Jewish-Christian Conflict," in *Social History of the Matthean Community*, ed. David L. Balch (Minneapolis: Fortress, 1991), 38-61; and L. Michael White, "Crisis Management and Boundary Maintenance: The Social Location of the Matthean Community," in *Social History of the Matthean Community*, 211-47.

them about the dangers of failure or of the loss of mission that results in their uselessness as disciples. Rather, this verse presents the serious possibility that the disciples, despite the declaration that they are the "salt of the earth," may be perceived as "foolish" and useless because of their identification with Jesus, which may result in rejection and hostile treatment that are described in persecution language. Nonetheless, the emphatic affirmation to the disciples remains, "You are the salt of the earth," suggesting that, even though their function may be hindered and considered useless by such treatment, they still must function in salt-like ways, no matter where they may be cast. In other words, by listening again to the text of Matt 5:13 with careful attention to its grammatical and contextual features, there is another way of reading this verse and saying that is contrary to most interpretations and readings and that offers an alternative answer to the question, "Can salt really lose its saltiness?" Instead of understanding this as a passage that warns its readers or wondering how to work around what puzzles us as readers, such a reading recognizes that the answer for Jesus's disciples to that question, "Can salt really lose its saltiness?" is an emphatic "Never!" For the call of Jesus' disciples is to live out whom they are called to be … wherever they are "sent" or thrown.

Hearing Voices

Identity and Mission in Mark[1]

Kent Brower

Introduction

In the opening words of his gospel, Mark sets out in summary form two linked foci: this story is about God's good news and it is about the identity of Jesus and his followers.

All of the Gospels set the story of Jesus's coming in line with God's good purposes. While the others begin with birth narratives (Matthew and Luke) or Jesus's pre-history (John), Mark is more direct. Mark's opening word, ἀρχή, is used at one level simply to state that the story has started. But because the same word also opens the LXX in Gen 1:1 and is linked as it is with the phrase τοῦ εὐαγγελίου Ἰησοῦ Χριστοῦ, it hints that the same God who brought order out of chaos is doing a new thing in the face of Roman occupation of the land and the disastrous spiritual leadership given by the temple elite to God's holy people.

The opening line is succinct yet comprehensive: this is τὸ εὐαγγέλιον. This is the narrative theme, but it also encapsulates the whole story of God's big purposes in Christ.[2] The story stretches back to creation, the covenant with Noah, the call of Abram, and the whole story of Israel. Thus, Mark sees the story of Jesus in continuity with what God has already done. Mark makes this

---

[1] Sections of this essay depend heavily on Kent Brower, *Mark: A Commentary in the Wesleyan Tradition* (Kansas City, MO: Beacon Hill, 2012). In a strange way, this is fitting because the commentary was written under the general editorship of George Lyons, in whose honor I offer this essay.

[2] See Richard Bauckham, *Jesus and the Eyewitnesses* (Grand Rapids: Eerdmans, 2006), 12–38.

connection by occasional citations of scripture and, more often, through allusions to texts and echoes of themes. His figural interpretation[1] is profound and pervasive. To make this point, Mark evokes the Isaianic restoration eschatology motif through the use of the term "gospel" right from the start, referring to the good news announced to the exiles by the exilic prophets. According to Isa 43:19, God announces his purposes through the prophet in the context of the return from exile. "See, I am doing a new thing! Now it springs up; do you not perceive it? I am making a way in the desert and streams in the wasteland." Now, Mark re-reads the promise of Isaiah in a fresh and almost unimaginable way. This new thing is the mission of God centered on Jesus, and enacted and embodied within the people of God.

The second focus of Mark is on the identity of the one on whom the whole story turns: Ἰησοῦς Χριστός υἱός θεοῦ[2] and the mission he undertakes of proclaiming τὸ εὐαγγέλιον τοῦ θεοῦ (1:14), which was that πεπλήρωται ὁ καιρὸς καὶ ἤγγικεν ἡ βασιλεία τοῦ θεοῦ (1:15). The meaning of this line is central to Mark's whole narrative. In compact language, the Markan Jesus announces that "God is now fulfilling his agelong purpose,"[3] not in some distant future, but now. In Jesus's coming God's purposes have reached the decisive moment.[4]

The announcing and effecting of God's reign, the assertion that this is the self-revelation of God,[5] is Jesus's mission. The

---

[1] See Richard B. Hays, *Echoes of Scripture in the Gospels* (Waco, TX: Baylor University, 2016). Hays calls this a figural interpretation of scripture.

[2] While the inclusion of the phrase 'Son of God' in this sentence on textual grounds alone may be questioned, on Markan narratological and theological grounds, the phrase is coherent with the rest of the story. See Peter M. Head, "A Text-Critical Study of Mark 1:1: The Beginning of the Gospel of Jesus Christ," *NTS* 37 (1991): 621-29, who argues against inclusion. See Brower, *Mark*, 43-44.

[3] R. T. France, *The Gospel of Mark*, NIGTC (Carlisle: Paternoster, 2002), 93.

[4] While *kairos* on its own does not indicate this decisive occurrence, in this context it indicates that the decisive moment has arrived (see, e.g., France, *The Gospel of Mark*, 91).

[5] See Bruce Chilton, *God in Strength: Jesus' Announcement of the Kingdom*, SNTSU B.1 (Freistadt: F. Plöchl, 1979), 297.

mission is based on Jesus's identity; it is also the mission of his followers, based on their identity. Right from the first line, Mark's readers know who this person is. This story, centered on Jesus of Nazareth, is about the Messiah, a term that evokes exciting and dangerous hopes in people who have been longing for a deliverer. But the term, although central to Mark's identity of Jesus (1:1; 8:29; 13:35; 13:21; 16:61; 15:32), is so loaded that the Markan Jesus never uses it of himself. Peter confesses it as Jesus's identity (8:29), but Mark immediately has Jesus flesh out its meaning in a righteous sufferer direction (8:31), again evoking an exilic theme of vindication through suffering, echoing both the servant songs in Isaiah and the vision of the one like a son of man in Daniel.[1] Mark sees the coming of Jesus and his ministry as the beginning of God's previously announced purposes. Mark leads his readers inexorably through his narrative to the conclusion that this person participates fully in the divine identity: Jesus is indeed God with us (see 1:11; 3:11; 5:7; 9:7; 13:32; 14:61; 15:39).[2]

With this as background, this essay focuses on identity and mission through giving attention to instances in Mark in which a voice is heard or a call is given. Mark explicitly uses the word φωνή six times, two of which are the voice from heaven (1:11; 9:7), two of which are from unclean spirits (1:26; 5:7) and two of which are in the crucifixion scene (15:34, 37). Two call narratives (3:13-15; 8:34-38) are used by Mark for forming identity and defining mission. Connecting lines will show how the narrative, which begins with Jesus's identity as Son of God and concludes with the voice of the centurion from the foot of the cross offering the same assessment (15:39), draws Jesus's followers into God's mission and purposes.

---

[1] See Robert S, Snow, *Daniel's Son of Man in Mark* (Eugene, OR: Pickwick, 2016).

[2] Whatever the conclusions reached on textual grounds about 1:1, the absence or presence of these words in this line make no difference to the overall theology of Mark: this is *the good news about Jesus Messiah, Son of God.*

The Voice in the Wilderness (Mark 1:3)

The first voice is in Mark 1:3, a voice crying in the wilderness. The description of this voice points toward the identity of the one who is to follow in terms of a Malachi base text but attributed to Isaiah. In Malachi, the messenger prepares the way for Yahweh to come in judgment of Israel (Mal 2:17–3:5). Mark has made a subtle yet significant alteration. Instead of ἐπιβλέψεται ὁδὸν πρὸ προσώπου μου as in Mal 3:1, Mark 1:2 changes "my" to "your" (πρὸ προσώπου σου). As a result, the words point to Jesus. On one level, the change simply makes the text fit with the story, as John prepares the way for Jesus. But at another level, Mark is saying that what is attributable to Israel's God in Scripture is attributable to Jesus Messiah, Son of God. This motif is repeated throughout Mark. The implications of this for Mark's Christology are important. [1]

The voice, then, confirms the identity of Jesus as Messiah, Son of God. But it also announces the preparation of the people for the mission of God.[2] Decades ago, Willi Marxsen noted that the wilderness geographical location is used by Mark with theological intent.[3] Placing the opening scene of Mark in its Isaianic framework immediately evokes the theme of exile and restoration. The return from exile would be the resumption of God's good purposes for the nations, so directly articulated in Isa 40–66.

N. T. Wright has made a strong case that, for many in the late Second Temple period, the sense of being in exile had not ended. The contours of the story are well-known and will not be repeated here. Suffice it to say that in the late Second Temple period, a ferment of discontent was never far below the surface, particularly in Judea. Many still longed for a Davidic Messiah (the Herodias never fitted the bill and were therefore never fully

---

[1] Morna D. Hooker, *A Commentary on the Gospel according to St Mark* (London: A. & C. Black, 1991), 36, writes, "God's advent in salvation and judgment has taken place in Jesus."

[2] See Thomas R. Hatina, *In Search of a Context: The Function of Scripture in Mark's Narrative*, JSNTSup 232 (Sheffield: Sheffield Academic, 2002), 182.

[3] Willi Marxsen, *Mark the Evangelist: Studies on the Redaction History of the Gospel*, trans. James Boyce et al. (Nashville: Abingdon, 1969), 38.

accepted as leaders and certainly not the Davidic heir), for a temple that was undefiled by the presence of the Romans and their collaborators, and in which God could again dwell. Some even abandoned the temple, considering it to be hopelessly corrupt. Several pretenders to messiahship rose and fell; some communities separated themselves from the rest of society and considered themselves to be the righteous remnant, the new covenant community, that would prepare for the presence of God.[1] Wright argues that, in general, they were still awaiting a restoration that would signal the return of Yahweh to his people. Sometime in the future, "Israel's God would return to his temple at last, the temple that the coming king will build. Then, and only then, the new Genesis will come about."[2]

This is the context in which the voice speaks in the wilderness. The Baptist is seen as the fulfillment of the Isaianic voice, who comes to announce the imminent end of the exile and the coming of the one who is to bring this about. Mark's interweaving of Mal 3:1 with Isaiah allows Malachi, with its theme of purification, to be read within the Isaianic framework. "Thus, the voice is not only announcing that the time of the exile is over, but also expecting the people to be purified for the mission of God."[3] For Wright and a growing number of scholars, Jesus "understood himself to be bringing about that return and restoration of Israel in order to fulfill the ancient divine plan,"[4] which Mark sees as the kingdom of God.

In Mark's view, the arrival of the kingdom of God is now in the words and deeds of Jesus, the Messiah. The renewal movement is underway, including the beginning of the re-creation of the

---

[1] See 1QS 8:8–14 where Isa 40:3 is cited in the context of the self-definition of the Qumran community as the new covenant community.

[2] N. T. Wright, "Yet the Sun Will Rise Again: Reflections on the Exile and Restoration in Second Temple Judaism, Jesus, Paul, and the Church Today," in *Exile: A Conversation with N. T. Wright*, ed. James M. Scott (Downers Grove, IL: IVP Academic, 2017), 44.

[3] Brower, *Mark*, 50.

[4] Wright, "Yet the Sun Will Rise Again," 80.

people of God. As Ben Meyer noted a generation ago, John's role was "to assemble by baptism the remnant of Israel destined for cleansing, and acquittal and so, climactically, for restoration."[1] They were to be the purified people of God, whose sins were forgiven, and who were prepared for God's mission.

The Voice from Heaven (Mark 1:11)

The second voice is the voice from heaven in Mark 1:11 that concludes Jesus's baptism scene and the work of John. Mark's sequence is important. The people have already been cleansed and restored (see Mal 4:5), so that they might fulfill the mission of God. Mark brings Jesus from Galilee to be baptized by John along with the whole Judean countryside and all the people of Jerusalem, thus subtlety, but clearly, linking Jesus to the people being prepared by John for the coming of the Lord. A further point of identity and mission emerges. John has announced that the coming one βαπτίσει ὑμᾶς ἐν πνεύματι ἁγίῳ (Mark 1:8). John's work—baptism with water—is preparatory, but it is "from below" as it were, rather than from above. Jesus functions again as YHWH does, since he is the one who puts God's Spirit in the people, thereby acting in fulfillment of Ezek 36.[2]

But how is this to be? John's baptism is intended to establish the condition upon which God could again be among his repentant and forgiven people, not to be understood in an individualist sense, but in the sense of a return to their calling. As Andy Johnson points out, it is as if "God's people, already repentant and prepared, are now pleading in the words of Isa 64:1, 'If only you would tear open the heavens and come down'! And that is what God does. God's Spirit rips open the heavens and comes down right into Jesus

---

[1] Ben F. Meyer, *The Aims of Jesus* (London: SCM, 1979), 128.

[2] The cleansing with water has become a preparatory rite of repentance in the public activity of John, whereas the gift of the Holy Spirit is reserved for a second stage, the activity of Jesus. See Adela Yarbro Collins, *Mark*, Hermeneia (Minneapolis: Fortress, 2007), 146.

(1:10),"[1] who is the baptizer with the Spirit because he is the bearer of the Spirit.

This voice is for Jesus of Nazareth, as it is explicitly directed to him, not the crowds. In Mark's sequence, the voice confirms to Jesus who he is and appoints him for his mission. For Mark, Jesus really is the human embodiment of Israel's God in whom the Spirit dwells.[2] The intertextual mix in Mark 1:11 of Ps 2:7, Gen 22:2 and Isa 42:1 is a rich re-reading of the Isaianic background in which Jesus is the locus of the action of Israel's God on God's mission. I. H. Marshall showed years ago that, "As the Son of God, Jesus is the Messiah, and the task to which he is appointed is that of the Servant."[3] To be sure, as Richard Hays notes, Mark's narrative "holds these elements in taut" without offering a conceptual resolution.[4] But the scene is crucial for Jesus's identity and for the mission he is to undertake.

> In this initial scene…, God the Father, through the Spirit, initiates a 'gracious gash in the universe,' and inhabits the body of the Son who becomes the primary locus of God's holy presence.[5]

The incarnational and Trinitarian shape of this scene seems clear to those who have eyes to see.

The Voice in the Synagogue (Mark 1:24)

The next voice we hear is that of the unclean spirit in the synagogue, which seeks mastery over Jesus through knowledge of

---

[1] Andy Johnson, *Holiness and the* Missio Dei (Eugene, OR: Cascade, 2016), 55–56.

[2] This incarnational identity is made explicit in John 1:14, but is no less clear in Mark.

[3] I. H. Marshall, "Son of God or Servant of Yahweh? – A Reconsideration of Mark 1:11," in *Jesus the Saviour: Studies in New Testament Theology* (Leicester: IVP, 1990), 130 (a reprint from *NTS* 15 [1968–69]: 326–36).

[4] Richard B. Hays, *Reading Backwards* (Waco, TX: Baylor University, 2014; London: SPCK, 2015), 27.

[5] Johnson, *Holiness and the* Missio Dei, 55.

his name: οἶδά σε τίς εἶ, ὁ ἅγιος τοῦ θεοῦ.¹ This hostile but accurate description of Jesus from the spirit world is the first identity of Jesus that is known to the disciples.

Most scholars have given scant attention to this title. But in an important corrective, Arseny Ermakov has shown how crucial this title is for Mark. Ermakov argues that the Second Gospel redefines the title away from its Second Temple usage. It no longer simply describes special people and angelic beings. Ermakov writes, Jesus is not a holy man of God, he is not one of the guarding angels of the holy throne of YHWH. For Mark, Jesus, the Holy One of God, is the centre of a contagious holiness that infects the people of God in the last days. Jesus is and does what Jewish prophetic literature expects YHWH to be and to do. In Markan Christological thought, the title 'the Holy One of God' points to the divine identity of the man Jesus.²

At the heart of Ermakov's article is the conviction that this title points to the "exclusiveness of Jesus and his mission. He belongs to God, acts on God's side, battles evil and unclean cosmic opposition in order to release and restore the people of God." That restoration with the Holy One of God in the midst of his people "restores the holiness and purity of the nation and (re)creates the new holy people of God.... It is the powerful presence of the Holy God himself."³

Those around Jesus, then, are being re-created as the new holy people of God, with Jesus, the Holy One, in their midst.

> The disciples are in the company of Jesus, the one with ἐξουσία who is the Holy One of God. They are part of God's holy people because they are with the Holy One.⁴

---

[1] This title for Jesus is rare (see John 6.69 — *We have come to believe and know that you are* ὁ ἅγιος τοῦ θεοῦ).

[2] Arseny Ermakov, "The Holy One of God in Markan Narrative," in *HBT* 36 (2014): 181.

[3] Ermakov, "The Holy One of God in Markan Narrative," 180.

[4] Kent Brower, *Holiness in the Gospels* (Kansas City, MO: Beacon Hill, 2007), 65–66.

The implications of that relationship are worked out in the rest of the narrative.

The Call and Identification of the Holy People of God (Mark 3:13-15; 3:31-35)

Mark's narrative moves from the beginning of the mission of God to the gathering of the (re)new(ed) people centered on the Holy One of God. Two particular scenes stand out in definition of the people of God and their mission.

The first is the call of the Twelve. On the face of it, the story is simply about Jesus calling and naming his twelve apostles. But within the story so far, it is far more significant. To this point, we have heard the voice in the wilderness, the voice from heaven, and the voice in the synagogue. Jesus proclaims the arrival of the kingdom of God and invites people to repent and believe the good news. His first act is to call four disciples: the healings, exorcisms, forgiveness of sins, and exercise of sovereign authority over the Sabbath round out Jesus's identity. All the unclean spirits know who Jesus is: ὁ υἱὸς τοῦ θεοῦ (Mark 3:11). Finally, we come to this passage where Jesus calls and creates the Twelve to symbolize the whole of God's holy people, on the mission of proclaiming and effecting the good news. Without that narrative context, the call of the Twelve is reduced to a story about when the twelve apostles are called and who they are.

Attention here is warranted because the scene is about who is calling as well as who is called. Mark tells us that ἀναβαίνει εἰς τὸ ὄρος (3:13) Since Jesus is not named, an antecedent from the previous passage is required: ὁ υἱὸς τοῦ θεοῦ ascends the mountain. The intertextual background is likely Exod 24[1] where God calls

---

[1] Joel Marcus, *Mark 1–8: A New Translation with Introduction and Commentary*, AB 27 (New York: Doubleday, 2000), 266, is only one of several who suggest a new-Moses typology here. But the likelihood of a new-Moses motif is diminished by Mark 9:2–9. There Mark excludes both a new-Moses and a returned-Elijah identity for Jesus. Both Elijah and Moses appear (9:4) along with the transfigured Jesus. Jesus is designated the beloved Son by the voice from heaven (9:7).

Moses and the leaders have fellowship with YHWH on the mountain.[1] If this is so, then the picture here is not of God calling Moses and creating a people, but of Jesus, the Holy One of God, calling and re-creating the holy people of God centered on God. The Twelve represent God's newly reconstituted people.

The threefold reason for the appointment is set out. Crucially they are called to be with him. God's people are holy only in relation to the holiness of God; theirs is a derived holiness. Being with the Holy One of God is central to their identity.[2] Second, they are to announce the good news, and are ἔχειν ἐξουσίαν ἐκβάλλειν τὰ δαιμόνια (Mark 3:15). They are called to enter into the cosmic dimension of the struggle that Jesus himself enters.

The second scene centers on Jesus's family. Opposition is growing and spreads even to Jesus's blood relations. They become outsiders and wish to take Jesus home (see Mark 3:19b-21, 31-35). Their separation from Jesus and his mission is highlighted by Mark's language here: they are ἔξω ἑστῶτες (3:31). Meanwhile, a crowd of unlikely followers are those who are αὐτὸν κύκλῳ καθημένους (3:34). The response of Jesus to his family is blunt: τίς ἐστιν ἡ μήτηρ μου καὶ οἱ ἀδελφοί; (3:33) They are those who do τὸ θέλημα τοῦ θεοῦ (3:35). This is Mark's only use of this phrase, but its meaning emerges from the narrative: it refers to God's mission (1:14-15) through Jesus, the Holy One of God (1:24).

Jesus's statement is a breath-taking challenge to barriers. His deliberate inclusion of women within the circle around him (see Mark 15:41) is countercultural but characteristic. Those on the outside—the unclean, the marginalized including women, the demonized, tax collectors and sinners—have been brought into the circle of the restored people who do the will of God. In turn, the identity of the people of God is determined rather straightforwardly: They are those who do God's will.

---

[1] Collins, *Mark*, 215.

[2] In Mark, Jesus's disciples illustrate the risk of independent mission (Mark 9:14-29) or acting as gatekeepers (see 9:38-40; 10:13-14). The authority and power to carry out this mission come from God.

The Voice of Legion (Mark 5:11)

The fifth voice is another identification from the spirit world: Legion calls Jesus υἱὸς τοῦ θεοῦ τοῦ ὑψίστου (Mark 5:7). At first sight, the inclusion of this story might seem surprising. We have already heard the unclean spirit (1:24), and have read the summative declaration (3:11). The previous story has Jesus acting as Yahweh is depicted in scripture with mastery over the sea, but the disciples are still unclear about Jesus's identity. For Mark, this episode adds to the answer to the disciples' question from the preceding story, Τίς ἄρα οὗτός ἐστιν (4:41).[1] Mark's purpose becomes clearer once we follow his narrative clues.

The location is interesting. Not only is it Gentile territory; it may have been near the barracks of a Roman garrison, probably accounting for the swine nearby. The self-identification of the demon, Λεγεὼν ὄνομά μοι, ὅτι πολλοί ἐσμεν (Mark 5:9), is also highly evocative. No first century reader of Mark could avoid evoking an image of the Roman military. That power undergirded the multi-faceted domination of Rome over her territories in economic and social terms that, metaphorically, bound the client states and their inhabitants just as surely as Legion held this man in captivity in a death-dominated place.[2] This environment is hostile: this man bound in a place epitomising impurity and opposition to the kingdom of God.

On the one hand, the liberating word of Jesus transforms this demonized man from a dangerous opponent serving the forces

---

[1] See John R. Donahue and Daniel J. Harrington, *The Gospel of Mark*, SP 2 (Collegeville, MN: Liturgical, 2002), 165.

[2] See Brower, *Mark*, 145–48. The Book of Revelation is overtly set against the context of the Rome, symbolically depicted as Babylon through a creative re-reading of selected prophetic texts. See Peter Oakes, "Revelation 17.1–19.10: A Prophetic Vision of the Destruction of Rome," in *The Future of Rome: Roman, Greek, Jewish and Christian Perspectives*, ed. Jonathan Price and Katell Berthelot (Cambridge: Cambridge University, forthcoming). See also Richard Bauckham, *The Theology of Revelation*, New Testament Theology (Cambridge: Cambridge University, 1993) and Dean Flemming, "'On Earth as It Is in Heaven': Holiness and the People of God in Revelation," in *Holiness and Ecclesiology in the New Testament*, ed. Kent E. Brower and Andy Johnson (Grand Rapids: Eerdmans, 2007), 343–62.

of evil into a witness to the work of God in Jesus (ὅσα σοι ὁ κύριος πεποίηκεν; Mark 5:19). This is important in itself. On the other hand, the implications are far broader. The kingdoms of this world — in this case, the Roman Empire — are a mere parody of the kingdom of God. The exorcism of Legion and the fate of the swine, which plunge into the sea over which Jesus returns in perfect calm, shows Jesus to have authority over all of creation and to be triumphant over all powers, again a divine identity. The liberating power of the good news announced and effected by the Messiah on the mission of God is far more than spiritual liberation.

Mark uses a narrative inclusio of the two sea crossings to advance his portrayal of Jesus's divine identity and authority. Jesus calms the sea (Mark 4:37–41), and then returns to Galilee on a calm sea (5:21). Through this story, Mark reminds readers that the good news is not restricted to Galilee nor to the realm of the spiritual.

This is also descriptive of the mission of Jesus's followers. Jesus, the Holy One of God, enters the worst imaginable context of impurity: swine, idolatry, oppression, and unclean spirits. His holiness does not need to be protected. It is his intrinsic character. Shortly after this, Jesus's followers, who are holy only in relation to him, are sent out on mission and to share in his authority. Like Jesus, they enter into the haunts of evil and oppression and, through the derived power and authority of the Holy One, people are transformed (Mark 6:7–13, 30). Their mission is his mission is God's mission because Jesus is the embodiment of God's mission.

The Call to Cross-bearing Servanthood (Mark 8:34–38)

The gradual revelation of the identity of Jesus culminated in the revelatory confession by Peter that Jesus is the Messiah. But the content of Jesus's messiahship was in stark contrast to the expectations of the disciples. Jesus reinterprets as a suffering-son-of-man messiahship. The revelation of Jesus's identity has gone hand in hand with that of the identity of the (re)new(ed) people of God, starting with his call of the four, and ending with the global redefinition of the family of God: whoever does the will of God (Mark 3:34).

This redefinition did not, as yet, have content to it. On the one hand, it was corporate – the gathered people around the Holy One of God on the mission of God were those who were doing the will of God. To this point, their engagement with the mission of God (Mark 6:7–13, 30–32) has been a success. But after the confession of Jesus's identity, both his path and that of his followers take a decidedly bleak turn. The content of following on the way is unveiled to them on the theological and geographical journey from Caesarea Philippi to Jericho (8:34–10:52).

Immediately after the first passion prediction (Mark 8:31-33), Jesus's explicit teaching to his disciples begins. But Mark clearly intends that all of his readers should be listening; he brings the crowd on the scene not just to hear Jesus's teaching, but to receive it. This is for all would-be followers. Thus, it is intensely personal as well as corporate.

The call is stark: ἀράτω τὸν σταυρὸν αὐτοῦ καὶ ἀκολουθείτω (Mark 8:34). Dietrich Bonhoeffer famously noted that "when Christ calls a man, He bids him come and die."[1] This is more than abandoning selfishness. Jesus calls would-be followers to give their lives ἕνεκεν ἐμοῦ καὶ τοῦ εὐαγγελίου (8:35). "They are to be more than mere martyrs for a cause. They are to be participants in the announcement of the good news along with Jesus."[2] This is the cost of following Jesus in doing the will of God in the mission of God. The fate of disciples mirrors Jesus's own fate. The proclamation of the kingdom is costly.

By addressing the crowds, the Markan Jesus dispels any notion that cross-bearing servanthood is reserved for the inner circle, however inscribed. There are no part-time disciples. Rather,

> discipleship calls for the total commitment of the entire
> person to Jesus and his message of all who would follow

---

[1] Dietrich Bonhoeffer, *The Cost of Discipleship*, trans. Reginald H. Fuller (London: SCM, 1959), 9.
[2] Brower, *Mark*, 235.

him…. [I]t is an open and unreserved commitment to the mission and person of Christ. If we intend to participate in the mission of the Son of Man, we cannot set arbitrary limits.[1]

The Voice from Heaven (Mark 9:7)

Our penultimate section focuses on the second instance of a voice from heaven.[2] Together with the confession at Caesarea Philippi, the transfiguration forms matching stories that disclose Jesus's identity and reveal the direction of God's mission.

Mark tells the story from the perspective of the disciples. To be sure, the three should already have known Jesus's identity. But they have not perceived what they have seen nor understood what they have heard (see 8:13–21). At crucial points (5:36; 14:33) Jesus takes Peter, James, and John with him. Now he leads them up a high mountain.[3] The revelation that the disciples are about to receive is a glimpse beyond the apparent weakness of the suffering Son of Man, on the one hand, and the fear of cross-bearing discipleship on the other. It will allow them to see the bigger picture of God's ultimate purposes, somewhat like the opened eyes of the seer in Rev 4:1.

The voice from the cloud speaks, but all attention is focused on Jesus. Here is the "sign from heaven" that the Pharisees demanded in Mark 8:11, but it is not given to "this generation" (8:12). Rather, it comes to his followers. The crowds may think he is John the Baptist or Elijah or one of the prophets (8:28). But he is none of these. In Mark, John fulfills the role of Elijah, and he appears on the mountain. A prophet like Moses was expected, but Jesus is neither Moses nor the prophet like Moses. Although Moses'

---

[1] Ibid, 239–40.

[2] We have now come to the end of what Dorothy Lee calls a "procession of voices." Dorothy Lee, *Transfiguration*, New Century Theology (London: Continuum, 2004), 11.

[3] Lee, *Transfiguration*, 15 calls this a mountain of God, a "thin place," as a metaphor of Celtic spirituality would call it, "at the boundary between heaven and earth, 'on the outskirts of heaven.'"

face shone when he descended from Sinai, this "text seems to imply that Jesus' transfigured state is part of the revelation, rather than a result of it."[1] For Mark, the transfigured one is of an order different from Moses: He is God's beloved Son. Significantly, here the voice does not address Jesus, but the three disciples. The voice from heaven has already confirmed Jesus's identity for Jesus himself and Mark's readers (1:11). Now, the voice confirms Jesus's identity to the disciples: Οὗτός ἐστιν ὁ υἱός μου ὁ ἀγαπητός. They are emphatically commanded: αὐτοῦ ἀκούετε (9:7).

The heavenly voice confirms that the path announced by Jesus is God's intended purpose. Although Peter' confession that Jesus is the Messiah is correct, Jesus's messianic identity must be nuanced: he is the Son-of-Man-must-suffer kind of Messiah. Peter speaks for all the disciples when he rejects this re-definition (Mark 8:31–33). But when Jesus calls would-be disciples to take up the cross after him, he is making clear the way of God, not any human direction. Jesus's way of the Messiah is the way for would-be disciples.

The transfiguration clearly confirms that the identity of the suffering Son of Man, who will be the Crucified One, and the glorious, beloved Son of the Father, the Holy One of God, are identical. The transfiguration is linked to the cross, where the identity of Jesus as Son of God is finally disclosed. He is the one hanging on a Roman cross.

> Mark's point is not just that Jesus engages radically with human suffering but rather that the beloved Son, revealed in heavenly glory and beauty on the mountain, is the harbinger of God's future, and the suffering Son of Man, dying in desolation on the cross, are one and the same person.[2]

---

[1] Collins, *Mark*, 417.

[2] Lee, *Transfiguration*, 32. As Craig Evans, *Mark 8:27–16:24*, WBC 34B (Waco: Word, 2001), 38, writes, "Only Jesus, not the great prophet Elijah or the great lawgiver Moses, can accomplish God's redemptive plan."

All this is confirmed by the voice from the cloud. But this time the voice is not for Jesus. Rather, it is for the three disciples. Disciples of Jesus need to heed his interpretation of Messiah, because he is the beloved Son who announces the will of God (see Mark 3:31–35).

The Voice at the Cross (Mark 15:39)

The final voice for our consideration comes from the cross. Jesus's voice is heard at least once[1] when he cries with a loud voice, cites Ps 22:2, and then, Ἰησοῦς ἀφεὶς φωνὴν μεγάλην ἐξέπνευσεν (Mark 15:37). It is this, ὅτι οὕτως ἐξέπνευσεν (15:39a), that leads to the culminating statement of Jesus's identity by the Roman centurion, Ἀληθῶς ὁ ἄνθρωπος οὗτος υἱὸς ἦν θεοῦ (15:39b). The focus of this final section is on the centurion's statement.[2]

The centurion's confession (Mark 15:39) is controversial.[3] Three translations are possible: "Surely this man was the Son of God!" (NIV), "Truly this man was God's Son!" (NRSV), or "Truly this man was a son of a god!" in keeping with Luke's version: "Surely this was a righteous man" (Luke 23:47 NIV). Seeking to ascertain precisely what the centurion said and meant is a fruitless quest with no definitive conclusion possible. Fortunately, this debate is interesting, but, in the end, irrelevant.

The crucifixion scene must be read at two levels. On the level of the events, it is unremittingly bleak: in addition to the horror of the scene itself, the foreboding darkness at noon, the cry from the cross, and the death of the messiah. But at the readers' level, the story is deeply ironic, culminating in the words of the centurion. In the passion narrative "we are not dealing with strict history but rather a creatively and theologically driven (or focused)

---

[1] Some argue that Mark 15:37 refers to 15:33.

[2] I have written extensive elsewhere on the so-called "Cry of Dereliction." See my "Elijah in the Markan Passion Narrative," *JSNT* 18 (1983): 85–101; and *Mark*, 397–402.

[3] For a comprehensive discussion, see now Brian K. Gamel, *Mark 15:39 as a Markan Theology of Revelation: The Centurion's Confession as Apocalyptic Unveiling*, LNTS 574 (London: Bloomsbury T&T Clark, 2017). See also Brower, *Mark*, 403–5.

literary retelling of Jesus' death. Historical figures become literary figures"[1] without in any sense diminishing the historical reality of the crucifixion. The centurion's role in the drama is exactly that — the crowning confession of Jesus's identity in Mark's narrative precisely as Jesus hangs on the cross and dies.

Everything that happens on that day is the action of God. The darkness at noon is over the whole earth, and the rending of the temple veil from top to bottom can only be a divine activity. For Brian Gamel, the rending of the temple curtain is decisive:[2] it is the "apocalyptic action of God."[3] On the historical level, the event is unconnected physically to the crucifixion. Its inclusion is theological, and readers know that is God's action. Significantly, the verb σχίζω is the same one used in 1:10. Gamel explains the rending as "a theophany so that in the divine abandonment of Jesus God is most fully present."[4] On the literary level, the centurion "is not just saying more than he understands – he understands more than he should know."[5] His confession is "stunning and unexpected."[6] But the darkness at noon over the whole earth is also the indisputable action of God. Even the placement of Jesus's death cry, "after the darkness at noon and before the rending of the temple veil"[7] is enclosed within divine action. This whole crucifixion story, including the cry of dereliction is within the action of God.

The deep irony comes from the juxtaposition of the story elements. It culminations in the irony that Jesus is confessed as the Son of God, a title that Caesar claims for himself, by a Roman centurion. "A pagan from a distant land becomes the first human in the gospel to grasp the height and depth of Jesus' identity. In doing so, he unwillingly fulfills the triumphant ending of the psalm whose searing words have punctuated the Markan death scene (cf.

---

[1] Gamel, *Mark 15:39 as a Markan Theology of Revelation*, 52.
[2] Ibid., 176.
[3] Ibid., 110.
[4] Ibid., 111.
[5] Ibid., 68.
[6] Ibid., 106.
[7] Brower, *Mark*, 400.

15:24, 29-32, 34)."¹ These words "locate Jesus' true identity in the divine sphere, something no other human character had hitherto done in Mark's gospel."² In contrast, the high priest witnesses the same thing but rejects Jesus's true identity as ὁ χριστός, ὁ υἱὸς τοῦ εὐλογητοῦ (14:61) as blasphemous.

This high christological reading is supported by the literary brackets of Mark 1:1 and 15:39. God again acts, but now "the confession is not the prospective announcement by God stating Jesus' being and mission, but the retrospective confirmation that Jesus has been precisely the Son of God in the whole gospel story and supremely so in the death scene. Jesus was never more truly Son of God than when He died."³

Conclusions

The voice from heaven speaks twice in Mark (1:11; 9:7), identifying Jesus as the embodiment of Israel's God who is renewing and recreating his people for his mission. Other voices are also used by Mark for identifying Jesus and his mission as well as the people of God.

This essay situates the coming of Jesus firmly within the expectations of God's restoration of the people of God for a divine mission in God's created order. Jesus's identity as the Son of God, the Holy One of God, is the basis for Jesus's proclamation and the initial calling of disciples. Jesus sets about the re-creation of God's people for mission, leading to Jesus's summoning them to the mountain. The wider identity of God's people is, in turned, stripped of ethnocentricity: the people of God are those who do the will of God (Mark 3:35). Successful mission (6:7-13, 30-31) and the pivotal recognition of Jesus's identity as Messiah (8:27-30) follow, but the

---

[1] Joel Marcus, *Mark 8–16: A New Translation with Introduction and Commentary*, AB 27A (New Haven: Yale University, 2009), 1068.

[2] Gamel, *Mark 15:39 as a Markan Theology of Revelation*, 52.

[3] Brower, "Let the Reader Understand: Temple and Eschatology in Mark," in *The Reader Must Understand: Eschatology in Bible and Theology*, ed. K. E. Brower and Mark Elliott (Leicester: IVP Apollos, 1997), 233.

disciples struggle to accept the significance for themselves that follows on from Jesus's identity. They resist following in cross-bearing servanthood. But the voice from heaven commands them to listen to the beloved son. Jesus is the one who is thinking divine thoughts, not human thoughts, and the way of discipleship is to follow the suffering-son-of-man messiah on the way. The journey ends on a Roman cross in the holy city of Jerusalem and culminates in the confession of the centurion that the identity of Jesus of Nazareth in the redemptive purposes of God was seen most clearly in the deeply ironic death scene in which the very structure of the story confirms that, for Mark, the Pauline statement that "God was in Christ reconciling the world to himself" (2 Cor. 5:19) is visible in the death scene itself.

A generation ago, it was fashionable to argue that New Testament Christology moved from functional to ontic as it was translated from Jewish to Gentile contexts.[1] But thanks to careful attention to gospel narrative, a more nuanced understanding of the Second Temple background, and fresh approaches through narrative intertextuality, the picture of Jesus in the Gospels is now seen to be the genesis of the incarnational and Trinitarian doctrines of the church fathers. And like those first disciples, we are called into a relationship with the Holy One of God so that we might be part of God's mission within God's vast creation.

---

[1] See, e.g., Reginald H. Fuller, *The Foundations of New Testament Christology* (London: Lutterworth, 1965), 173. For a coherent description of the state of play at that time, see Ralph P. Martin, *Mark: Evangelist and Theologian* (Exeter: Paternoster, 1972).

Reading Three of Mark's Stories Featuring Women with Care[1]

Kara J. Lyons-Pardue

*– a daughter who has always known herself
to be loved by God and by her dad –*

For Christian readers of Scripture who seek to read the Bible with eyes of faith, there are some stories that confound our best attempts to make theological meaning or apply the messages to our life. The Old Testament is the most common object of pious Christian shoulder shrugs or excuse-making. For example, stories of Hagar (Gen 16:1-16; 21:9-21) or the Levite's concubine (Judg 19) — famously termed "texts of terror" by pioneering feminist interpreter Phyllis Trible — are tales full of senseless violence and tragedy for the featured female characters.[2] Although the First Testament is the more frequent target of frustrations over brutality toward women, children, and the stranger, stories in the New Testament are near matches or, at minimum, leave the reader perplexed. This paper operates under the conviction that these discomfiting passages (1) are better dealt with head-on than ignored; (2) have much in common and share points of illumination with more traditionally satisfying passages, so that reading in concert is helpful; and (3) are preserved in Scripture as a form of testimony, perhaps even as protest, that bear witness to injustice and exclusion. Even in the

---

[1] I presented an earlier version of this piece at Fresno Pacific University (March 28, 2019) as part of the Janzen Lectureship in Biblical Studies. I am grateful for the warm welcome and the feedback I received in that process.

[2] Phyllis Trible, *Texts of Terror: Literary-Feminist Readings of Biblical Narratives* (Philadelphia: Fortress, 1984).

absence of explicit condemnation of wrongdoing, bearing witness can be its own form of activism.

This essay takes its scope from the intersections of three terms in Mark's Gospel: daughter (θυγάτηρ), little daughter (θυγάτριον), and little girl (κοράσιον). In the whole New Testament, the only two occurrences of the diminutive form of daughter, θυγάτριον, are found in Mark. In varying configurations, at least two of these terms appear in each of three Markan pericopae: the intercalated story of Jesus's healings of the hemorrhaging woman and Jairus's daughter (Mark 5:21-43), the beheading of John the Baptist (6:14-29), and Jesus's encounter with the Syrophoenician woman (7:24-30). These daughters in Mark 5—7 have been the focus of recent studies by Sharon Betsworth and F. Scott Spencer. [1] And, although a variety of approaches to women and gender in Mark have become increasingly a focus of scholarly studies,[2] these treatments come after many centuries of scholarly neglect.

My claim is that Mark's use of diminutives, whether "little daughter" or "little girl," has the effect of establishing empathy on the narrative level and forging connections between these three

---

[1] Sharon Betsworth, *The Reign of God is Such as These: A Socio-Literary Analysis of the Daughters in the Gospel of Mark*, LNTS 422 (New York: T&T Clark, 2010); and F. Scott Spencer, *Dancing Girls, Loose Ladies, and Women of the Cloth: The Women in Jesus' Life* (New York: Continuum, 2004), 47-75. His focus in the third chapter is the story of Herodias and her daughter, but he finds connections between that account and others in this three-chapter span in the Markan Gospel: "where women lead men" (51). He positions his study among those in a line of feminist-critical treatments that have reinvestigated biblical stories about women (48-49). Joel Marcus also connects the three pericopae (*Mark 1-8*, AB 27 [New York: Doubleday, 1999], 403), as does Susan Miller (*Women in Mark's Gospel*, JSNTSup 259 [New York: T&T Clark, 2004], 73).

[2] E.g., Miller, *Women in Mark's Gospel*; Hisako Kinukawa, *Women and Jesus in Mark? A Japanese Feminist Perspective* (Maryknoll, NY: Orbis, 1994); Joan L. Mitchell, *Beyond Fear and Silence: A Feminist-Literary Approach to the Gospel of Mark* (New York: Continuum, 2001); James A. Kelhoffer, "A Tale of Two Markan Characterizations: The Exemplary Woman Who Anointed Jesus's Body for Burial (14:3-9) and the Silent Trio Who Fled the Empty Tomb (16:1-8)," in *Women and Gender in Ancient Religions: Interdisciplinary Approaches*, ed. Stephen P. Ahearne-Kroll et al, WUNT 263 (Tübingen: Mohr Siebeck, 2010), 85-98.

disparate stories. It is true that "little girl" may overstate the smallness inferred by the diminutive. The term κοράσιον, for example, certainly refers to an unmarried young woman within a range of ages, probably through her early teenage years.[1] Yet in each story in which these feminine diminutives appear, callousness or abuse of power stands in sharp contrast to the readers' triggered response of compassion for the vulnerable children. Several Old Testament echoes — some faint whispers, others blaring loudly — form a backdrop that reinforces the contrast between righteous care for daughters and their exploitation or devaluing. Finally, the act of remembering and telling, here enshrined in Scripture, is itself an act of defiance to the silencing or hiding of women's stories of pain and mistreatment, which endures to this day.

---

[1] See references to Esther and the other women in King Artaxerxes's (LXX)/Ahasuerus's (MT) harem, who are called κοράσια (Esth 2:2-3, 7-9, 12 LXX), at least until their turn to "go in to" (εἰσελθεῖν) the king (2:12). The seven-times wed — but still a virgin, as none of the marriages are consummated — Sarah in LXX Tobit is called κοράσιον twice (6:12, 14). In Ruth, the widow gleans among the κοράσια (young women/servant girls) of Boaz (Ruth 2:8, 22-23; 3:2 LXX), but is not herself described as a κοράσιον (as a widow). In some texts, the line between maiden and maid, so to speak, is unclear (LXX 1 Sam 9:11-12). In others, κοράσιον clearly refers to a slave girl or hired girl (1 Sam 25:42 LXX). In this way, it is analogous to παῖς, which can refer to someone's small child (e.g., Matt 2:16; Luke 2:43) or to a slave or servant (e.g., Matt 8:6; Luke 12:45; Acts 3:13). In fact, παῖς is used of Jairus's daughter in Luke's rendition, paralleling Mark 5:21-23, 35-43 (Luke 8:51, 54).

Table 1: The instances of θυγάτηρ, θυγάτριον, and κοράσιον in Mark

	θυγάτριον	θυγάτηρ	κοράσιον
INTERCALATED STORIES OF JAIRUS AND THE WOMAN WITH A HEMORRHAGE (Mark 5:21–43)			
Mark 5:23 (Jairus to Jesus)	τὸ θυγάτριόν μου ἐσχάτως ἔχει my little daughter has [reached the] end		
Mark 5:34 (Jesus to Woman with a Hemorrhage)		θυγάτηρ, ἡ πίστις σου σέσωκέν σε· Daughter, your faith has saved you;	
Mark 5:35 (People from Jairus's household to Jairus)		ὅτι ἡ θυγάτηρ σου ἀπέθανεν· because your daughter died.	
Mark 5:41 (Jesus to Jairus's daughter)			τὸ κοράσιον, σοὶ λέγω, ἔγειρε Little girl, I say to you, get up!
Mark 5:42 (Narrator, about Jairus's daughter)			εὐθὺς ἀνέστη τὸ κοράσιον καὶ περιεπάτει immediately the little girl arose and was walking around

| | θυγάτριον | θυγάτηρ | κοράσιον |

ACCOUNT OF JOHN THE BAPTIST'S EXECUTION (Mark 6:14–29)

	θυγάτριον	θυγάτηρ	κοράσιον
Mark 6:22 (Narrator, about Herodias's daughter)		εἰσελθούσης τῆς θυγατρὸς αὐτοῦ Ἡρῳδιάδος after <u>his daughter Herodias</u> entered	
(Narrator, about Herod's speech to the child)			εἶπεν ὁ βασιλεὺς τῷ κορασίῳ the king said to the little girl
Mark 6:28 (Narrator, about the executioner's actions)			ἔδωκεν αὐτὴν τῷ κορασίῳ he gave it to the little girl
(Narrator, about the child's actions)			τὸ κοράσιον ἔδωκεν αὐτὴν τῇ μητρὶ αὐτῆς the little girl gave it to her mother

| | θυγάτριον | θυγάτηρ | κοράσιον |

STORY OF JESUS'S ENCOUNTER WITH THE SYROPHOENICIAN WOMAN (Mark 7:24–30)

	θυγάτριον	θυγάτηρ	κοράσιον
Mark 7:25 (Narrator, about the Syrophoenician woman)	ἧς εἶχεν τὸ θυγάτριον αὐτῆς πνεῦμα ἀκάθαρτον whose little daughter was having an unclean spirit		
Mark 7:26 (Narrator, about the Syrophoenician woman's intention)		ἵνα τὸ δαιμόνιον ἐκβάλῃ ἐκ τῆς θυγατρὸς αὐτῆς in order that he might cast the demon from her daughter	
Mark 7:29 (Jesus to the Syrophoenician woman)		ἐξελήλυθεν ἐκ τῆς θυγατρός σου τὸ δαιμόνιον. The demon has departed from your daughter.	

Reading Three Stories of Little Daughters in Light of Power and Vulnerability

At first glance, one of these stories seems quite unlike the others. The lengthy account of John the Baptist's beheading gives the impression of a horror story, not a tale of good news. Further, although Jesus is the main actor in the healing narratives in chapters 5 and 7, Jesus is not present in the account of John's death. Whereas there is positive resolution for both Jesus and his supplicants in the healing stories, the same outcome does not transpire for John. Mark does not soften or moralize the story of John's execution, which he recounts with comparatively great detail. We tend to think of the woman with the hemorrhage, Jairus's daughter, the Syrophoenician woman and her daughter as victims who become exemplars of faithfulness. In contrast, Herodias and her daughter are usually read as villains.[1]

Beyond the common vocabulary in focus, the three passages have in common a remarkable degree of omniscience on the part of the narrator. Mark knows the hemorrhaging woman's intentions (Mark 5:27-28) and personal history (5:25-26). In the tale of John's demise, Mark recounts things happening away from the main narrative plane of action and courtly happenings to which commoners would have had no access (6:17-29). The narrator has access both to Herod's preferences (6:20, 26), fears (6:20), and internal judgments (6:14b, 22, 26), as well as Herodias's schemes (6:19, 24). Finally, Mark is able to describe Jesus's unspoken wishes as he travels to Tyre (7:24b) and internal sensations (5:30).

The first set of stories, the intercalated stories of Jesus's healings of the woman plagued by a hemorrhage for twelve years and of the twelve-year-old daughter of Jairus, is the only one of these three pericopae that contains each of the three terms under study: θυγάτηρ, θυγάτριον, and κοράσιον. For my reading, its tone establishes our reading priorities for the remaining two episodes featuring "little daughters." It is, in fact, the middle pericope,

---

[1] For example, Betsworth states of Herodias and her daughter: "This evil mother and daughter are juxtaposed in the Gospel with the stories of faithful parents and daughters, and the contrast is quite vivid ..." (*Reign of God*, 126). Other interpreters emphasize especially the complex situation of Herodias and her daughter, even as they note their negative characterization (e.g., Spencer, *Dancing Girls*, 52-57, 67).

featuring a royal banquet, scandalous behavior, and ending with the death of Jesus's forerunner, that most needs our interpretive attention: we will, therefore, save it for last. For if Mark is telling us a story in which some little girls are very, very good and others are very, very bad, then we need not proceed much farther than the morality of nursery rhymes in which little girls are supposed to be sugar, spice, and everything nice. Indeed, one requires little more than the conventional virgin/whore paradigm to make sense of Mark's theological vision of womanhood and family life if Herodias's daughter is merely to be read as devious. But if Mark stands in a trajectory of biblical story-telling in which narratives are caught up in a larger story of God's redemption in the world and testimonies are preserved because they are worth hearing and sensing reverberations, we may have more interpretive work to do.

In Mark 5:22-23, the synagogue leader Jairus approaches Jesus and begs him for help,[1] describing his little daughter (τὸ θυγάτριόν μου) as near the end of her life. He entrusts the fate of his vulnerable child to Jesus, inviting Jesus to come lay his hands on her so that she might live. Jesus obliges (5:24). It is difficult to determine the degree of authority and notoriety we should ascribe to Jairus. Being a synagogue leader (ἀρχισυνάγωγος) of a small village would

---

[1] Mark 5 has something of a pleading theme, as Jesus has already had several encounters with entities who "beg" or "urge" (παρακαλέω) him. The word appears four times outside of the chapter (Mark 1:40; 6:56; 7:32; 8:22), but the concentration of five uses in chapter 5 alone indicates a thematic emphasis. In 5:10, the man possessed of Legion begs (παρεκάλει)—apparently on behalf of the unclean spirits—not to be sent far away. Jesus's response to this petition is unclear, because before he has the opportunity to respond, the unclean spirits speak for themselves (5:12). They begin to plead (παρεκάλεσαν) to be sent into the nearby swine, a request that Jesus grants. Then, after seeing the man who was formerly demon-possessed and learning the dire fate of the herd of swine, the townspeople beg (παρακαλεῖν) Jesus to leave their region (5:17), which he does (5:18-20). The man who had experienced the exorcism then pleads (παρεκάλει) with Jesus that he might follow him as a disciple (5:18); Jesus denies his request (5:19). When, in 5:22-23, Jairus falls at Jesus's feet and begs him again and again (παρακαλεῖ αὐτὸν πολλά) to come and heal his daughter, Jesus's response to the last entreaty of this chapter is not guaranteed.

not require anything like aristocratic status. Nevertheless, it places him as a person of prestige within the sphere of his local community.¹ As such, he is perhaps the only person of any elevated status in his community whom Mark records as approaching Jesus with a request for healing intervention.² Jairus's daughter is clearly a treasured and valued member of her family, a family that was likewise valued within their community. When she dies (5:35), Jesus encounters an assembly of mourners, gathered to weep over her passing (5:38-39). The sincerity of their mourning may be in question, as they are able to laugh at Jesus, who insists that the dead girl is only sleeping (5:39-40). Once Jesus has the girl's parents, three of his disciples, and the dead little girl alone in the room, he addresses her directly.³

Jesus's terms of address to the dead girl mirror the diminutive characteristics of her father's description of her. Mark retains Jesus's Aramaic in transliteration—ταλιθα—which he says is in translation, "Little girl [τὸ κοράσιον]" (Mark 5:41). Jesus's command to the little girl—κουμ—Mark glosses into Greek as "I am saying to you, 'Arise!'" Not only are there terminological connections between what the girl is commanded to do, ἐγείρω, and prior successful healings Jesus has undertaken already in Mark's narrative (1:31; 2:9, 11-12; 3:3), but it also betokens a crucial event in Jesus's own future (14:28; 16:6). A further indication of the significance of Jesus's pronouncement is sometimes excluded from translations, perhaps perceived as redundant, "I am saying to you [σοὶ λέγω]" (5:41). In Mark, Jesus most often uses that phrase to

---

[1] On this, see Betsworth, *Reign of God*, 111.

[2] Of course, news of Jesus travels to royal circles, as we find out in the next chapter (Mark 6:14). Jesus has encounters and debates with leaders of various Jewish groups (e.g., 7:1-5; 10:2-12; 12:18-27) and rises to the attention (albeit negative) of the high priestly caste (14:1-2, 53, 55-65). Still, none of these people come to Jesus as supplicants.

[3] Betsworth elaborates, "Mark also emphasizes the centrality of the girl by referring to her directly seven times in 5.39-42.... The repetition of 'child' and 'girl' keeps the focus of Jesus' action on the daughter" (*Reign of God*, 110).

introduce significant teaching,[1] and only one other time in a healing story.[2] Here, Mark's translation of Jesus's words to the little girl grants them significance; this significance is reflected in the outcome, as well. Immediately, the little girl gets up[3] and begins to walk around. The ensuing amazement is extreme (ἐξέστησαν … ἐκστάσει μεγάλῃ; lit.: "they were amazed with great amazement").[4]

It is only in verse 42 that we learn the age of the "little girl," twelve years-old. Jairus's "little daughter" is on the cusp of womanhood. The detail of "twelve years" (ἐτῶν δώδεκα) is significant, of course, because it points us back to the story lodged in the middle of that of Jairus's quest to secure Jesus's intervention

---

[1] This is in no way a phenomenon limited to Mark's telling of Jesus's story, but it is a characteristic way that Jesus speaks throughout the canonical Gospels. However, I will only survey Mark for the following reflections. Frequently, Jesus introduces important claims when teaching with some combination of λέγω and σύ (always in the dative, usually in the plural, ὑμῖν): Mark 3:28; 8:12; 9:1, 13, 41; 10:15, 29; 11:23, 24, 33; 12:43; 13:30, 37; 14:9, 18, 25. It is intriguing then, at the tomb, that the young man confirms to the women that Jesus has been raised and has gone into Galilee "just as he told you," as the phrasing confirms that things that Jesus "says to you" (as here) come to be: καθὼς εἶπεν ὑμῖν (16:7).

[2] In the story of Jesus's healing of the man with paralysis, he instructs the man, "I am saying to you [σοὶ λέγω], arise [ἔγειρε], pick up your mat, and go to your home" (Mark 2:11). The first three words in Greek of that instruction are exactly the same as Mark's translation of Jesus's Aramaic phrase: σοὶ λέγω, ἔγειρε (5:41).

[3] The word ἀνίστημι is used to describe her "getting up." Like ἐγείρω, the word is used both in mundane (e.g., Mark 1:35; 2:14; 7:24; 10:1) and christologically significant (e.g., 8:31; 9:9–10, 31; 10:34; 16:9) ways in Mark. Marcus also notes this linguistic foreshadowing (*Mark 1–8*, 372).

[4] Such amazement is a hallmark of Mark's narration of Jesus's activities (Mark 2:12; 3:21; 6:51; 16:8). A variety of terms beyond these two from the ἐκ + ἵστημι stem connote an emphatic response of wonder, sometimes tipping into the realm of fear (θαυμάζω; θαυμαστός; ἐκθαμβέω; ἀπορέω). Intriguingly, the term used here can be used pejoratively as well (see 3:21). Jesus's command that they must remain silent about the amazing restoration of their daughter to life (5:43) is typical in miracle stories. This is certainly, and famously, so in Mark (e.g., 1:44; 7:36; 8:30), but also conveyed by the other Synoptic Gospels (e.g., Matt 9:30; Luke 8:56). See, e.g., Wilhelm Wrede, *The Messianic Secret*, trans. J. C. G. Greig (Cambridge: James Clarke, 1971).

on behalf of his "little daughter" (ἦν γὰρ ἐτῶν δώδεκα). Mark has apparently kept these stories entangled together because there is something further to be understood about Jesus within the intercalation, or sandwiching, that each story on its own could not have conveyed. If their arrangement were not sufficient to indicate that they should be read in concert, the minute detail of the twelve years clinches their connection, both to one another[1] and, symbolically, to God's purposes for redeeming humankind.[2]

My summary of Jesus's healing of Jairus's daughter bypassed the lengthy episode sandwiched inside it. While Jesus is following Jairus to his home, initially, he is intercepted by what seems to be an inconsequential touch (Mark 5:24, 30–31). We meet a woman who has been living with an unceasing flow of blood for twelve years (5:25). Any help she sought from physicians had only worsened her conditions, and she had expended all her resources while seeking their help (5:26). So, after hearing about Jesus, she trusted that touching his clothes would be sufficient for her healing (vv. 27–28). Her story deserves a longer hearing—one that our treatment cannot afford her but that Jesus himself gives her (5:33) when she tells him "the whole truth" (πᾶσαν τὴν ἀλήθειαν)—but when Jesus responds to her, he affirms her faith and calls her "daughter" (θυγάτηρ). In fact, although it is ultimately clear that salvation (i.e., the total restoration of her whole self) comes through Jesus, Jesus's pronouncement of that restoration credits the woman: "Daughter, your faith has saved you" (5:34, emphasis mine). This

---

[1] Indeed, Mark uses the conjunction γάρ to speak of the age of the restored daughter (Mark 5:42). It is not obvious how this usually causal conjunction relates to the preceding statement. A child can often walk (the preceding clause: "and she began to walk around"/καὶ περιεπάτει) at twelve *months*, not years! If γάρ is functioning causally, Mark might be explaining the preceding statement by adding that the "little girl" was not a baby who could not walk on her own. Given its position near the conclusion of a carefully intercalated story pair, it is possible that a causal conjunction intimates that something in the situation and the resulting amazement had to do with the twelve-year connection between Jairus's daughter and the woman with a hemorrhage.

[2] Betsworth catalogues a variety of interpretations on the significance of the number twelve (*Reign of God*, 6–7, 108–9).

woman, whose ability to participate fully in the religious life of her people and whose economic life has been upended by her particular illness,[1] is made right. Her full reestablishment to bodily health was something she sensed internally (5:29, 33), but her reinstatement fully as a member of her community and of God's family is something that Jesus conveyed with the title, "Daughter" (θυγάτηρ). Jesus's urgency to figure out what happened to the power that went out from him (5:30, 32) and to convey peace to the trembling woman echoes that of Jairus's concern for his own beloved daughter. These two daughters, one young and full of potential, evidently embraced by her community, and the other whose

---

[1] The precise diagnosis of this woman and its implications for ritual purity are the subject of scholarly debate. See, e.g., Betworth, *Reign of God*, 5, 102 n 23. Marcus argues against those who see more strict restrictions on women with vaginal discharge as a later rabbinic development—thereby taking the Temple Scroll as reflecting reality rather than merely utopian—"As a *zābâ* [lit. "oozer"; a woman with discharge beyond her period] the woman would probably have been quarantined, since *zābôt* and *niddôt* [menstruants] seem to have been treated in this way in Second Temple and later Judaism" (*Mark 1–8*, 357). In response to various ways to parse the law's applications, Spencer makes two important points. First, "[t]he fact is, none of these limitations has any relevance to the woman's case in Mark 5. She's by the Sea of Galilee, nowhere near the temple" (*Dancing Girls*, 59). And, second, "[h]owever we parse the Torah restrictions, the most telling point against a purity-oriented interpretation of the bleeding woman's story is that Mark says nothing about it" (60). Candida Moss draws from ancient understandings of physiology to note an important connection between Jesus and the woman: "[T]he curious flow of power from Jesus can tell us much about the physiological composition of the Markan protagonist. While many scholars have concentrated on the parallels between the woman with the flow of blood and Jairus's daughter, they have neglected the obvious comparison between Jesus and the woman. In the narrative, the flow of power from Jesus mirrors the flow of blood from the woman. Like the woman, Jesus is unable to control the flow of that emanates from his body. Like the flow of blood, the flow of power is something embodied and physical; just as the woman feels the flow of blood dry up, so Jesus feels physically the flow of power leave his body. Both the diseased woman with the flow of blood and the divine protagonist of Mark are porous, leaky creatures" (Candida Moss, "The Man with the Flow of Power: Porous Bodies in Mark 5:25–34," *JBL* 129 [2010]: 516). See also Moss's collection of scholarly sources on the purity debate (508 n 3).

potential seems utterly spent, financially and physically, are reintegrated as valued "daughters."

As we turn our attention to the final pericope in chapter 7, which features a "little daughter" (θυγάτριον), we encounter a Syrophoenician woman. Her ceaseless advocacy for her daughter, who remains off-stage in the narrative,[1] beset by unclean spirits, reflects — within Mark's depiction — the proper concern and care for one's daughter, one's child. The Evangelist's narration at this point echoes the tenderness we noted from Jairus's lips, as Mark calls the daughter of the Greek[2] Syrophoenician woman "little daughter" (θυγάτριον). After hearing about Jesus, who did not want to be found, the woman seeks him out. Mark describes her posture as one of honor, she prostrates herself at his feet (Mark 7:25). Mark tells us that she asks[3] Jesus to exorcise the demon from her daughter (θυγάτηρ).

Given the established care for "daughters," whether small or grown, that is evident in chapter 5, and Jesus's impressive resumé of exorcisms (Mark 1:26, 34, 39; 3:11; 5:13; 9:25; including vicarious ones: 6:13), a reader might expect that his most speedy and direct route back to the solitude he desires would be to follow the woman, or ask her to retrieve her little daughter, and then cast out the demon. But instead he deflects (7:27).[4] In doing so, he makes a statement that grants priority to children over dogs, seemingly privileging metaphorical children over the real daughter in real

---

[1] Jairus's daughter begins her narrative off-stage, too (see Mark 5:23), but is later at the center of the scene, although she never speaks (5:40-43).

[2] Mark calls her Ἑλληνίς, "Greek woman," by which he indicates her non-Jewish status.

[3] Although many modern English translations identify her request (Mark 7:26) as "begging" (NRSV, NIV, CEB, NLT, ESV), the Greek term is better rendered "asking" (ἐρωτάω) in her request (see NET, NASB, YLT), in contrast to Jairus's "urging" or "pleading" (cf. παρακαλέω in 5:22-23).

[4] About Jesus's initial refusal, Sharon H. Ringe says, "Christological biases aside, it is not the response that would be anticipated from any practitioner of healing when confronted with a situation of need" ("A Gentile Woman's Story, Revisited: Rereading Mark 7.24–31," in *A Feminist Companion to Mark*, ed. Amy-Jill Levine [Cleveland, OH: Pilgrim, 2001], 87).

need. Now, such a comment is arguably derisive and devaluing of the woman and her daughter. Many interpreters have taken up this question,[1] including this one.[2] But it is worth noting that the conversation is not over, not for Jesus nor for the intrepid mother.

Again, in this story, Jesus listens to the perspective of a woman, as he had with the woman who had been hemorrhaging for twelve years. In this instance, instead of the healing already having been completed and needing only a final word of affirmation from Jesus, here, Jesus's deferral is undone by what he hears from the woman. The woman, instead of decrying Jesus's canine inference, lets it stand. "Even the little dogs [κυνάριον] under the table," she says, "eat the children's tiny crumbs [ψιχίον]" (Mark 7:28). Instead of scarcity, if all that is needed is a crumb from the right source, then there is plenty.

Unlike Jesus's response in Matthew's telling (Matt15:28),[3] and unlike Jesus's response to the woman with the flow of blood (Mark 5:34),[4] there is no specific acknowledgment of the Syrophoenician mother's faith in this pericope. However, Jesus's words affirm that the woman's speech brought about the change of fate for her daughter.[5] Jesus says, "Because of this statement, go!" Her speech provokes Jesus to change course and grant her request, which he tells her he has done, as he sends her away (7:29). When she returns home, she confirms that what he said was true: she finds

---

[1] Betsworth includes an expansive list of treatments of this passage (*Reign of God*, 11 n 56–58). Ringe also writes about the encounter from her experience as a reader ("Gentile Woman's Story," 80–81), as well as surveying non-majority approaches to the pericope (92–96).

[2] See my article: Kara J. Lyons-Pardue, "A Syrophoenician Becomes a Canaanite: Jesus Exegetes the Canaanite Woman in Matthew," *JTI* 13, no. 2 (Nov. 2019): 235–50.

[3] Jesus's response to the woman's retort is, "O, woman, your faith is great!" (ὦ γύναι, μεγάλη σου ἡ πίστις·)

[4] Before he bids her to go, Jesus says to the formerly bleeding woman, "Daughter, your faith has saved you" (θυγάτηρ, ἡ πίστις σου σέσωκέν σε·)

[5] This confirms Ringe's argument that the woman's response is both the heart and focus of the pericope, which she demonstrates structurally ("Gentile Woman's Story," 82–83).

her daughter whole and untroubled by the demon that threatened her (7:30). Even though the child was off-stage for the entire episode in which her future hung in the balance, Betsworth argues that Mark's narration attempts to keep her in focus by the ongoing use of diminutives, including the aforementioned "little dogs" (κυνάριον) and "tiny crumbs" (ψιχίον).[1]

The females generate different initial responses from Jesus: from a willingness to heal, even despite scorn from the supposed mourners, in the instance of Jairus's little daughter; to an unconscious and then recognized healing in the case of the woman with a hemorrhage; all the way to an initial resistance to healing the Syrophoenician woman's possessed daughter. However, the result in each case is that Jesus listens and brings restoration. The healing that comes to each of the daughters would not have happened without Jesus's intervention. And in the cases of the "little daughters," Jesus's intervention required that a person of greater power would pursue a remedy on their behalf. The girls' vulnerability is highlighted, dependent not merely on the decision of the healer, but also on a guardian to advocate for them.

Turning, then, to the daughter whose story is told in the intervening chapter between the two other accounts of daughters, an equivalent situation of vulnerability is easy to miss (Mark 6:17–29). In the account of Herod Antipas, his wife Herodias, her daughter, and their designs on John the Baptist, we are not informed regarding any infirmity that leaves the girl physically vulnerable, for sure. Nevertheless, the forces of intrigue and power-imbalance in the Herodian court are patent, which puts this κοράσιον on the side of susceptibility rather than power.

In many ways, the story was never about the Herodian daughter. The forces at play that divide Herod Antipas's allegiance between his wife Herodias (Mark 6:17-19) and John the Baptist (v. 20) are well underway already when the "opportunity" (εὔκαιρος)

---

[1] Betsworth, *Reign of God*, 130–31.

comes for Herodias to disentangle herself.[1] It is only in verse 22 that the daughter[2] enters the scene at that courtly banquet and dances in a way that pleases Herod and his dining companions. Herod's response to the dance initiates the chain of events that unleashes a disastrous outcome for John the Baptist.

It is John's victimhood, not that of the dancing girl, that draws the narrative focus within the pericope (Mark 6:29). Yet in Mark's detailed narration, there are some hints of recognition that the victimization is more widespread. Herodias's child is described as daughter (θυγάτηρ) and little girl (κοράσιον) when she is first introduced (6:22). The term "little girl" or "maiden" is used again of her twice (6:28). This term, which Jesus and the narrator have applied to Jairus's vulnerable daughter (5:41–42), describes Herodias's daughter three times in this pericope.

The girl is thrust into a situation that has little to do with her and that, ultimately, uses her as an instrument to bring about the desired outcomes of adults. These adults are figures in her life who should be—as evidenced in the other pericopae under discussion— seeking her best, but instead involve her in their own deadly intrigue. The girl's continual deference to her mother exemplifies

---

[1] One of my reasons for choosing language of entanglement is because of the semantic range of the term that describes Herodias's attitude toward John the Baptist in Mark 7:19: ἐνέχω. It is probably best translated that "Herodias *harbored a grudge* against him [John]," but the term ἐνέχω can indicate *entanglement in* a situation. In many ways, it is possible that Herodias's own vulnerability to the decisions of her (second) husband, held in the sway of his own impressionability to John's preaching, was the spark that drove her to eliminate the secondary cause of endangerment to her position. The main cause of her vulnerability, Herod himself, would have been a more difficult target. Her position was, indeed, an entangled one.

[2] Mark identifies the daughter variously. In Mark 6:22, the Greek seems to call her "his daughter Herodias" (τῆς θυγατρὸς αὐτοῦ Ἡρῳδιάδος). But, as the description is embedded within a lengthy genitive absolute construction (καὶ εἰσελθούσης τῆς θυγατρὸς αὐτοῦ Ἡρῳδιάδος καὶ ὀρχησαμένης; genitive endings underlined), the string of genitives might be configured variously in translation. We know from other historical sources that her name was Salome (Josephus, *Ant.* 18.136), but Mark never calls her by that name (see Marcus, *Mark 1–8*, 396).

her familial fidelity and position of absolute dependence, as a child (Mark 6:24, 28). When Herod offers to give to the girl "whatever you might wish" (6:22–23), she—after consultation (6:24)—takes on her mother's suggestion as her own desire ("I want," θέλω; 6:25). The girl's reward for dancing, then, is immediately handed over to the person who truly desired it, her mother (6:28). Ostensibly, the girl is left with nothing, when she might have requested up to half of the king's kingdom (6:23).

While the girl's request echoes her mother's instruction, it seems to intensify her mother's suggestion in a disturbing fashion, demanding that Herod behead John "at once" (ἐξαυτῆς).[1] Yet there are other clues in Mark's narration that we should see her as a vulnerable pawn being used in various ways by both parental figures.[2] Herod takes pleasure from her dance. Many read Herod's and his guests' pleasure in sexual terms, as the lecherous exploitation of a minor and a step-daughter.[3] But victim-blaming runs rampant, even in biblical interpretation, and some of those same interpreters make the mistake of putting the blame on the girl, calling her dance itself "erotic," rather than recognizing that it is only Herod's perception of it as "pleasing" that the narrator expresses.[4] After making his showy promise, the king feels regrets. But in granting the request, Herod thinks not of the girl, but of his

---

[1] Marcus calls it her "own macabre touch" (*Mark 1–8*, 402).

[2] An audience member at my lecture (see footnote 1) raised a valuable critique of this point. Previously, I had considered Herodias's own vulnerability as a woman born into this dysfunctional Herodian family. Her male relatives seemed to pass her around like a commodity and not a person. Therefore, her access to real, free choice regarding her situation was likely negligible. The audience member, however, pressed me further: What if, in such a context, the goal of teaching her daughter survival techniques *required* exposure and desensitization to violence? That is, Herodias's actions could be aiming to secure not only survival but increasing her daughter's opportunities within the Herodian world in the long term. The suggestion is at once tragic and plausible. Such awareness can and should inform modern readers' interpretations, even as there is no evidence of sympathy in the Evangelist's characterization of Herodias.

[3] E.g., Marcus, *Mark 1–8*, 396, 401.

[4] Ibid., 397.

honor before his guests, when granting her request. Her mother's thoughts are on her grudge, not the grisly request she puts in the mouth of her child. The diminutive κοράσιον is used twice in verse 28: the "little girl" is handed the platter holding the decapitated head, which she in turn delivers to her mother.

It is hard to imagine a scenario in which the girl is not traumatized by the bloody violence, which she witnesses up close. The narrative never mentions the girl again. She falls out of the narrative scope just as quickly as she entered. Yet, the experience of this κοράσιον stands in contrast to the story of a cherished κοράσιον in the previous chapter (see Mark 5:41–42), and the "little daughter" whose wholeness remained the Syrophoenician mother's singular mission throughout her interaction with Jesus, even as the young girl remained off-stage. Although Herodias's daughter seems to occupy the spotlight of the narrative for a time, the adults on whom she relies never consider either her needs or her protection.[1]

Old Testament Allusions Set the Stage for the Stories of Daughters in Mark

These stories of little daughters and little girls each have points of commonality — either ones that evidence coherence or disjuncture — with stories in the Old Testament. The allusions vary in directness; that is, some potential resonance may remain merely as a connection that readers could make, but need not make to understand. Other allusions show intentional engagement by the author and contain an aspect of necessary information or perspective that enriches the story. In fact, in confirmation of my impulse to read these texts as engaging with a wide range of textual forebears, F. Scott Spencer — when treating merely the story of

---

[1] It is worth noting again that one could suppose that Herodias's actions seek to secure her place in Herod's good graces and, therefore, the ongoing protection of her daughter. Women, even elite or royal women, were subject to the whims of the men in their lives (e.g., Suetonius, *Nero* 34). That "protection," however, ends up requiring Herodias to use her daughter's dancing as leverage, and permitting the daughter's potential traumatization to bring about the desired, but violent, outcome.

Herodias and her daughter in Mark 6:14-29—comes up with a list of "intertextual associates" that offer allusive potential that includes Judith (LXX), Jezebel, Jephthah's daughter, and Queen Esther.[1]

One of the most shocking stories of father-daughter interactions found in Scripture, which can be contrasted to Jairus's advocacy and care for his "little daughter," is the story of Jephthah in Judg 11. The narrative devotes two verses to his vow itself, that is, that if the Lord should deliver a victory over the Ammonites to Jephthah, he will sacrifice the first thing that exits his house to meet him as a burnt offering to the Lord (Judg 11:30-31). It is a careless pledge, but one that he feels obliged to keep (11:35), because he leads a decisive victory over his opponents, recounted in another scant two verses (11:32-33). Jephthah returns home to his house at Mizpah, and his daughter comes out to greet him jubilantly. Both the Hebrew and the Greek versions of the story emphasize that this daughter was his only child, thereby elaborating that Jephthah had no other sons nor daughters, but the LXX adds that she was beloved by him (αὕτη μονογενὴς αὐτῷ ἀγαπητή; 11:34). The text reinforces her youth, stating she was a virgin and had never "known" a man (11:37, 39); she was, in the terms of our Markan texts a κοράσιον, a little girl, although the LXX denotes that by using the term for virginity (παρθένια; 11:37-38).[2]

The contrasts between Jephthah and Jairus are numerous. Were it not for the story's further connections to Herod, perhaps it would be unfair to even juxtapose the stories. But in what follows, I aim to show a web of continuities and discontinuities that may add illumination to our readings of Mark's "little daughters." Jephthah's young daughter is able-bodied, indicated by her dancing to welcome her father home (Judg 11:34)—just as Herodias's daughter seems healthy as she dances for her stepfather the king (Mark 6:22)—whereas Jairus's daughter is infirm to the point of death (5:23). Jephthah is the illegitimate son of a Gileadite who is shunned

---

[1] Spencer, *Dancing Girls*, 49.

[2] She goes to the mountains for two months, with other young women, and they weep for her virginity (ἔκλαυσεν ἐπὶ τὰ παρθένια αὐτῆς; Judg 11:38).

until his half-brothers think he might give them a better chance at triumph over their many opponents, so they offer him a chance to rise in their tribe if he leads them in battle (Judg 11:1-11). And Jephthah just keeps winning (11:21-22, 32-33). We know, not from Mark, but from widespread historical record that Herod Antipas survives the "Game of Thrones"-style battle to survive in the household of Herod the Great, ruling as tetrarch for more than 40 years (4 B.C.E.-39 C.E.). We are not told, in contrast, how Jairus rose to prominence and became a local synagogue leader (Mark 5:22), but it was not likely through battle nor high-level political machinations. Jephthah leaves his home to fight and returns to find his daughter where he wishes she were not (Judg 11:35), whereas Jairus's going and coming are all concerned with rescuing his daughter from her ailment (Mark 5:21-24, 35-38).[1] Nevertheless, we need not rely on authorial intent to gain insight by placing this pair of father- (or step-father-) daughter stories in contrast to one another. Jairus illustrates what actual fidelity to one's duty entails: He exemplifies a love for his daughter that is willing to go to great lengths to secure her wellbeing. Jephthah and Herod fail miserably on these counts.

Jezebel stands as a potential analogue or allusive foil for the women in at least two of our episodes. As a queen who seeks to impose her will on her ruling husband by seeking to inflict violence on her opponents (1 Kgs 18:4, 13), Herodias ticks many boxes of parallels to Jezebel's character. Yet, their outcomes are starkly different. Herodias's death wish for the prophetic figure John results in his execution, whereas Jezebel's own grisly death results from her quest to inflict harm on God's prophets, particularly Elijah (who notably does not die at all; 2 Kgs 2:1-12).

In the second case, Mark tells us just enough details that might tie the Syrophoenician mother to Jezebel — geographical

---

[1] The motif of travel is not present in the Herodian narrative.

origins,[1] her active pursuit of her desires (1 Kgs 19:2), and the macabre connection to dogs (1 Kgs 21:23; 2 Kgs 9:10) — only to have them overturned. The mother does not seek her own power, but the restoration of her child. She is not manipulative, but evidences steadfast trust in Jesus's power to heal. As I have explored elsewhere, the Gospel writers may be playing with allusive connections between the Syrophoenician woman (or Canaanite woman, in Matthew's telling) and two Old Testament women known to be from the area surrounding Tyre.[2] Although readers may fear that Jesus's encounter with this gentile woman who barges into his desired repose bears the threat Jezebel posed for Elijah, the Syrophoenician woman instead evidences a kinship with the widow of Zarephath, from a village between Tyre and Sidon. That widow already stands as a contrast to Jezebel within the narrative of 1 Kings. From the narrative details available, the Syrophoenician woman, like the widow, is outside the protection of an adult male. The widow of Zarephath is ultimately concerned to protect her son, particularly after an illness (1 Kgs 17:17), just as the Syrophoenician mother advocates doggedly for her own child. A scarce supply of bread, real rather than metaphorical in the 1 Kings account, is cause for concern starting with the widow's first interaction with God's prophet (17:11–12). It is only in the resolution of the Syrophoenician woman's predicament that we see the scale tip decisively in favor of her resemblance to the Zarephath widow, not to Jezebel.

In the category of intentional allusion by the author, the story of John's beheading contains a direct allusion to Esther. When Herod promises up to half his kingdom to a girl for a dance, there are parallels to Artaxerxes,[3] who promises an extravagant half of his kingdom to Esther. The wording is nearly identical.

---

[1] While she is the daughter of Ethbaal, the King of the Sidonians (1 Kgs 16:31), neither ethnic or cultural term that describes "Syrophoenician" or "Canaanite" (Matt 15:22) woman is ever used of Jezebel.

[2] See my article, Lyons-Pardue, "Syrophoenician Becomes a Canaanite."

[3] This is the king's name in the LXX; it is Ahasuerus in the MT. Hereafter, "Artaxerxes" is the name used in this essay, as the LXX form is in reference.

Table 2: Wording similarities between Mark 6:23 and LXX Esther 7:2
    ... δώσω <u>σοι ἕως ἡμίσους τῆς βασιλείας μου</u> (Mark 6:23).
    ... I will give to you up to half of my kingdom.
    ... ἔστω <u>σοι ἕως τοῦ ἡμίσους τῆς βασιλείας μου</u> (LXX Esth 7:2).
    ... let it be to you up to half of my kingdom.

Further, there are parallels between Herod Antipas's malleability and frivolity and that of the king in the story of Esther. In both, the so-called "supreme" ruler is visibly susceptible to whims, his own or of people in his close circle (Esth 1:10–22; Mark 6:21–26), whether advisors or consorts. In the case of Artaxerxes in Esther, Haman exploits his overly trusting nature is exploited by Haman (Esth 3:1–11), but then conveniently employed to undo Haman and protect the Jewish people (7:1–10). His weakness as a leader initially causes trouble, but then is used for good. In Mark's telling of John's beheading, the inverse trajectory is apparent: although Herod was initially swayed by John's perspective and ways of teaching, at least to some degree, it is the proposal of a "little girl" (with her strings being pulled by her mother) that ultimately persuades him to turn on John (Mark 6:26). Although these broader story elements are inverted between the two narratives, some of the storytelling features are parallel. That is, particularly in Artaxerxes's promise to Esther, there is a repetition of his offer that intensifies it. The same can be said of several aspects of the Herodian courtly conversations as Mark reports them. In each case, a weak king takes a stand as a result of maneuvers — whether for good or ill in the narrator's perspective — by a vulnerable woman or women in his midst.

The allusions — whether necessary or possible — to episodes from Israel's Scriptures that we find in our stories of little daughters are significant and should shape our readings of Mark's account. At the same time, the resonances are quite varied; I would not wish to argue for a purposely systematic pattern of allusion in each of these cases. Nevertheless, readers or hearers of these "little daughter" stories might invoke a multiform backdrop of scriptural precedent to make value-judgments on stories that remain ambiguous or ambivalent in their basic telling. The onus is on the interpreter to identify the allusive connections and draw conclusions about their implications.

The Power of Remembering and Telling

There are stories throughout Scripture in which modern readers wish for more resolution than the text affords us. Whether an act of violence or prejudicial behavior goes by without explicit refutation (not to mention seeming approval) or whether a particular marginalized person begins and remains on the margins, readers may wish the Bible said more. Some of the gratuitous cases in Israel's Scriptures that include women were referenced in my introduction—the Levite's concubine and Hagar—but there are many more names we can reference offhand that convey pain and mistreatment by their mere mention: Lot's daughters, Leah, Tamar, Bathsheba, or Vashti. The psalmist utters curses on enemies unchecked. There are legal restrictions that seem to penalize disability. In the New Testament, one matter of particular importance is early Christians' practices of slavery.[1] Most passages that mention slaveholding take for granted its perpetual existence; slaves and masters were part of the matrix of human life (e.g., Matt 25:14-30; Eph 6:5-9). In Philemon we can read a great deal of affection and empathy on Paul's part toward Onesimus, the present or former slave (Phlm 10, 12, 16-19). But Paul never rejects the institution of slavery in general, nor does he condemn it outright in Onesimus's case. The letter has an opaque backstory and an unclear resolution, allowing centuries of Christian interpreters to speculate, some of them in damaging ways.

In our texts under discussion, at least two of the three lack the resolution or moral evaluation that many contemporary readers crave. What happens to Herodias and her daughter? Surely their grasp at control—whether we deem it overtly wicked or an understandable, but not justifiable, evil—did not satisfy ultimately.

---

[1] See Jennifer A. Glancy, *Slavery in Early Christianity* (Minneapolis: Fortress, 2006).

Did the daughter grow to resent her parental neglect and abuse by over-exposure? And what of Jesus's interaction with the Syrophoenician woman? Did he feel remorse for the canine insinuation? Did the woman begrudge Jesus his comment? What became of the daughter after she was released from her demonic possession? What are we, as readers, supposed to make of their interaction?

The story of Jephthah's daughter, whether or not it is to be engaged as necessarily-allusive backdrop to the stories of parents and daughters in Mark, illustrates how the telling of the story, even without an explicit condemnation of the actions of the protagonist, demonstrates its availability for such debate and denouncement, upon inspection of the details provided. As I noted previously, the relative time the narrator spends explicating Jephthah's battle (a mere two verses) in contrast to the time invested in narrating his vow and subsequent interaction with his daughter, and, finally, his daughter's retreat into the mountains, illustrates that this is not meant to be just one among his catalogued battle victories. His actions stemming from his vow and concerning his only child are under scrutiny. Certainly, the story serves to explain an ongoing practice among the people of Israel as the final verse indicates (Judg 11:40). But the foregoing story includes enough detail and pathos to guarantee a response, whether of pity, reverence, or (likely) indignation. It is not only modern, feminist interpreters who look to cast blame on Jephthah; rabbis criticized his simplistic adherence to a hasty vow.[1]

One cannot resolve a scarcity of details or the resulting sense of lack of resolution. Nevertheless, by focusing on and taking as characters of value these minor or only partially described people (who are often women), we unlock an important function of these stories. The preservation of these stories, their unvarnished telling, and their exposure to an amplified audience is, in itself, advocacy

---

[1] See Midrash Tanhuma Buber Bechukotai 5, ed. Samuel A. Berman, The Sefaria Library, https://www.sefaria.org/Midrash_Tanchuma%2C_Bechukotai.5?lang=bi.

for attention, which can lead to justice. The retention and selection of these accounts, ugly as some may be, are themselves an invitation for later generations to bring critiques and develop ethical responses to them for their own time.

As victims of abuse and violence attest commonly today, there is something worthwhile about telling one's story. In cases of childhood exploitation, often there is no available fix or even anything that resembles justice to be retrieved. Yet, many victims report a retrieval of their own sense of power through the ability to have their story heard and their experience validated. Scriptural storytelling can function similarly: truth and justice are in telling and listening to difficult stories. Yet the texts cannot receive an automatic stamp of holy approval, but must be face the interpretive rigor of a community of readers. The text acts as a faithful witness to a community's experiences. As readers, we can, through devoting our readerly attention to detail and depending on the Spirit, seek aims of justice that the text does not achieve nor mandate on its own.

This interpretive strategy — that is, taking seriously details that stories provide, even if scarce about marginal or minor figures, and resisting the impulse to import intentions that are not clearly stated in the narration — have the capacity to open up new vistas of meaning potential in biblical texts. It constitutes a way of attending to the diversity of persons within and entry points into a story. The implications of such a reading strategy also puts the ethical onus on interpreters to use literary clues, the broader witness of Scripture, and a community's theological imagination to make stronger and more liberative claims about the biblical text. The simplest implementation of this reading strategy simply requires Bible readers to take note of more minor characters, particularly women, children, and members of other disenfranchised groups, and to recognize that each is a valued child of God.

Conclusion

The vulnerability and possibilities for misuse and exploitation of daughters are on display in three Markan pericopae. Also textually accessible in close proximity is the value that loving parents place in their children—attributes of care that are not shown in the courtly episode of Herod, Herodias, and her daughter that results in the death of John the Baptist. Those tragic interactions result in losses and dehumanization beyond those felt by John and his followers, whether the text reports it overtly or not. Jesus's treatment of the daughters he encounters, whether a "little girl" or a "daughter" who has bled for twelve years, is one of value. In the moments in which that value seems uncertain from Jesus's perspective, in the case of the Syrophoenician woman's unrelenting petitions on her daughter's behalf, the mother's own intervention is enough to reorient him.

LISTENING AGAIN INTRACANONICALLY

Gospel Themes as "Glue" for Pauline Ecclesiological Images[1]

Andy Johnson

Introduction

Among the images for the church in the Pauline corpus are the church as the body of Christ (1 Cor 12:12-27; 6:15; 10:17; Rom 12:4-5; cf. Col 1:18; 3:15; Eph 1:22-23; 2:16; 4:4, 12-16), the temple of God/Holy Spirit (1 Cor 3:16-17; 6:19; 2 Cor 6:16; Eph 2:19-22), the new creation (2 Cor 5:17; Gal 6:15), and the new humanity (Col 3:9-11; Eph 2:15; 4:22-24). Aspects of the story of Jesus congeal into gospel themes that bear an analogy to these ecclesiological images. Reading the Pauline letters in light of these themes enables us to recognize an organic—albeit implicit—connection between Paul's ecclesiological images.[2] These gospel themes provide a kind of "glue" that organically connects the ecclesiological images of the church as Christ's body, God's temple, new creation, and new humanity. The purpose of this paper is to describe that gospel "glue" and sketch out that implicit organic connection between these ecclesiological images, showing that the image of the church as the body of Christ is the one "place" where they all converge and

---

[1] It is an honor to dedicate this essay to my friend, George Lyons, to whom I am grateful for providing many of us a faithful model of engaging in careful exegesis and exemplary teaching in service to the church (and for his rather direct involvement in providing me with my first teaching assistant, his daughter Kara Lyons-Pardue!).

[2] In what follows, when I refer to Paul, I mean the canonical Paul associated with the Pauline corpus. I am tabling the historical question as to whether the historical Paul wrote the disputed letters of Colossians and Ephesians.

overlap.¹ In doing so, I hope to underscore the inseparability of Christology and ecclesiology in the Pauline corpus.

The essay proceeds as follows. I begin by describing some broad canonical background and some general first-century cultural assumptions that bear on the way one might understand certain elements of the Gospels' narrations of the story of Jesus. In particular, I discuss the way that Genesis depicts creation as God's cosmic sanctuary and how this is connected to first-century conceptions of the Second Temple. I also briefly describe a popular understanding in the Greco-Roman world of the way the human body was related to the cosmos as a whole. In light of this background, I then highlight ways in which the Gospels—specifically Mark and John—portray Jesus as the temple of God, the locale of the new creation, and the new/true human being.² In the last part of the essay, I offer a sketch of how the "glue" of the preceding discussion suggests implicit organic connections between the related Pauline ecclesiological images.

Canonical Background and Cultural Assumptions regarding Cosmos, Temple, and Body

Creation as God's Well-Ordered Cosmic Sanctuary/Temple
The theme of creation as God's cosmic sanctuary/temple has become commonplace in contemporary biblical studies.³ Genesis

---

¹ I stress that: (1) I am *not* arguing that Paul was aware of these gospel themes and *consciously* used them to forge his ecclesiological images; and (2) I only offer an *initial sketch*, not a detailed exegetical argument, as to how these images may be held together *implicitly* by the gospel "glue" I describe.

² Some combination of these themes could also be developed from the Gospels of Matthew and Luke, e.g., the themes of Jesus as temple (see Nicholas Perrin, *Jesus the Temple* [Grand Rapids: Baker Academic, 2010]) and Jesus as the new/true human being or "the last Adam" (see Brandon C. Crowe, *The Last Adam: A Theology of the Obedient Life of Jesus in the Gospels* [Grand Rapids: Baker Academic, 2017]).

³ E.g., see G. K. Beale and Mitchell Kim, *God Dwells Among Us: Expanding Eden to the Ends of the Earth* (Downers Grove, IL: IVP, 2014), 17–28; J. Richard Middleton, *New Heaven and a New Earth: Reclaiming Biblical Eschatology* (Grand Rapids: Baker Academic, 2014), 46–49. This sub-section and some of the following

begins with God creating the physical world as God's cosmic sanctuary or temple to become a "theater of his glory."[1] Although creation is "very good" in the beginning (Gen 1:31), it is not "perfect,"[2] in the sense of some sort of static perfection. Rather, God calls and enables humanity from the outset to become a participant in God's mission to bring creation to its intended destiny of flourishing with abundant life. This is related to God's creation of humans in God's own image.

When Gen 1 and 2 are read against their ancient Near Eastern background, both depict humanity as, in Middleton's words, "the authorized cult statue in the cosmic temple, the decisive locus of divine presence on earth, the living image of God in the cosmic sanctuary."[3] In Gen 2:7, the holy God graciously breathes God's breath/Spirit into humanity—God's own previously inert cult statue—thereby enabling humanity to re-present God's gracious presence (like priests) in God's cosmic temple and to rule over it (like kings) in a way that creation would flourish with well-ordered life (Gen 1:28; 2:15) and reach its intended destiny. It reaches its intended destiny when the entirety of the renewed creation is soaked with God's unmediated holy, life-giving presence/glory (Rev 21:11, 22; 22:3-5; cf. 1 Cor 15:28) making all of it God's now completed cosmic temple/sanctuary.

The Jerusalem Temple as a Microcosm of God's Macrocosmic Sanctuary of Creation

This theology of creation as the temple/sanctuary of God was portrayed in the structure and furnishings of the moveable

---

are adapted from my *Holiness and the* Missio Dei (Eugene, OR: Cascade, 2016), 3-5, 48-49.

[1] Middleton, *New Heaven and a New Earth*, 46-49.

[2] On this way of putting the matter, see Terence E. Fretheim, *Creation Untamed: The Bible, God, and Natural Disasters*, Theological Explorations for the Church Catholic (Grand Rapids: Baker Academic, 2010), 9-38.

[3] Middleton, *New Heaven and a New Earth*, 49.

tabernacle in the wilderness and in Israel's first temple.[1] Both had symbolism indicating that they represented creation as a whole, creation rightly ordered with God on the throne dwelling with God's people in a way that mediated God's beneficent presence safely.[2] By the time of the Second Temple, this connection between the temple as God's dwelling place and the ordered cosmos was widely assumed.[3] As was the case with some Greco-Roman temples,[4] it was understood as directly connected to the cosmos itself.[5] It was "the point from which creation proceeded," the "meeting place of heaven and earth,"[6] a microcosm of a rightly ordered creation as a whole.

---

[1] In this paragraph, I adapt material from my "The 'New Creation,' the Crucified and Risen Christ, and the Temple: A Pauline Audience for Mark," *JTI* 1 (2007): 181–82.

[2] J. J. M. Roberts, "Temple, Jerusalem," *NIDB* 5:501–502; Beale and Kim, *God Dwells Among Us*, 51–64.

[3] E.g., *J. W.* 5.5.5 §§ 212–14, 219; *Ant.* 3.6.4 § 123; 3.7.7 §§ 180–87. Citing extensive literature, C. H. T. Fletcher-Louis argues that "this [temple centered cosmic] ideology was as axiomatic for late second-temple theology as is a concept such as covenant *which we now recognize to be everywhere assumed even when not explicit*" ("The Destruction of the Temple and the Relativization of the Old Covenant: Mark 13:31 and Matthew 5:18," in *Eschatology in Bible and Theology*, ed. Kent E. Brower and Mark W. Elliott [Downers Grove, IL: IVP, 1997], 160, my italics). See also G. K. Beale, *The Temple and the Church's Mission: A Biblical Theology of the Dwelling Place of God*, NSBT 17 (Downers Grove, IL: IVP, 2004), 29–80.

[4] E.g., in the opinion of Dio Cassius (*Roman History* 53.27.2), the rounded form of the Pantheon in Rome appears to have been built to resemble the heavens, suggesting that it may have been intended to function as an embodiment of the universe. Pausanias describes Apollo's sanctuary at Delphi as the "navel of the world" (*Descr.* 10.16.3). In addition, throughout the Roman Empire, temples of Mithra functioned as "replicas of the cosmos" (Leroy A. Campbell, *Mithraic Iconography and Ideology*, EPRO 11 [Leiden: Brill, 1968], 49–50).

[5] Jon Levenson, *Sinai and Zion: An Entry into the Jewish Bible* (Minneapolis: Winston, 1985), esp. 89–184.

[6] Levenson, *Sinai and Zion*, 118, 123.

The Human Body as a Microcosm of the Macrocosmic Cosmos in the Greco-Roman World

In the Greco-Roman world the cosmos itself could also be portrayed as a body. In tandem with this, the human body could also be associated with the cosmos and understood to be "a microcosm—a small version of the universe at large."[1] In light of such conceptuality, the Gospel accounts of God raising the human body of Jesus might suggest that God had begun the redemption of the universe in microcosm. In the words of David Toolan, the risen body of the Lord would signal "the fleshing out of the Creator's dream for the universe" in that, "[i]f he be raised up, it means that all things are raised up."[2] In other words, if the Gospels are heard in light of this available conceptuality of the connection between the human body and the cosmos, one might imagine that what God did for the body of Jesus in microcosm, God has started doing—as imperceptible as it most often is—for the entirety of the cosmos in macrocosm.

With this background material in place, we turn our attention to the Gospels to highlight ways in which they portray Jesus as the temple of God, the locale or microcosm of the new creation, and the new/true human being.

Gospel Themes

Jesus's Body as Eschatological Temple and Microcosm of New Creation in Mark

In his activities prior to coming to Jerusalem in the Synoptic Gospels, we might well describe Jesus as a moveable tabernacle housing God's holy presence, in whose body some functions of the temple were localized.[3] As "the Holy One of God" (Mark 1:24), Jesus becomes the locale of forgiveness (2:1-12), healing (e.g., 1:29-

---

[1] Dale B. Martin, *The Corinthian Body* (New Haven: Yale University, 1995), 16.

[2] David Toolan, *At Home in the Cosmos* (Maryknoll, NY: Orbis, 2001) 208, 213.

[3] On which, see Perrin, *Jesus the Temple*.

34), and cleansing (e.g., 1:39-44). In a similar way that the blessings of God's holiness were understood to radiate outward from the sanctuary (ναός) of God in Jerusalem, Jesus's body becomes the site of the holy presence of God, from which flow salvation, shalom, and life (e.g., Mark 5:23, 28, 34). Like the divine fire of the temple's altar, Jesus was not defiled by impurity but instead cleansed and sanctified those whom he encountered.[1]

After arriving in Jerusalem in the Gospel of Mark, what Jesus does and says in the temple lands him in serious trouble. In 11:12-21 Jesus's cursing of the fig tree, followed by his words and actions in the temple, amount to a cursing of the temple and symbolize its coming destruction,[2] which he explicitly predicts (13:2). After the parable of the vineyard (12:1-9), told against the Temple leadership, Jesus's explanatory words from Ps 118:22 regarding the rejected stone becoming the cornerstone (12:10) imply his own vindication as the new eschatological temple housing God's presence (or at least as its foundation). Not surprisingly, then, even though they are characterized as "false witnesses" in Mark 14:56-59, "many" people testified that Jesus had said he would destroy the Jerusalem temple and build another not made with hands, a charge echoed by those deriding him at the cross (15:29).

Given this imagery of Jesus's body as God's eschatological temple, it is not surprising that the way Mark narrates Jesus's death in 15:33-39 involves the temple. Although Mark's narration of Jesus's death may certainly be read in other ways, a good case can be made for reading it in such a way as to maximize the effect of its

---

[1] "If an inappropriate or unclean offering was accidentally placed on the altar, the fire was so powerful that it incinerated the impurity and sanctified the item. ... The process of holiness is dynamic, almost chemical in that the very nature of the offering is transformed by contact with holy power" (Hannah K. Harrington, *Holiness: Rabbinic Judaism and the Graeco-Roman World* [New York: Routledge, 2001], 53).

[2] See, e.g., Kent E. Brower ("'Let the Reader Understand': Temple and Eschatology in Mark," in *Eschatology in Bible and Theology: Evangelical Essays at the Dawn of a New Millennium*, ed. Kent E. Brower and Mark W. Elliot; [Downers Grove, IL: IVP, 1997], 119-43).

literary symmetry with Jesus's baptism.¹ In Mark's narration of Jesus's baptism (1:9-11), Jesus's entrance into the narrative was marked by the movement of the Spirit, who was portrayed as ripping open (σχιζομένους) the heavens and descending into (εἰς) him (1:10). Jesus's exit here in 15:37-39 is marked by a literary symmetry regarding the activity of this same Spirit. At his death in 15:37, Jesus breathes out the Spirit (ἐξέπνευσεν).² As a result of the Spirit's movement,³ the heavens are ripped open again (ἐσχίσθη), this time in the form of the heavens painted on the outer temple curtain, symbolizing that the temple was a microcosm of the cosmos (15:38).⁴ God's Spirit/Presence is thus portrayed as moving out of Jesus into the temple, not as moving out of the Holy of Holies. Since the idea that the temple was a microcosm of the cosmos was implicitly but graphically portrayed by means of this outer curtain, its ripping signifies not only a final sign of God's sure judgment on the temple, but also the end of the old order of things it modeled.⁵

---

¹ For a fuller treatment and defense of the possibility of reading Mark's narration of Jesus's death and resurrection in the way suggested in this section, see my "The 'New Creation,'" 181-90.

² Since ἐκπνέω was not commonly used as a euphemism for dying in the *koinē*, the audience would likely judge ἐξέπνευσεν to have more significance than just to convey that Jesus died. For an argument that Matthew's "ἀφῆκεν τὸ πνεῦμα" (27:50) and John's "παρέδωκεν τὸ πνεῦμα" (19:30) may also be taken as referring to Jesus "releasing" or "handing over" the Spirit rather than simply being euphemistic ways of referring to Jesus dying, see my "You Wonder Where the Spirit Went": The Spirit and the Resurrection of the Son in Matthew and John," *JTI* 12 (2018): 58-75.

³ This takes the beginning καί in 15:38 as expressing result (BDF §§ 442, 458, 471).

⁴ For similar arguments, see David Ulansey, "The Heavenly Veil Torn: Mark's Cosmic *Inclusio*," *JBL* 110 (1991): 124-25); and Howard M. Jackson, "The Death of Jesus in Mark and the Miracle from the Cross," *NTS* 33 (1987): 24). For a representative argument for the tearing of the inner curtain instead, see Morna Hooker, *The Gospel according to Saint Mark*, BNTC (London: Black, 1991), 377-78.

⁵ So also D. Rudman, "The Crucifixion as *Chaoskampf*: A New Reading of the Passion Narrative in the Synoptic Gospels," *Bib* 84 (2003): 103-7, esp. 107, and cf. Beale, *Temple and the Church's Mission*, 190.

But the Spirit does more than simply signal the end of the old cosmos. By means of that same breathed-out Spirit, God raises the body of the one in whom the functions of the temple had already been localized throughout Mark's narrative. In doing so, God replaces the microcosm of the old order (i.e., the Jerusalem temple) with the microcosm of the new order (i.e., the risen body of Jesus). Hence, one might conclude that the now risen body of Jesus (although remaining absent in Mark) becomes the new temple which functions as microcosm of the new creation. One might arrive at a similar conclusion based on the assumption of some in the Greco-Roman world that the human body is a microcosm of the cosmos. That is, the now risen body of Jesus is the microcosm of the new cosmos inaugurated by the making-alive Spirit in the darkness of the tomb.

The theme of Christ's body as a new temple with Christ's resurrection as the catalyst for a new creation can also be seen in John, but with the added element of Christ being raised as the new humanity.

Jesus's Body as Eschatological Temple, Microcosm of New Creation, and New Humanity in John

John's language and imagery suggesting that Jesus takes over the functions of the Jerusalem temple and becomes the eschatological temple is even more pronounced than that in the Synoptic Gospels.[1] In John, Jesus is clearly depicted as the moveable tabernacle (σκηνή) of the Father's glory (1:14). In 2:19-21 Jesus refers to his own body as the temple/sanctuary (ναός), the Holy of Holies housing the glory/visible holiness of Israel's God. "Destroy this ναός," he says, "and in three days I will raise it" (2:19), with the narrator then informing us in verse 21 that "he was speaking about the temple (ναοῦ) of his body (σώματος)."[2] As "the Holy One of

---

[1] On the way Jesus takes over the functions of the temple in John, see Alan Kerr, *The Temple of Jesus' Body: The Temple Theme in the Gospel of John*, LNTS 220 (Sheffield: Sheffield Academic, 2002); Perrin, *Jesus the Temple*, 53-55.

[2] All translations of Scripture in this essay are my own.

God" (6:69), he is the one in whose face, to use Paul's words, "shines the light of the knowledge of God's glory" (2 Cor 4:4), and, like the Second Temple, he was indeed the "meeting place of heaven and earth"[1] with "the angels of God ascending and descending upon the Human One" (1:51). So the theme of Jesus's dying and being raised as God's eschatological temple, and therefore as a microcosm of God's new creation, could be developed here as well, particularly since the theme of creation's renewal is implicitly present throughout John's narrative.[2] In particular, John's allusions to Gen 1–3 in his account of the passion and resurrection and his evoking the tradition of creation's renewal on the eighth day by emphasizing twice that Jesus's resurrection was on "the first day of the week" (20:1, 19) suggest that Jesus's resurrection did indeed inaugurate a new creation of which he is its embodiment.

But, more specifically, John's symbolism also suggests that Jesus lives, dies, and is raised as the new humanity/new Adam of this new creation.[3] In order to describe the way John does this, we will focus on his allusions to Gen 1–3 in his depiction of Jesus's passion, death, and resurrection.

The clearest allusion to these early chapters of Genesis is that of John's language in 20:22, which draws from Gen 2:7. However, before that passage, John makes implicit connections between Jesus and Adam, not least of which is his association of a garden with the setting of Jesus's crucifixion, burial, resurrection, and ascension.[4] John begins his passion narrative in a garden (18:1) and includes a

---

[1] Levenson, *Sinai and Zion*, 118, 123.

[2] See especially, Jeannine Brown, "Creation's Renewal in the Gospel of John," *CBQ* 72 (2010): 275-90. For a recent, critical investigation of the presence and significance of creation imagery in the Fourth Gospel, see Carlos Raúl Sosa Siliezar, *Creation Imagery in the Gospel of John*, LNTS 546 (London/New York: Bloomsbury/T&T Clark, 2015).

[3] The rest of this section has been heavily adapted from my "'You Wonder Where the Spirit Went,'" 66-75.

[4] Crowe offers a less detailed argument, complementary to the following one, regarding the significance of John's garden imagery in depicting Jesus as the new Adam (*The Last Adam*, 195).

subtle reminder that Jesus had been "handed over" in that garden (18:26).[1] More importantly, John tells us in 19:41 about what appears to be a different garden: "Now in the place where he was crucified, there was a garden (κῆπος) and in the garden (κῆπος) there was a new tomb in which no one had yet been laid." This signals to the hearers that this latter garden is the scene of Jesus's burial, resurrection and ascension since the setting does not change until after Jesus tells Mary that he is ascending to the Father in 20:17.[2] John reminds his hearers that we are still in this garden when Mary identifies the risen Jesus as "the gardener" (ὁ κηπουρός; 20:15). Given other possible allusions to Gen 1–3, such language invites hearers to make a connection with the garden of the original creation in Gen 2.[3]

A common objection to this possibility is that Gen 2:8 LXX refers to the garden of the original creation with the word παράδεισος, rather than κῆπος, as here in John.[4] However, the force

---

[1] John Suggit suggests that Judas's act of betrayal in this garden can be compared to Adam's "first great act of disloyalty" in the primordial garden ("Jesus the Gardener: The Atonement in the Fourth Gospel as Re-creation," *Neot* 33 [1999]: 166).

[2] John does not narrate the ascension as an observable event (cf. Acts 1:9-11). However, his assertion in this verse that he is ascending to the Father might well be taken as implying that Jesus's ascension is about to take place off the narrative stage. Earlier in the narrative, he had promised his disciples that when he returned to the Father, he would send the Holy Spirit (John 14:26). Given his actions of breathing that very Spirit into his disciples in 20:22, the clear implication is that he has indeed returned to the Father off the narrative stage between the time of his words to Mary Magdalene in 20:17 and his bestowing of the Spirit in 20:22. Jesus's own words in 20:17 imply that, in John's Gospel, this return to the Father is to be understood as his ascension.

[3] The word for gardener (κηπουρός) only occurs here in the NT. Mary's statement may be a classic example of Johannine "misunderstanding" that functions as an ironically correct designation of the new gardener of the new creation initiated in this garden (so Suggit, "Jesus the Gardener," 167; Anthony Moore, *Signs of Salvation: The Theme of Creation in John's Gospel* [Cambridge: James Clark, 2013], esp. 54-93; contra Siliezar, *Creation Imagery*, 174-90).

[4] E.g., Raymond E. Brown, *The Death of the Messiah: From Gethsemane to the Grave: A Commentary on the Passion Narratives in the Four Gospels*, 2 vols., ABRL (New York: Doubleday, 1994), 1:149, 2:1270; Siliezar, *Creation Imagery*, 180-83. In

of this objection is lessened by observing that: (1) in a context where the MT references the garden of Eden, Ezek 36:35 LXX uses κῆπος; (2) both words can be used synonymously in the LXX (Eccl 2:5; Sir 24:30-31); (3) Josephus uses the words synonymously in discussing Gen 2.[1] So, then, the use of κῆπος rather παράδεισος does not preclude the possibility that John's narrative encourages hearers to make a connection between the primordial garden of the original creation and his garden in 19:41.[2]

Making such a connection might naturally lead to the expectation of there being a new gardener—a new Adam—in this new garden. That is, John's language invites us to consider making a connection between Adam, the first gardener, and Jesus.[3] Earlier in the passion narrative, in his pregnant statement in 19:5 as Jesus is standing before him in royal purple robes being mocked as messianic king, Pilate unwittingly depicts Jesus as the paradigmatic human being when he says: "Behold the Human (ὁ ἄνθρωπος)." Regardless of John's intention, it is difficult not to hear an echo of God's making/forming the Human (τὸν ἄνθρωπον) (Gen 1:27/2:7 LXX)[4] in God's image to be God's "authorized cult statue in the

---

addition to the three points made here, see Moore's detailed response to this objection (*Signs of Salvation*, 66-79).

[1] In discussing Gen 2:8, Josephus refers to the garden of Eden as a παράδεισον (*Ant.* 1.1.3 § 37) the first time he refers to it. From then on, he refers to it four times as ὁ κῆπος (*Ant.* 1.1.3-4 §§ 38, 45, 51).

[2] The significance of this connection could be understood somewhat differently than I attempt to articulate in this essay, e.g., as John's way of connecting Jesus's death and resurrection to the reopening/restoration of, or the way to, Paradise (e.g., E. C. Hoskyns, *The Fourth Gospel*, vol. 2 [London: Faber & Faber, 1940], 604; Moore, *Signs of Salvation*, 10, 58) or perhaps as John's way of signaling that what started in the primordial garden is brought to its eschatological consummation in what happens in this garden (Suggit, "Jesus the Gardener, 167).

[3] Some argue that John expects us to see Jesus as the new divine gardener who first planted and cultivated the garden in Gen 2:9 (e.g., M. L. Coloe, "Theological Reflexions on Creation in the Gospel of John," *Pacifica* 24 [2011]: 8; Moore, *Signs of Salvation*, 10). While this is not necessarily at odds theologically with simultaneously seeing Jesus as the Second Adam, I do not think it is the primary effect of the garden imagery.

[4] Gen 1:26 LXX also has the noun, ἄνθρωπον, but without the article.

cosmic temple."¹ Here, then, as Jeannine Brown puts it, "John shows in narrative fashion that God is inaugurating creation's renewal in Jesus, the 'second Adam.'"²

When Jesus dies, the Son's human corpse, the fleshly body of the second Adam, lies lifeless in the tomb. It is worth noting that John says that the garden was "in the place where he was crucified" (19:41), apparently indicating that the crucifixion did not take place inside the garden itself.³ Instead, Jesus dies outside the garden, as did the first Adam. But in a reversal of the first Adam's exit from the garden, this second Adam's lifeless body is brought into the garden (19:41) to receive the "eternal life" forfeited by the first Adam in the original garden (Gen 2:17; 3:19, 22-24). Like the latter's lifeless, dusty body (Gen 2:7), this second Adam awaits God's life-giving breath/Spirit who, according to John, "makes alive" (6:63). The first day of the old creation begins in darkness where the Spirit/wind of God is active⁴ before that day breaks into light (Gen 1:2-5). John's use of similar language in 20:1⁵ signals that here in the garden tomb the first day of a new creation is beginning; indeed, the

---

¹ Middleton, *New Heaven and a New Earth*, 49. For a summary of interpretations that connect Pilate's statement in a variety of ways with Adam, see M. D. Litwa, "Behold Adam: A Reading of John 19:5," *HBT* 32 (2010): 130-35. Whether or not Litwa's own proposal is ultimately convincing, he highlights numerous intratextual connections in John's narrative that provide support to the claim that hearers are to understand Pilate's statement as connecting and contrasting Jesus and Adam.

² Brown, "Creation's Renewal in the Gospel of John," 281.

³ That is, the wording of the Greek phrase (ἦν δὲ ἐν τῷ τόπῳ ὅπου ἐσταυρώθη κῆπος) suggests that the place of the Skull (Golgotha) was not itself a garden, but there was a garden located within its bounds. So, John is probably not locating the cross inside the garden and depicting it as the tree of life, as theologically appealing as that might be (contra Nicholas Wyatt, "'Supposing Him to Be the Gardener' (John 20:15): A Study of the Paradise Motif in John," *ZNW* 25 [1990]: 21-38, esp. 38).

⁴ Cf. καὶ σκότος ἐπάνω τῆς ἀβύσσου, καὶ πνεῦμα θεοῦ ἐπεφέρετο ἐπάνω τοῦ ὕδατος (Gen 1:2 LXX).

⁵ Cf. Gen 1:5 LXX (καὶ ἐγένετο ἑσπέρα καὶ <u>ἐγένετο πρωΐ, ἡμέρα μία</u>) with the timing of Mary's visit in John 20:1 (<u>Τῇ δὲ μιᾷ τῶν σαββάτων</u> Μαρία ἡ Μαγδαληνὴ ἔρχεται <u>πρωῒ σκοτίας ἔτι οὔσης</u>).

Second Adam is being brought to life and, hence, a new humanity is being inaugurated.[1]

John's allusion in 20:22 to Gen 2:7 is of a piece with this conceptuality. In Gen 2:7, God made/formed the human (τὸν ἄνθρωπον) and then "breathed" (ἐνεφύσησεν) into his lifeless body the breath of life so that he became a living being. Here in John 20:22, Jesus "breathed (ἐνεφύσησεν) into his disciples and said to them, 'receive the Holy Spirit.'"[2] Right before this, Jesus had said, "Just as the Father has sent me, I also am sending you" (20:21). This suggests that the way Jesus sends the disciples in 20:22 is in some sense analogous to how the Father had sent him. Hence, since Jesus is sending the disciples in mission by breathing the Holy Spirit into them, the implication is that the Son has just been sent as the Second Adam by the Father in a similar way. That is, inside the garden tomb, the Father had breathed the Spirit into Jesus's lifeless body, thereby inaugurating a new humanity.[3]

---

[1] It is important to note that John is loosely using creation imagery from Gen 1–3, not slavishly following the timeline in Genesis. In 20:22 he clearly draws on imagery from God's creation of humanity when he uses Gen 2:7 (where God brings the first Adam to life) in the narrative setting of "the first day of the week" (20:19). This makes it clear that adhering to the chronological order of the days of the week in Gen 1 is not his concern. Hence, to argue that John is not implying a connection to creation imagery with his language of "the first day of the week" since humanity was not created until the sixth day in Gen 1 (e.g., Siliezar, *Creation Imagery*, 170, n. 73) is wide of the mark.

[2] While almost all interpreters assume some link between John 20:22 and Gen 2:7, Siliezar develops a detailed argument that John intends his readers to recognize that he is making use of this Genesis text (*Creation Imagery*, 153–73).

[3] This interpretation does not negate the clear parallel to John 17:18 in which the Son's being "sent" is a clear reference to the incarnation itself. But, however we are to conceive of the Father's sending of the Son in the incarnation, it involves some sort of receiving of the Spirit in John's Gospel. The divinely human Son in John simply is the one whom the Father has saturated with the life-giving Spirit "without measure" (3:34). But from the standpoint of the narrative, the dead human body of Jesus in the tomb somehow must be "freshly resaturated" with that life-giving Spirit of the Father for Jesus to become the one who stands in the disciples' midst, breathes out that same Spirit on them, and sends them into the world. So, the way Jesus is sending the disciples in 20:22 is *in some sense analogous* to the way the Father had sent him, both in the incarnation per se (maintaining the

Here, in a second moment of the new creation, the second Adam, raised and "freshly re-saturated" with the Holy Spirit, "births" his brothers/sisters (John 20:17) into the new humanity that the Father began through the Spirit in that new creation's first moment inside the garden tomb. Hence, this post-ascension scene offers a vivid portrayal of the Spirit proceeding from the Father through the Son, and perhaps a narrative representation of Paul's "last Adam" in his role as a "making-alive Spirit" (πνεῦμα ζῳοποιοῦν, 1 Cor 15:45).

Hence, in Mark and John, the temple of God, new creation and new humanity all converge and overlap in one place, namely, the body of Christ. There is an organic connection between these themes. The same life-giving Spirit who inhabited the Son's body throughout his life and death raises and enlivens the crucifixion-marked (John 20:27), raised body of the Son, God's eschatological new temple, the microcosm of God's new creation. It is the body of this Spirit-saturated new human being, God's true authorized cult statue in his cosmic temple, through whom God is at work to bring his creation to its intended destiny. In the Pauline corpus, we might also recognize an analogous organic connection between Paul's corresponding ecclesiological images.

Pauline Images for the Church

The portrayals of Jesus in the Gospels of Mark and John as the eschatological temple of God, the locale or microcosm of the new creation, and the new/true human being bear an analogy to the primary images Paul uses to depict the church and suggest a particular relationship between those images. Their portrayals offer a kind of "glue" that organically connects Paul's ecclesiological images, suggesting that images of the church as the temple of God, new creation, and new humanity all converge and overlap in one place, namely, the image of the church as the body of Christ.

---

parallel with 17:18) and in his being sent from the tomb as the Second Adam whose very breath is the divine Spirit, sending and equipping his disciples for their mission in the world.

Body of Christ

We begin with the image of the church as the body of Christ. From a canonical standpoint—and I see no necessary reason to reject this as historically improbable—one might imagine that the words of the risen Christ in Paul's first encounter with him in Acts 9 provided the catalyst for Paul's depiction of the church as the body of Christ.[1] There, the risen Christ says to Saul, in reference to his persecution of the church, "Why are you persecuting me? ... I am Jesus whom you are persecuting" (Acts 9:4-5). Simply on the basis of the number of passages referring to the church as Christ's body/the body/one body in the Pauline corpus,[2] its importance to Paul for depicting the nature of the church is clear. In addition, although we would need to fill out its meaning with more detail, Paul's characteristic language of being "in Christ" means at least being "in the ecclesial body of Christ."[3] Hence, the sheer prevalence

---

[1] This is not to say that for Paul the church and Christ's cruciform risen body are simply identical without remainder. The image is more pliable than that in Paul's letters. Most probably he developed it in conjunction with the familiar image of the state or city being a political body to addresses issues of unity and diversity in the church (cf. James D. G. Dunn, *The Theology of Paul the Apostle* [Grand Rapids: Eerdmans, 1998], 550-51). But for Paul the church is not just any generic body of people; it is very specifically the body *of Christ*. Such words as we find in Acts 9, then, might have spurred Paul to develop this image that was useful not just for addressing issues of unity and diversity, but especially for depicting the church's life together as—ideally at least—corporately analogous to Christ's life of faithfulness to God and love for others.

[2] 1 Cor 12:12-27; 6:15; 10:17; Rom 12:4-5; cf. Col 1:18; 3:15; Eph 1:22-23; 2:16; 4:4, 12-16.

[3] Cf. Michael J. Gorman (*Cruciformity: Paul's Narrative Spirituality of the Cross* [Grand Rapids: Eerdmans, 2001], 36) and Dunn (*Theology of Paul the Apostle*, 401), both of whom call attention to the communal significance of "in Christ," and James W. Thompson (*The Church according to Paul: Rediscovering the Community Conformed to Christ* [Grand Rapids: Baker Academic, 2014]) who says that "the body of Christ is an extension of 'in Christ'" (52, cf. 71, 72).

of explicit and implicit references to this image makes it foundational among Paul's ecclesial images.[1]

But it is foundational for another reason as well. Depicting the church as the body of Christ explicitly indicates that it has, or should have, a specific character analogous to that of the cruciform One whose "story" in Phil 2:6-11 reveals both the true nature of divinity and the true nature of humanity.[2] The other ecclesial images (temple of God, new creation, new humanity) do not, in themselves, have this sort of specificity.[3] But these images do rely on that Christological specificity for their content in Paul's letters. For example, to say that the church is both the temple of God (the true God's public presence and face) and the new/true humanity relies for its content on the way that Christ in his very body revealed the true nature of Israel's God and of humanity. Hence, it is not surprising that images of the church as the Temple of God, new creation, and new humanity all converge and overlap in one place in Paul's letters, namely, the image of the church as the body of Christ.

Temple of God/the Holy Spirit

As we saw above, in the Gospels of Mark and John Jesus takes on the functions of the Jerusalem temple prior to his crucifixion and resurrection. As the "Holy One of God," he is the messianic bearer and mediator of the Holy Spirit. His body is a moveable tabernacle, the temple/sanctuary (ναός) housing the

---

[1] Dunn calls it "the dominant theological image in Pauline ecclesiology" (*Theology of Paul the Apostle*, 548), but Thompson flatly contradicts Dunn, claiming that "it is scarcely the central feature of Paul's ecclesiology" (*Church according to Paul*, 52).

[2] On this way of reading the "Christ hymn," see my "Missional from First to Last: Paul's Letters and the *Missio Dei*," in Missio Dei: *A Wesleyan Understanding*, ed. Keith Schwanz and Joseph Coleson (Kansas City, MO: Beacon Hill, 2011), 67-74; and esp. Michael J. Gorman, "'Although/Because He Was in the Form of God:' The Theological Significance of Paul's Master Story," *JTI* 1 (2007): 147-69.

[3] As illustrated, for example, by the claim of other Jewish communities to be God's eschatological temple (i.e., the community at Qumran [4Q174]).

glory/visible holiness of Israel's God. He is the public presence and face of the Holy God where one sees "the light of the knowledge of God's glory" (2 Cor 4:4). And it is his crucifixion-marked body that God raises as the new temple/sanctuary (ναός), saturated with the presence of the life-giving Spirit. Considering the "glue" of the preceding discussion, then, describing the church as the [cruciform] body of Christ already implies that the church is also the temple/sanctuary (ναός) of the Holy Spirit/God.

Not surprisingly, then, when addressing the issue of some of the male members of the church in Corinth having sex with prostitutes (1 Cor 6:12-20), Paul appeals to both ecclesiological images with two rhetorical questions. Anticipating his later discussion of the church as Christ's body in 12:12-27, he first asks, "Don't you all know that your bodies (σώματα) are members (μέλη) of Christ" (6:15)?[1] That is, the individual bodies of each person in the church are "members" of Christ's body. A few verses later, he asks, "Don't you all know that your body (τὸ σῶμα ὑμῶν) is a temple/sanctuary (ναός) of the Holy Spirit, which you have from God" (6:19)? Although this language is most often understood to refer exclusively to each individual's body as being a temple of the Holy Spirit, a comparison of Paul's language in the first rhetorical question with that of the second suggests that his language retains a corporate sense in 6:19.[2] That is, Paul's language here is best taken

---

[1] Cf. Paul's language in 1 Cor 12:12: "For just as the body is one and has many members (μέλη)...so also is Christ."

[2] Note that, when Paul wants to refer to each individual's body explicitly in 1 Cor 6:15, he uses the plural (σώματα). In contrast, in 6:19 he uses the singular for "body" followed by a second person plural pronoun (τὸ σῶμα ὑμῶν). It is certainly possible that this still refers to the individual bodies of those he is addressing in the audience, but he could have made that explicit by returning to the plural of bodies (σώματα) and pairing it with the plural of temples/sanctuaries (ναοί). Hence, it is equally possible, if not more likely, that "one's own body" against which one sins in committing sexual sin (6:18c) is the corporate body of Christ of which that one is a member (μέλη). After all, one might take 6:18c (whatever 6:18b means) as a pithy summary of the whole of chapter 5 where Paul is clearly concerned with what one man's sexual immorality is doing to the church *as a corporate body*. This is *not* to deny that Paul thinks that the Holy Spirit also

as inferring that the corporate body of Christ to which the individual bodies of those in the congregation belong as members is the temple/sanctuary (ναός) of the Holy Spirit/God (cf. 3:16-17). Here, then, the image of the church as Christ's body directly converges with the image of the church as a temple/sanctuary of God. To say that the church is the temple/sanctuary (ναός) of the Holy Spirit/God in places like Corinth or Ephesus (1 Cor 3:16-17; 6:19; 2 Cor 6:16; Eph 2:19-22), where public space is dominated by temples of gods/goddesses, is to claim that the community that is the body of Christ is indeed the public presence and face of Israel's God.[1]

New Creation

Again, given the "glue" of the preceding discussion, these two ecclesial images of body and temple also converge and overlap with another of Paul's ecclesial images: new creation. Since some in the Greco-Roman context of Paul's churches understood the human body to be a microcosm of the cosmos at large, depicting the church as the corporate body of Christ converges with imagining it as a microcosm of the cosmos. As the body of the cruciform, risen Christ, however, the church would be a microcosm of the new cosmos God had set in motion by raising Jesus; it would be a microcosm of a new creation. This also converges and overlaps with the imagery of the church as the temple of the Holy Spirit/God. As we saw, in raising the body of the one in whom the functions of the temple had been localized, the Spirit replaced the microcosm of the old order (i.e., the Jerusalem temple) with the microcosm of the new order (i.e., the risen body of Jesus). The risen body of Jesus then

---

inhabits individual Christians (e.g., Rom 8:11). Rather, it is to make the point that 6:19 is more likely making a direct connection between the church as the σῶμα of Christ and the church as the ναός of the Holy Spirit/God. Cf. John R. Levison, *Filled with the Spirit* (Grand Rapids: Eerdmans, 2009), 294-300.

[1] For a more detailed description of the intersection of the images of body and temple in 1 Corinthians, see Thompson, *Church according to Paul*, 66-73. For further discussion of these contexts in which the church is depicted as a temple of God/the Holy Spirit, see my *Holiness and the* Missio Dei, 135-37.

becomes a new temple that functions as the microcosm of the new creation as a whole, a new creation with its own "cross-shaped order" and corresponding new "purity map."[1] Hence, as the corporate body of Christ that becomes a temple of the Holy Spirit/God in its local context, the church also functions as a small version, or microcosm, of the cross-shaped new creation. It is no wonder Paul can say, "If anyone is in [the corporate body of the cruciform, risen] Christ, there is a new creation" (2 Cor 5:17; cf. Gal 6:15).[2]

New Humanity

The imagery of new creation with the church as the microcosm of God's cosmic sanctuary converges and overlaps with the imagery of the church as a new humanity, "the authorized cult statue" in God's cosmic temple. As we observed in the way John tells the story, he implies that when Jesus's body is raised from the tomb, the Second Adam is being brought to life and, hence, a new humanity is being inaugurated. Particularly since Paul explicitly depicts Christ as "the last Adam" (1 Cor 15:45), it is not at all surprising that a community depicted as the body of that same cruciform and risen Christ would also explicitly be depicted as the new humanity in the Pauline corpus (Col 3:9-11; Eph 2:15; 4:22-24).[3] All the above images overlap and converge in the first two chapters of Ephesians, chapters that one might say contain "the quintessence

---

[1] On this new "cross-shaped order" and its corresponding new "purity map" in both the gospels and in Paul's letters, see my *Holiness and the* Missio Dei, 67-70, 103-4, 145-47.

[2] N. T. Wright's discussion of the church as a "*microcosmos*" makes similar connections between the ecclesial images under discussion in this paragraph (*Paul and the Faithfulness of God*, Christian Origins and the Question of God. 4 [Minneapolis: Fortress, 2013], 1489-94, esp. 1492).

[3] Although Paul does not explicitly use the terminology of "the new humanity" in the undisputed letters, the conceptuality is clearly present in: (1) the comparison he forges in Rom 5:12-21 between "the one human being," Adam, through whom sin and death entered the world, and "the one human being," Jesus Christ, who brings life; and (2) his language of "our old humanity" as having been co-crucified with Christ in Rom 6:6.

of [the ecclesiology of] Paulinism" whether or not Paul wrote the letter.[1] There, at the end of Paul's thanksgiving prayer for his audience, he speaks of God having given Christ "as head over all things to the church, which is his body" (1:22-23).[2] This "integral and almost organic connection between Christ and the Church"[3] continues in 2:10 where Paul says: "For we are God's creation (ποίημα), created in Christ Jesus (κτισθέντες ἐν Χριστῷ Ἰησοῦ) for doing good works." Reflecting what Paul says in 2 Cor 5:17 and Gal 6:15, this community is a new creation because it is the corporate body of the crucified, risen Christ, the current locale or microcosm of the new creation. This is the same locale—the one corporate body of Christ—in which the one new humanity of this new creation has been created (2:15, cf. 4:24). And it is in his corporate body that the community, depicted as a "building," "is joined together and is growing into a holy temple (ναόν) in the Lord,"[4] a proper "dwelling place (κατοικητήριον) for God in the Spirit" (2:21-22).[5] It is, then, a microcosm of the new creation to be consummated in the future

---

[1] This language is, of course, a play on F. F. Bruce's well-known characterization of Ephesians as "the quintessence of Paulinism" (*Paul: Apostle of the Heart Set Free* [Grand Rapids: Eerdmans, 1977], 424) that is recently echoed by Wright (*Paul and the Faithfulness of God*, 729).

[2] Here Christ is not explicitly identified as the "head" of the body as in 5:23, but as "head" over all things, he is certainly assumed to be in authority over the church. But in view of Paul's language in 4:15-16, the image of Christ as head of the ecclesial body in Ephesians also conveys that he provides the telos of the body's growth as well as the unifying force which holds it together (cf. Stephen E. Fowl, *Ephesians: A Commentary* [Louisville: Westminster John Knox, 2012], 62).

[3] Fowl, *Ephesians*, 63.

[4] Given Jesus's designation as "the Holy One of God" in the Gospels (e.g., Mark 1:24; John 6:69), it is not surprising that the church's holiness is a constant concern in the Pauline corpus, on which, see my *Holiness and the* Missio Dei, 127-52. On ecclesial holiness in Ephesians, in particular, see George Lyons, "Church and Holiness in Ephesians," in *Holiness and Ecclesiology in the New Testament*, ed. Kent Brower and Andy Johnson (Grand Rapids: Eerdmans, 2007), 238-56.

[5] Cf. the way Paul transitions from describing the church as a generic building to describing it specifically as God's temple in 1 Cor 3:9-17. On the blending of the images of body, temple and building in this Ephesians passage, see Thompson, *Church according to Paul*, 208-10.

when "God brings all things in heaven and earth to their proper end through and in relation to Christ" (1:10),[1] i.e., when creation reaches its intended destiny of being God's completed macrocosmic temple/sanctuary.

To close this section, perhaps it is worth stating the obvious. That is, Christ's resurrection is the adhesive catalyst in the "glue" of this whole discussion. Apart from Christ's vindicating resurrection by God, a cruciform communal body would simply be a monument to a tragic death. It would not be the temple of Israel's life-giving God whose communal life is a microcosm of God's coming new creation, reflecting what it means to be truly human.

Conclusion

I have argued that aspects of the story of Jesus congeal into gospel themes that bear an analogy to the primary images Paul uses to depict the church. These gospel themes provide a kind of "glue" that allows us to recognize an organic connection between Pauline ecclesiological images of the church as God's temple, new creation, and new humanity, with the image of the church as the body of Christ being the one "place" where they all converge and overlap. Hopefully, this brief sketch opens the way for a more detailed exegetical treatment of the Pauline passages in which these ecclesiological images occur in order to offer a thicker description of the "glue" that holds these images together.

Enough has been said, however, to underscore the fact that ecclesiology is inseparable from Christology in the Pauline corpus. And that needs emphasizing, especially in evangelicalism in the US where what it means to be the church often seems to have little connection with the story and character of the Jesus of the Gospels. Lord have mercy. Christ have mercy.

---

[1] Fowl, *Ephesians*, 47.

Loving Neighbor, Loving One Another, and Loving Enemies

Three New Testament Ethics of Love

Thomas E. Phillips

In 2009, I borrowed a dedication that had stuck with me over the years in an otherwise long forgotten volume. Those remembered (and adopted and adapted) words simply said: "To George Lyons, from whom I learned the best and most."[1] Among the many things that I learned from George Lyons was the value of a critical (perhaps even cynical) perspective on popular expressions of religion and the absolute centrality of "other regard" in all matters of religious ethics. This essay is informed by both of those values, the necessity of both a critical mind and a loving heart. So, with apologies to the late Burt Lancaster and his Academy Award, let me begin with a little cynicism:

> Love is the only bow on life's dark cloud. It is the Morning and Evening Star. It shines upon the cradle of the babe, and sheds its radiance upon the quiet tomb. It is the mother of Art, inspirer of poet, patriot and philosopher. It is the air and light of every heart, builder of every home, kindler of every fire on every hearth. It was the first to dream of immortality. It fills the world with melody, for Music is the voice of Love. Love is the magician, the enchanter, that changes worthless things to joy, and makes right royal kings and queens of common clay. It is the perfume of the wondrous flower—the heart—and without

---

[1] Thomas E. Phillips, *Paul, His Letters, and Acts*, Library of Pauline Studies (Peabody, MA: Hendrickson, 2009; Grand Rapids: Baker Academic, 2010).

that sacred passion, that divine swoon, we are less than beasts; but with it, earth is heaven and we are gods.[1]

So says Elmer Gantry, the lead character and unredeemable rogue in Sinclair Lewis's scathing novel about the church. (Lewis was, of course, the Richard Dawkins of his time.) While I write neither to praise nor to bury Elmer Gantry, I would like to suggest that Elmer is not the last biblical interpreter to offer abstracted and idealized praises for the emotive concept of love without ever explaining — in specific and concrete terms — what that love entails for the various biblical writers.

In this essay, I want to do four things: (1) briefly explain (and invalidate) some popular contemporary scientific (evolutionary) challenges to the very notion of love (and altruism); (2) introduce two theorists, Pitirim Sorokin and Garth L. Hallet, each of whom provides important conceptual tools for thinking about the nature of love and its demands in the New Testament; (3) reexamine some of the New Testament's teachings about love in light of the categories provided by Sorokim and Hallet; and (4) offer my own concluding observations about the nature of love and its demands in the New Testament.

Is "Love" Even Possible?

Most of us have at least a passing familiarity with Richard Dawkins and his theories regarding the inherent selfishness of genes. In his best-selling book, The Selfish Gene, Dawkins argued that human beings are little more than convenient transportation systems for the genes within their DNA.[2] These genes, he argued, are engaged in an intense evolutionary battle for intergenerational survival. According to Dawkins, genes must behave selfishly; they

---

[1] Sinclair Lewis, *Elmer Gantry* (New York: Harcourt, Brace and Co, 1927; repr., New York: Dell Publishing, 1954), 63.

[2] Originally published in 1976, the book is now available in the 40th anniversary edition with a new introduction by the author. Richard Dawkins, *The Selfish Gene*, 4th ed., Oxford Landmark Science (New York: Oxford University, 2016).

have no choice, because unselfish behavior would mean their extinction. Selfish genes survive to reproduce; unselfish genes lose out in the competition for reproduction and thus for existence beyond the lifetime of their current host organism.

Although Dawkins has a very strong moral center of his own (he is a devout humanist and pacifist), some theorists have extended Dawkins's arguments about the unavoidable selfishness of all genes and have further argued for the unavoidable selfishness of all persons. Such popularized arguments for the inevitability of selfishness — whether conscious or unconscious selfishness — are not only challenged by our shared human observations of seemingly unselfish behavior, but they are also incompatible with recent evolutionary research on group selection and kinship theories. Essentially, these theories take one of two forms. On the one hand, kinship theorists first argue that individuals can behave unselfishly for the sake of closely related individuals (e.g., siblings) who possess closely related genes. They further argue that the altruistic person's behavior is therefore benefiting the altruist's genes, even though the behavior is not directly benefiting the altruist himself or herself. Or, on the other hand, group selection theories argue that groups favor altruistic individuals because groups with altruistic members are more prone to long term survival than are groups composed solely of selfish individuals. When such theories of kinship and group selection are taken into consideration, it is no exaggeration to say that arguments for the inevitability of human selfishness have been decisively swept away by a wide range of work in biology, psychology and sociology. The broom of sociobiology has seen to that. There is now broad consensus in the sciences that human beings can cooperate and that humans can express genuine empathy and altruistic regard for the other.[1]

---

[1] To review some of the scientific work in this area, see C. Daniel Batson, *The Altruism Question: Toward a Social-Psychological Answer* (Hillsdale, NJ: Lawrence Erlbaum Associates, 1991); Matt Ridley, *The Origins of Virtue: Human Instincts and the Evolution of Cooperation* (New York: Viking, 1996); Elliot Sober and David Sloan Wilson, *Unto Others: The Evolution and Psychology of Unselfish Behavior* (Cambridge:

I have taken this very brief foray into the sciences in order to set up the real question that interests me: If human beings truly can practice altruism, defined as genuine other-regard, and they really can practice love, then what can be learned about the extent and degree of the love promoted—and possibly even practiced—by the various New Testament writers and the Christian communities that they addressed?

Sorokin on Love and Altruism

If we want to learn about the extent and degree of the love envisaged and practiced in the New Testament, then I suggest that the often neglected work of a mid-twentieth century social-scientist and a slightly younger ethicist is particularly helpful—Pitirim Sorokin and Garth L. Hallett.

Sorokin, the late Harvard sociologist of love, came to the study of love through his own traumatic life experiences. He prefaced his classic inquiry into the nature of love with a brief autobiographical note that explained:

> In 1918 I was hunted from pillar to post by the Russian Communist Government. At last, I was imprisoned and condemned to death. Daily, during six weeks, I expected to be shot, and witnessed the shooting of my friends and fellow prisoners. During the subsequent four years of my stay in Communist Russia, I underwent other painful experiences and observed, to the heartbreaking point, endless horrors of human bestiality, death and destruction.[1]

Harvard University, 1998); and Thomas Nagel, *The Possibility of Altruism* (Oxford: Clarendon, 1970). For recent surveys of the question of love, altruism and the theoretical challenges to their existence, see Thomas Jay Oord, *Defining Love: A Philosophical, Scientific, and Theological Engagement* (Grand Rapids: Baker Academic, 2010) and Andrew Michael Flescher and Daniel L. Worthen, *The Altruistic Species: Scientific, Philosophical, and Religious Perspectives of Human Benevolence* (Philadelphia: Templeton Foundation, 2007).

[1] Pitirim Sorokin, *The Ways and Power of Love: Types, Factors, and Techniques of Moral Transformation* (Boston: Beacon, 1954; repr., Philadelphia: John Templeton Foundation, 2002), viii. For the details of Sorokin's life, see his autobiography,

Sorokin's concrete and very direct experiences with hatred and violence prompted him to think very deeply about concrete and direct expressions of love. Sorokin was a deeply committed humanitarian, but he sought to investigate love as a social scientist. His work on love, though over five decades old, remains a good starting point for contemporary investigations of love — particularly if one is interested in social science categories for measuring love and altruism.[1]

Sorokin's classic, The Ways and Power of Love, discussed five "dimensions" of love: intensity, extensity, duration, purity, and adequacy. Although Sorokin was emphatic that love could not be measured on a linear scale, he insisted that we could recognize expressions of love that were relatively higher and lower in the five dimensions that are briefly defined below.

Pitirim A. Sorokin, *A Long Journey* (New Haven: College & University Press, 1963) and Barry V. Johnston, *Pitirim A. Sorokin: An Intellectual Biography* (Lawrence: University of Kansas, 1996). Sorokin's work has seen a rebirth of interest in recent years, particularly through the work of Stephen Post and the Institute for Research on Unlimited Love. See Stephen G. Post, *Unlimited Love: Altruism, Compassion, and Service* (Philadelphia: Templeton Foundation, 2003). Sorokin's work remains important among professional social scientists even today. See, e.g., Joseph G. D'Ambrosio, "Love During Divorce: Development of the Sorokin Pyscho-Social Love Inventory (SPSLI)," (PhD diss., University of Louisville, 2012).

[1] As examples of those interested in measuring and assessing love and altruism, see Thomas Jay Oord, *Science of Love* (Philadelphia: Templeton Foundation, 2004); Thomas Jay Oord, *Defining Love: A Philosophical, Scientific, and Theological Engagement* (Grand Rapids: Brazos, 2010); and Stephen G. Post, *Unlimited Love: Altruism, Compassion, and Service* (Philadelphia: Templeton Foundation, 2003). As examples of those interested in the origins of love and altruism, see Thomas Nagel, *The Possibility of Altruism* (Princeton: Princeton University, 1970); Matt Ridley, *The Origins of Virtue: Human Instincts and the Evolution of Cooperation* (New York: Penguin, 1996); Elliott Sober and David Sloane Wilson, *Unto Others: The Evolution and Psychology of Unselfish Behavior* (Cambridge: Harvard University, 1998); A. Sutherland, *The Origin and Growth of the Moral Instinct* (New York: Longmans, Green, & Co., 1998); and C. Daniel Batson, *The Altruism Question: Toward a Social Psychological Answer* (Hillsdale, NJ: Lawrence Erlbaum Associates, 1991).

First, the intensity of one's love refers to the demands that any particular act of love places upon the one who expresses that love. For example, giving up one's seat on a crowded bus would normally be a relatively low intensity form of love, while risking one's life to rescue someone from a burning building would be a highly intense act of love.

Second, the extensity of one's love refers to the distance one's act of love extends beyond the individual himself or herself. Acts of love toward one's children or family would have low extensity, while acts of love toward strangers in a foreign land would have a high level of extensity. This extensity could be either genetic (in the case of family relationships), geographical (in the case of clan or nationalistic relationships), or ideological (in the case of religious or political relationships).

Third, the duration of love refers to the length of time commitment involved in the act of love. Some acts of love may transpire in a single moment in time (perhaps risking one's life by intervening in a violent situation), while other acts may require years or even a lifetime to complete (perhaps caring for a severely handicapped person).

Fourth, the purity of one's love in Sorokin's system relates to the motive behind the act of love. Sorokin's "pure love" operated without any "tainted motives" like the hope of a personal reward, pleasure, profit, or any other secondary motive. Sorokin's pure love arose solely from an uncorrupted desire to assist the other person. (Even the desire to avoid hell or to attain heaven was impure in Sorokin's analysis.)

Finally, the adequacy of love is concerned with the consequences of the act of love. Adequate love would benefit the recipient. Therefore, the adequacy of love was analyzed independently of the loving subject's intentions. Only the love's effect upon the recipient of that love was significant in this measurement.[1]

---

[1] Sorokin, *The Ways and Power of Love*, 15-19.

Importantly, for my purposes, Sorokin understood these different dimensions of love to exist in tension—perhaps even in competition—with one another. For example, an increase in the intensity of love tends to provoke a corresponding decrease in the extensity of love—and vice versa. People can love an "in-group" very intensely, but the very intensity of that love tends to diminish the group's love for those outside the group.

Of course, these observations may seem like common sense to many of us. But still, these basic relational insights have not been widely employed in the analysis of the New Testament's traditions about love. In a few moments, I will set myself to exactly that analytical task, but first I want to introduce another set of analytic tools for thinking about love in the New Testament and early Christianity—the tools and categories provided by Garth Hallett.

Hallett on Love and Self

Hallett has developed a scale for measuring the relationship between self-regard and other-regard in various expressions of love. Hallett's rubric spans an uneven spectrum, consisting of ethical orientations ranging from self-preference to self-denial. Hallett defined each orientation in terms of how the deciding self regarded his or her own needs and desires in relation to the needs and desires of other people.

Hallett's first category, self-preference, is represented by persons who accept that when "deciding between alternative lines of action, a person should take account of others' good but should give more weight to his or her own good than to the equal good, collective or individual, of others." Within this ethos, a potential benefactor would act in favor of the other "only when others seem likely to benefit much more, collectively or individually, from one option than [the potential benefactor] would from some other alternative." Hallett suggested that this ethic was taught by Thomas Aquinas and most subsequent Catholic moral theology.[1]

---

[1] Garth L. Hallett, *Christian Neighbor-Love: An Assessment of Six Rival Versions* (Washington, DC: Georgetown University, 1989), 3, also see 49-50.

Hallett's second category, parity, suggests that one should consider only the potential benefit received by all the involved parties, giving neither increased nor decreased weight to one's needs and wants. Under this ethos, one's relationship to the potential beneficiary—even one's self—is irrelevant. Hallett associated this approach with John Stuart Mill's utilitarianism and with many early and contemporary Christian thinkers (e.g., Justin, Origen, Augustine, and Reinhold Niebuhr).[1]

Hallett's third category, other-preference, is the inverse of self-preference, and asserts that individuals should give priority to the needs of others, either individually or collectively, over one's own wants and needs in situations of equal gain or loss for all parties. Under this ethos, one's own benefit can be considered—and even prioritized, but only when one option disproportionally benefits one's self in comparison to a much lower level of benefit received by the other. Hallett finds this ethos among a few early medieval thinkers, particularly Leo the Great.[2]

Hallett's fourth category, self-subordination, is stronger than other-preference, which allowed one's needs and desires to compete with those of other people. Under an ethos of self-subordination, one may choose benefit to one's self only when that benefit does not compete with benefit to others; the actor is not allowed to permit his or her interests to compete with the interests of other persons. Hallett associates this ethos with Karl Barth.[3]

Hallett's fifth category, self-forgetfulness, requires "a person [to] consider his or her own benefit only in relation to others'." One's own well-being is not given "any independent weight." Within this ethos, "other-regard" and the common good are the only considerations to be valued. Hallett finds this ethic in John of the Cross, Ignatius of Loyola, and Jürgen Moltmann.[4]

---

[1] Hallett, *Christian Neighbor-Love*, 3–4, 50–52.
[2] Ibid., 4–5, 52–53.
[3] Ibid., 5, 53–55.
[4] Ibid., 5, 55–61.

Hallett designates his sixth and final category, self-denial, as the "most extreme understanding of Christian altruism." In this ethos, "a person should never seek his or her own good save as a means to other's good; so far as maximum benefit to others permits, self-service should be minimized." This ethos not only places no value upon one's own benefit; it goes beyond that principle and calls for the actor to actively deny her or his own benefit. Hallett finds traces — perhaps only rhetorical flourishes — of this ethos in several Christian thinkers (e.g., Ambrose, Chrysostom, Thomas à Kempis, Catherine of Siena, Calvin, and Luther).[1]

There are two brief asides for us to consider before continuing. First, I mentioned the asymmetrical character of Hallett's paradigm and the astute listeners among you probably observed that one could accomplish symmetry within Hallett's model simply by adding three more categories — other-subordination, other-forgetfulness, and other-denial — that would be parallel to the categories of self-subordination, self-forgetfulness, and self-denial in Hallett's model. Hallett acknowledges the potential — indeed, the reality — of these "other-unfriendly" relationships between the self and the other, but he argues that other-subordination, other-forgetfulness, and other-denial are such weak forms of other-regard that they are essentially and primarily self-regard. As such, they should not be considered forms of "altruism."

Second, some contemporary theorists would be troubled by Hallett's strong distinction between the self and the other, arguing that the "self" is always a social construction. While neither Hallett nor I would deny the social construction of the "self" (and of all reality), I am not — and neither, I think, is Hallet — ready to dissolve the important ethical distinction between the self and the other. For what benefits me — or at least what I perceive to benefit me — can (and often does) compete with what benefits -or is perceived to benefit — others.

Now, let us move on to the New Testament.

---

[1] Ibid., 6, 55–61.

Love in the New Testament

Let me begin by describing my project regarding the New Testament. First, I want to look at specific commands and specific reports of human-to-human love in the New Testament. Love between humans and the divine is excluded from my focus in this project — as are theological concerns about the origin of love; I am concerned only with the directives toward and expression(s) of human-to-human love in the New Testament. I am particularly interested in what Sorokin's calls the extensity of love. Specifically, whom do the New Testament writers command their readers to love? And whom do the New Testament writers report that they and their readers actually do love?

Second, I want to use Hallett's taxonomy of the relationship between the loving self and the loved other to examine the relationship between the loving self and the loved other in New Testament's commandments regarding, and expressions of, love.[1] I will look primarily at three major New Testament traditions: the synoptic, Johannine and Pauline traditions.

The Synoptic Tradition

Assuming the classic two-source theory (Mark and "Q" as written sources for Matthew and Luke), we will begin with Mark's Gospel. Mark's Gospel speaks directly about love only in a dialogue between Jesus and the scribe who asked Jesus about the two greatest commandments, a dialogue which is also reported in both Matthew and Luke. At first blush, therefore, Mark seems to offer little unique insight into love. In Mark, Jesus frames the command to love in terms of the familiar call for parity in love, "loving your neighbor as you love yourself" (12:31, 33). Although in Mark's

---

[1] In regard to Sorokin's other four categories, one could argue that Hallett's scale for the examination of the relationship between the loving self and the loved other are simply differently framed ways of talking about Sorokin's concern for the purity of love. As I see it, the task of evaluating the duration, intensity, and adequacy of the loved expressed in the NT is more difficult and will be left for another time.

account the interpretation of this commandment to love one's neighbor comes from a scribe and not from Jesus himself (12:33, cf. 12:31), the scribe's interpretation of the command simply endorses the command's ethic of loving parity toward one's neighbor. Unfortunately, neither Jesus's recitation of the second great commandment nor the scribe's elaboration on that recitation provides any substantive definition of the neighbor who is to be loved.[1] However, Bruce Malina is almost certainly correct to suggest that few people in the Greco-Roman world—and most certainly almost no Jewish scribes—would have defined their neighbor as an otherwise unrelated person who just happened to exist in geographical proximity to themselves.[2] In Mark, therefore, we find an ethic of loving parity with limited, but poorly defined, extensity.

The redactions of this Markan exchange in the Gospels of Matthew and Luke take significant editorial license with Mark's account. On the one hand, Matthew—in keeping with his editorial habits—significantly abridges Mark's account. Matthew omits the scribe's largely affirming commentary on Jesus's citation, a deletion quite probably motivated by Matthew's general hostility toward the Jewish scribes (it wouldn't do to have Jesus commended by a dreaded scribe; see Matt 23:1-36). In spite of Matthew's abridgment, he left the "neighbor" as undefined, as did his Markan source (Matt 22:37-39). Interestingly, Matthew's only other reference to loving one's neighbor, where Matthew inserts this commandment among others listed by a "rich younger ruler" (Matt 19:19//Mark 10:17-22; Luke 18:18-23), also leaves the neighbor undefined. On the other hand, Luke, like Mark, recites this command to love one's neighbor only once (the rich young ruler makes no mention of loving his neighbor in either Mark or Matthew). Still, in his redaction of

---

[1] Joel Marcus is correct to suggest that the "immediate Markan context provides no clue as to the meaning of 'neighbor'," but that Mark's Gentile perspective probably would imply the inclusion of Gentiles—even if only Gentile Christians (*Mark 8-16: A New Translation with Introduction and Commentary* [AB 27A; New Haven: Yale University, 2009], 839).

[2] See Bruce J. Malina, "Neighbor," *NIDB* 4:251-52.

Mark's dialogue between Jesus and the scribe, Luke removes all ambiguity about the neighbor's identity. Luke replaces the scribe's interpretation of the commandment with a self-serving question from Jesus's dialogue partner. In Luke, the Markan scribe (Mark 12:28) becomes a lawyer (Luke 10:25) who seeks to justify himself by interrogating Jesus. The lawyer asked, "And who is my neighbor?" (10:29). Jesus answered this question with the parable of the good Samaritan, which essentially commanded the lawyer to go out and become a neighbor to his enemies. Even though an earlier account in Luke's Gospel left the reader with little doubt of the mutual contempt that existed between Jews and Samaritans in general (even Jesus's disciples wanted to fry a Samaritan village, 9:51–56), this particular Samaritan became a neighbor to the (presumably Jewish) man who fell among thieves.[1] By placing the parable of the good Samaritan in this context, Luke has transformed Mark's commandment for loving parity toward one's undefined neighbor into a commandment for loving parity toward one's enemies.

The Markan and Markan-derived traditions about love, therefore, demand an ethic of loving parity toward one's neighbors, neighbors who are not well defined in the Gospels of Mark and Matthew, but who are essentially transformed into enemies in Luke's Gospel. All three versions of the Markan-derived commandment promote parity toward one's neighbor, but Mark and Matthew extend this parity to the undefined neighbor, while Luke clearly defines this neighbor as one's enemy.

The love commands in Q are quite similar to the Lukan redaction of Mark's love traditions. The Q traditions require loving one's enemies (Luke 6:27–36; Matt 5:43–48). The Q commandment regarding love in Matthew and Luke specifically pits an extensive love toward enemies against a narrow endogenous love toward

---

[1] On Jesus's reframing of the question from "Who is my neighbor?" (Luke 10:25) to "Who became a neighbor?" see Thomas E. Phillips, "Subtlety as a Literary Technique in Luke's Characterization of Jews and Judaism," in *Literary Studies in Luke-Acts*, ed. Richard P. Thompson and Thomas E. Phillips (Macon, GA: Mercer University, 1998, 313–26).

one's own people group. Each evangelist includes a series of rhetorical questions that demeans a non-extensive love. For example, Matthew asks, "If you greet only your brothers and sisters, what more are you doing than others?" (Matt 6:47) and Luke asks, "If you love those who love you, what credit is that to you?" (Luke 6:32). When considered from an earthly, temporal perspective, both evangelists require a high degree of other-regard in these commands. The scale of this love reaches at least to self-subordination and possibly all the way to self-forgetfulness. In the immediately preceding verses, both evangelists require their readers to give to everyone who begs from them — and apparently without regard for one's own needs (Matt 5:42; Luke 6:30). Luke even includes an explicit prohibition against expecting anything in return (6:35). This self-forgetfulness is likely empowered by Q's insistence that believers need not be anxious since God will supply their needs (Matt 6:25-32; Luke 12:22-30). However, when viewed eschatologically — as the context strongly suggests that one should — the purity and selflessness of the love toward enemies are less pronounced. Immediately after calling his readers to disregard any concern for return from the recipients of their love, Luke reassures these same readers that their eschatological reward will be "great" (Luke 6:35). Matthew's sayings about loving one's enemies do not include any explicit reference to eschatological rewards (as do Luke's), but Matthew's next three sayings about almsgiving, prayer and fasting all conclude with explicit promises of eschatological rewards (Matt 6:4, 6, 18).[1]

---

[1] Several other synoptic traditions demand self-denial from believers and could be added to this discussion. For example, the Markan-derived sayings about cross-bearing and self-denial (Mark 8:34 — 9:1; Matt 16:24-28; Luke 9:23-27) clearly teach self-denial, but that self-denial seems to be directed toward God and not toward human beings. The same kind of divinely aimed love and self-denial is found in Q (Luke 14:25-27; 17:33; Matt 10:37-39). Traditions of such love toward God are outside the scope of this investigation, although it is interesting to note that these seem to teach a "God-preference" to the immediate detriment ("hate" or "love less") of the other — even closely related others — and to the eschatological advance of the believing self…. Troubling, indeed.

The Q-derived traditions about love, therefore, are characterized by profound extensity—directly calling for love of one's enemies. They are also marked by great purity in the short term, falling in the range of self-subordination to self-forgetfulness on Hallett's scale. However, when these same traditions are viewed in eschatological perspective—as their context encourages their readers to read them, these Q-derived traditions are quite impure and display a strong emphasis upon reward and self-advantage.

The Johannine Tradition

Perhaps the simplest commands about love are found in John's farewell discourse. The Johannine Jesus gave his disciples a new commandment, that they love one another (John 13:34). The practice of this "in-group" love was to distinguish Jesus's followers as his disciples in the eyes of the unbelieving world (13:35). This "in-group" love was modeled on Jesus's love for his disciples, his "friends" for whom he laid down his life (15:12-13). Thus, the Johannine Jesus could summarize his solitary command simply as "love one another" (15:13). And, to be sure, this Johannine ethic is thoroughly endogenous. Jesus, the community's exemplar, limited his intercession to his followers and specifically refused to pray for the world (17:9).

The Johannine letters follow the gospel's tradition of endogenous love. In positive terms, the epistles repeatedly characterize their community as those who accept the commandment to love another (1 John 3:11, 23; 4:7, 11-12; 2 John 5). Occasionally, the letters—unlike the gospel—stray from the language of "loving one another," but even in these cases the letters use the conceptually identical language of loving brothers and sisters (1 John 2:10; 4:21), loving the children of God (1 John 5:2), loving some particular person within the Johannnine community (3 John 1), or loving the chosen lady, that is, the Johannine church (2 John 1, 3 John 6). As in the case of the gospel, the readers of the letters are distinguished from the world by their "in-group" love for another (1 John 3:10, 17-18; 4:20) and they are specifically forbidden from loving the world (1 John 2:15). Also, as in the gospel, the Johannine community of the letters knows what love is because they have seen love demonstrated by Jesus—who laid down his life for them—and they are called to imitate that example by laying down their own lives for their brothers and sisters (1 John 3:16).

In the Johannine tradition, therefore, the command to love rates very low on the extensity scale (just loving other believers), but very high on the intensity scale (giving up one's life). This love is also quite pure. Believers are called to practice self-denying love without any immediate or clearly articulated promise of eschatological reward.[1]

The Pauline Traditions

Let me state my thesis regarding the Pauline traditions upfront: I think that Paul's genuine letters stand very close to the Johannine tradition of loving one another and that the deutero-Pauline letters are nearly indistinguishable from the Johannine tradition. In Paul's letters, the apostle calls for Christians to practice "brotherly love" toward one another (1 Thess 5:13) and to prefer one another in honor (Rom 12:10). Paul repeatedly claims to love his readers (1 Cor 16:24; 2 Cor 2:4; 11:11; 12:15; Phil 4:1; 1 Thess 2:8; 3:6). He repeatedly claims both to have experienced love from his readers (2 Cor 8:7-8; Phil 1:16) and to have seen his readers loving one another (1 Thess 4:9-10; Phlm 5, 7). Paul implores his readers to love other Christians (2 Cor 2:8; 8:24) and even prays that they will do so (1 Thess 3:12), but Paul never clearly calls for his readers to love outsiders or non-believers.

Even Paul's great love chapter, 1 Corinthians 13, with its eloquent call for self-denying Christian love (even to the point of

---

[1] The best comparison of the Johannine tradition's love for one another and the synoptic tradition's love for enemies is Martin Hochholzer, *Feindes- und Bruderliebe im Widerstriet? Eine vergleichende Studie zur synoptischen und johanneischen Ausprägung des Liebesgebots* (Frankfurt am Main: Peter Lang, 2007). Hochholzer argues that there was no ancient parallel to the synoptic tradition's love for enemies (just as Matt 5:43 would seem to imply), but that the Johannine tradition's love for one another had roots within Judaism's sense of election.

flames [13:3]!), falls squarely within the context of the Corinthian community's breakdown of internal cohesion. The Corinthians were not fighting with unbelievers over spiritual gifts; they were fighting with their Christian siblings over these issues (1 Cor 12−14). The Corinthians needed to love one another. In keeping with this conception of endogenous Christian love, Paul discouraged Christians from eating food without regard for their Christian siblings—siblings whom Christ loves and for whom Christ died (Rom 14:15).

The only seeming exceptions to Paul's preference for "in-group" love are his two citations of the command for believers to love their neighbor (Rom 13:9; Gal 5:14), but the context of these citations is crucial for understanding Paul's understanding of Christian love. Both times when Paul cited this command to love one's neighbor, he—like Luke—used the immediate context to define the identity of the neighbor who was to be loved. Earlier, we saw that Luke defined the neighbor as one's enemy. In Luke's Gospel, the command was given and the subsequent verses were used to define the neighbor as one's enemy. In Paul, the citation of the command functions very differently. In Luke, the command to love is primary and the definition of the neighbor serves as commentary on the command. In Paul, the preceding command to love another (Gal 5:13, Rom 13:8) is primary and the command to love one's neighbor is given to validate Paul's previously stated directive to love one another. In both instances, Paul's citation of the command to love one's neighbor is used in support of Paul's more central concern to establish a Christian community that "loves one another" and therefore fulfills the law (Rom 13:8, 10; Gal 5:13-14). In these contexts, the command to love one's neighbor is used to bolster Paul's demand for an "in-group" love toward one another. The command to love one's neighbor serves as little more than a theological "support text" from the Old Testament and Jesus tradition in support of Paul's concern for endogenous love. In both of these cases, the neighbor to be loved is clearly the Christian sibling—as in the Johannine tradition.

The "in-group" love in Paul's letters is, as in the Johannine tradition, quite intense. Paul listed the abuses that he has willingly endured—and will continue to endure—for the Corinthian church (2 Cor 11:7-11; 12:15). Paul reports having benefited from the sacrificial giving of some his converts (Phil 2:25-30; 4:15-17; 2 Cor 11:9) and he even insists that the Galatians would have torn out their eyes for him (Gal 4:15). In most respects, therefore, the conception of love in the authentic Pauline letters is nearly identical to the self-denying endogenous, in-group, love of the Johannine of the tradition. The only exception to this in-group ethic of Christian love is Paul's tortured love for his other in-group, his fellow Jews (Rom 9–11).

In the deutero-Pauline tradition, Paul's emphasis upon endogenous love is intensified, often taking on even more explicitly Johannine language. Ephesians offers thanks that Christians practice "love for all the saints" (Eph 1:15) and insists that the body of Christ is held together by love (4:15-16). Not surprisingly, therefore, Christians are urged to bear with "one another in love" (4:2). This love rests on the theoretical model of Christ "who loved us and gave himself up for us" (5:2, 25), but its practice appears far less self-sacrificing as husbands are charged to love their wives as their own bodies (5:28) and the husband loves himself (5:33). In Ephesians, therefore, we observe a command for love that is extensive and self-sacrificing in theory, but that is practiced as in-group parity. Colossians contains many of the same tendencies, although in less pronounced forms. Colossians boasts about the love expressed among all the saints (Col 1:4) and likewise sees this love as the source of Christian unity (2:2; 3:14). The command for husbands to love their wives is placed neither within the conceptual framework of Christ's self-sacrificing love nor within parity promoting comparison of self-love (3:19). The love in Colossians is endogenous to be sure, but its intensity remains ill-defined. The lone reference to love in 2 Thessalonians is likewise endogenous— "the love every one of you has for each other" (2 Thess 1:13), as are the few prevailing references to love in the Pastorals (love for family

[Tit 2:4] and love for fellow Christians [Tit 3:15]). Poor Demas dared practice an extensive love for the world (2 Tim 4:10), but that love was just as disastrous for Demas as it would have been for a character in the Johannine narrative. The goal of Christian instruction in 1 Timothy is love (1:5), but that is an entirely undefined love.

In the Pauline tradition, therefore, we see a pretty clear trajectory — a largely in-group, non-extensive, but self-sacrificing love in Paul's authentic letters with both a less extensive and less intensive in-group love in the post-Pauline letters. In Paul's authentic letters, Christians behave sacrificially toward one another; in Ephesians, Colossians, and 2 Thessalonians Christians are bound tightly together by their in-group love, but a love that is characterized more by parity than by self-sacrifice; in the Pastorals, love is an in-group phenomenon with little content — or even Christological foundations.

Before concluding, a brief note on the General Epistles is appropriate. In Hebrews, love is helping God's people (Heb 6:10). In James, love is apparently showing regard for economically disadvantaged co-religionists (Jas 2:1–13). In 1 Peter, love is emphatically endogenous, as the Petrine letter urges believers to love another deeply (1 Pet 1:22; 4:18), to love the family of believers (2:17), to love believers as siblings (3:8), and even to greet fellow believers with a kiss of love (5:14).[1]

What Then Are We to Make of All This?

I begin with an apology. I have only surveyed the surface of a vast and deep sea of data. Of course, this investigation could be expanded and deepened by looking beyond the mere linguistic appearances of the word "love" (primarily ἀγαπάω) in the New Testament. And, of course, the explicitly theological piece regarding divinity as both a source and recipient of love is important.

---

[1] The best introduction to the love directives within the Pauline and General Epistles remains Victor Paul Furnish, *The Love Command in the New Testament* (Nashville: Abingdon, 1972), 91–131, 159–93.

However, my goal has been small — to examine the commands and claims regarding human to human love in the major witnesses of the New Testament. With that examination complete, a few things now seem clear.

First, in-group, endogenous love is the primary stated norm within the New Testament, particularly in the central witnesses of Paul and John. The biggest challenges to this tradition are found in the Q tradition and in Luke's redactional material, with their emphases upon love for one's enemies. The Markan and Matthean command to love one's neighbor may challenge the early Christians' preference for in-group love, but the degree of that challenge depends upon how one chooses to define those authors' highly ambiguous use of "neighbor." Perhaps the most surprising observation about this prevalence of endogenous, in-group, love within the New Testament is Q's willingness to criticize this tradition so directly (what credit is it to love only those who love you?).

Second, where in-group love is most plausibly challenged (Q and the Markan traditions), the increase in the extensity of the love sees a corresponding decrease in both the intensity and purity of the love. The intense self-sacrificing love of the Johannine and Pauline traditions shrinks to a far less intense directive for loving parity in Mark and Q. Neither John nor Paul directly associates his call for endogenous Christian love with any promise of reward, neither temporally nor eschatological, However, Q makes direct promises of eschatological reward for acts of Christian love that extend to one's enemies.

Third, and perhaps least surprisingly, the relationship between the various aspects of love in the New Testament corresponds quite closely to the relationships that Sorokin's research predicted, but this is a topic for another day. My goal here has merely been to present the New Testament evidence within a framework provided by Sorokin and Hallett.

LISTENING AGAIN TO THE LETTERS

Love Empowered Knowledge

How the Way of the Cross Determines Behavior in 1 Corinthians 8

David A. Ackerman

Paul engages the Corinthian church in spiritual development in 1 Corinthians 8–10 with the goal of healing any division within the church and strengthening the bond of love between believers. Paul's broader concern in chapters 5–11 is with how the church should live out its faith in Christ in a hostile environment full of immorality and idolatry. He offers group boundaries that define a new community that is maturing in the Spirit and has the "mind of Christ" (1 Cor 2:6-16). Paul offers himself as an example with the use of an inclusio in 4:17 and 11:1 that calls the church to imitate his way of life in Christ. He devotes a significant part of the letter in chapter 9 to giving himself as an example of giving up one's rights in order to live out the call of the gospel. The Corinthian believers, however, were living too much like the world. Their divisive selfishness led Paul to describe them as immature and fleshly (3:1-3). Such descriptions contrast with his beginning remarks in the letter, which remind them of the way of the cross (1:18–2:5) and offer a pattern for how they should live as the church of God. Being a new community in Christ involves orientation to the divine paradox of the cross in attitude and action. Paul deals with their attitude in chapters 1–4 and their actions in 5:1–11:1. Evidently, the Corinthians advocated individual freedom to the detriment of community cohesiveness (6:12; 10:23). They were acting too much like their pagan neighbors and failed to grow into a holy ethic.

In the second major argument of the letter, Paul deals with two issues that early Christians faced in the pagan Greco-Roman culture. These are given in two similar imperatives: "flee sexual immorality" (φεύγετε τὴν πορνείαν; 6:18) and "flee idol worship" (φεύγετε ἀπὸ τῆς εἰδωλολατρίας; 10:14). The New Testament indicates that early churches throughout the Roman Empire struggled against the influence of immorality and idolatry. Many of the new believers may have been involved with these practices and struggled to put on "the new self, created to be like God in true righteousness and holiness" (Eph 4:24) and "walk in love, as Christ loved us and gave himself up for us, a fragrant offering and sacrifice to God" (Eph 5:2). Food sacrificed to idols was to be avoided, according to the apostolic decree in Acts 15:20 (cf. Acts 15:29; 21:25). The combination of πορνεία ("sexual immorality") and εἰδωλολατρία ("idol worship") is also a significant issue addressed in Rev 2:14, 20. Similar problems are addressed in the late first-century document, the Didache, which states, "Now about food: undertake what you can. But keep strictly away from what is offered to idols, for that implies worship of dead gods" (6:3).[1]

One possible link between these two problems is the issue of authority (ἐξουσία; "power" or "freedom"). This word is found in both sections (1 Cor 7:37; 8:9).[2] The spiritual issue is one of control: Who is Lord of the Corinthians' lives? Their devotion was incomplete—compromised with the values around them—and too focused on matters of the flesh (3:3). This compromise was keeping them from maturing in their faith and was affecting their fellowship with one another. Paul reminds them of his teaching about the cross and expects them to mature by having this same "mind of Christ" (2:16). The work of the Holy Spirit in them should be clearly evidenced by loving relationships within the church (see chs 12–13). In chapters 8–10, Paul deals with the general topic of idol worship, but his deeper concern is that the Corinthians learn to love one another so that they can overcome the temptations around them and be stronger together to fulfill God's purposes for them as the

---

[1] See C. K. Barrett, "Things Sacrificed to Idols," in *Essays on Paul* (Philadelphia: Fortress, 1982), 40–59.

[2] The term and issue also appears in other materials within the broader Pauline corpus: Rom 9:21; 13:1, 3; Col 1:16; 2:10; 15; and 2 Thess 3:9.

body of Christ. He is concerned that everyone in the church develop a life of holiness through complete devotion to Christ. This holiness will be evident in love that considers the needs of everyone in the church, especially those who have come out of the pagan environment.

The Challenge of Culture

Paul begins a new topic in 1 Cor 8:1, as indicated with "now about" (περὶ δέ). He may be offering his response in chapter 8 to questions from the Corinthians' letter (7:1) as well as to his perspective about the cultural and religious environment observed during his eighteen month stay in the city (Acts 18:1-17). The term εἰδωλόθυτον describes food sacrificed at a pagan temple. The topic of εἰδωλόθυτον has been foreshadowed in the lists of vices in 5:10-11, and Paul includes idolaters (εἰδωλολάτρης) in the list in 6:9. Different types of food were offered as part of idol worship. Paul refers both to meat as part of the sacrifice and also to food in general (βρῶμα); therefore, meat was not the only problem (8:13).[1] Three things typically happened to sacrificed meat: (1) the god's portion (μωρία) was burned on the altar; (2) a certain part was allotted to worshipers for consumption; and (3) a third part was put on a table (τραπέζομα) and dedicated to the god but consumed by worshipers or priests.[2] Often the leftovers were sold by the priests to help supplement their income.[3]

Paul knew well the religious context of Corinth, having spent eighteen months ministering there (according to Acts 18), particularly in the marketplace. Many of the problems in the church at Corinth can be linked to the syncretistic environment of the city of Corinth. Sacrificial meals were common in the Hellenistic cults

---

[1] Many different types of food were sacrificed to gods including grain, wine, honey, and animals; Peter D. Gooch, *Dangerous Food: 1 Corinthians 8-10 in Its Context*, SCJ 5 (Waterloo, ON: W. Laurier University, 1993), 53-54.

[2] Wendell Willis, *Idol Meat in Corinth: The Pauline Argument in 1 Corinthians 8 and 10*, SBLDS 68 (Chico, CA: Scholars, 1985), 16-17; Gooch, *Dangerous Food*, 22.

[3] See L. Bruit Zaidman and P. Schmitt Pantel, *La religion grecque dans la cité grecque à l'époque classique* (Paris: A. Colin, 1991), 19-77.

and associations, and these included interaction on the social level.¹ Archeological evidence supports the significant presence of numerous cults, temples, and shrines in the vicinity of Corinth that could have influenced the beliefs and morality of the church. Dining facilities have been found at the temple of Demeter and Core located on the road to the Acrocorinth. Cultic meals were probably eaten in these dining rooms. The cult of Demeter and Core, which had a strong presence in Corinth, was related to the cultivation of food with attention given to the yearly agricultural cycle, the burial and rebirth of dead seeds, and the growth and harvest of abundant food.² This cult was also related to the Eleusinian mysteries that incorporated the eating of religious food as one of the central rites of initiation. The use of food in the worship of Demeter at Eleusis suggests similar practices at Corinth. Since food was a sacred part of the worship of Demeter, any food eaten within the precincts of the temple most likely would have been dedicated to her.³ The temple of Askelpeion (located on the northern wall of Corinth) and the fountain of Lerna found nearby also suggest the availability of idol food in Corinth. The dining facilities found there may not have been part of the worship of Asklepios, but these possibly played a part through the incubation and pursuit of health.

The typical diet of the poor during this period did not usually consist of meat because of its expense. One could afford this luxury only on a special occasion such as a religious feast or if someone was economically affluent. The typical diet of the time consisted of grain products, porridge, olives, and occasionally fish.⁴

---

[1] Willis, *Idol Meat*, 47–61.

[2] For archeological evidence of the presence of Demeter and Core worship in Corinth, see N. Bookides and J. E. Fischer, "The Sanctuary of Demeter and Core," *Hesperia* 41 (1972): 283–331; N. Bookides and R. S. Stroud, *Demeter and Persephone in Ancient Corinth* (Princeton: ASCSA, 1987).

[3] Gooch, *Dangerous Food*, 1–13.

[4] See P. Garnsey, "Mass Diet and Nutrition in the City of Rome," in *Hourir la plebe*, ed. A. Giovanni (Basel: Herder, 1991), 67–101. Peter Tomson writes, "In antiquity meat was expensive and very difficult to keep. . . . [I]t was eaten only at special events such as festivals and ceremonies, certainly by the lower classes. . . .

Gerd Theissen identifies five occasions when the poorer citizen could have eaten meat: (1) special celebrations of victory, funerals, or to win the public's goodwill; (2) sacrificial meals for particular days; (3) the great religious feasts; (4) participation in one of the many associations; and (5) an invitation to dine at a temple. For lower status people, eating meat was typically associated with some type of ceremonial occasion.[1]

Eating food sacrificed to idols was a significant part of the social interaction of many people in cities such as Corinth. Many social events besides cultic worship were held at the dining halls associated with various temples. Sacrifice was often part of many social meals, especially those during some type of social transition (e.g., births, weddings, funerals, and reunions). Willis writes, "The assessment of the cult meals as occasions of good company, good food, and good fun makes it obvious why the Corinthian Christians would not have wanted to miss out."[2] Eating at sacrificial meals was a civic responsibility, and failure to do so brought social isolation.[3] Gooch assesses,

> If Corinthian Christians following Paul's advice were to attempt to avoid any situation where they would be asked to eat food explicitly identified as idol-food, then it is very likely that they could not accept invitations to frequent and important occasions.... It would not be possible to maintain social relationships with those outside the Christian circle without major adjustment and the serious possibility of misunderstanding and hostility.[4]

The Foundation for Holy Living

[F]ish, bread, vegetables, cakes and fruit were the regular diet" (*Paul and the Jewish Law: Halakha in the Letters of the Apostle to the Gentiles* [Van Gorcum: Assen/Maastricht; Minneapolis: Fortress, 1990], 189).

[1] Gerd Theissen, *The Social Setting of Pauline Christianity: Essays on Corinth*, trans. and ed. by John H. Schütz (Philadelphia: Fortress, 1982), 127–28.

[2] Willis, *Idol Meat*, 63.

[3] Joop F. M. Smit, "1 Cor 8, 1-6: A Rhetorical *Partitio*," in *The Corinthian Correspondence*, ed. Reimund Bieringer (Leuven: Leuven University, 1996), 582.

[4] Gooch, *Dangerous Food*, 37, 46.

Paul's call to holiness appears to be rooted in concepts found in the Hebrew Bible, especially the Holiness Code of the Pentateuch, although he also interacts to some extent with the conservative morality of his day.[1] One of ancient Israel's reoccurring problems was its worship of idols. The worship of idols violated the basic foundation of the covenantal relationship between Israel and Yahweh. Idolatry was strictly forbidden in many places in and outside the Pentateuch (Exod 20:4; 34:17; Lev 26:1; Deut 7:25; 11:16; 16:22; Ps 81:9). The concept of moral holiness in the Hebrew Bible is founded upon the core principle of the holiness of God (Lev 11:44-45; 19:2; 20:7, 26; 21:8). The reason for not making or worshiping idols is that, "I, the LORD your God, am a jealous God." Yahweh demanded exclusive worship, and anything less brought judgment. The Deuteronomist historian saw that the worship of idols led to the destruction of Israel in the promised land (Deut 4:27-28). The answer to the danger of idolatry came in the form of complete devotion to Yahweh (Deut 6:4-5, 12-15). The orthodox view was that idols were useless and worthy of destruction (Deut 7:25). The monotheism found in the Shema, the confessional statement to be taught to children after the conquest of the land of Canaan (Deut 6:4-9), shows the effort to combat the worship of idols: "Hear, O Israel, the Lord our God, the Lord is one. You shall love the Lord your God with all your heart, soul, and might."

Paul echoes the thought of the Shema (Deut 6:16) in 1 Corinthians 10:1-13. In 8:4-6, he modifies the idea from Deuteronomy 6:4-5 by adding "one Lord, Jesus Christ, through whom all things exist and through whom we exist." In the context of the idolatry present in Corinth, this statement is a reminder to the Corinthians of their exclusive loyalty to Jesus as Lord (1 Cor 12:3). It was the blood of Jesus shed on the cross that brought about the new covenant (11:25). The new covenant, like the covenant established at the foot of Mount Sinai, called for total devotion to God. The

---

[1] Thomas L. Brodie, "The Systematic Use of the Pentateuch in 1 Corinthians," in *The Corinthian Correspondence*, ed. Reimund Bieringer (Leuven: Leuven University, 1996), 441-57.

Corinthians were in danger of violating the new covenant with Christ by their participation in idolatry (10:15-17). Based on this danger, Paul warns them, "Flee from idolatry" (10:14). The danger of not fleeing from idolatry was to incur the Lord's jealousy, just as ancient Israel experienced (10:22; cf. Deut 4:24; Josh 24:19; 1 Kgs 14:22). The kingdom of the holy God does not consist of immorality or idolatry (1 Cor 6:9-10; 15:50).

Both Deuteronomy and Paul recall the incident at the foot of Mount Sinai described in Exod 32 when the Hebrew people cast a golden calf and then bowed down and worshiped it, thereby violating the central tenet of Israel's law code. Paul uses this incident in 1 Cor 10:1-13 to support his call to loyalty to Christ. Since Johannes Weiss, this has been recognized as a midrash on the incident from the exodus of the Hebrews from Egypt and their journey through the desert.[1] Paul quotes Exod 32:6b in 1 Cor 10:7, emphasizing the testing of the Lord and the consequences of destruction by serpents. Paul also alludes to incidents both leading up to this event at Mount Sinai and following it, including the crossing of the Red Sea (Exod 13:21; 14:22), the giving of manna and water from the rock (Exod 16:4-35; 17:6; Num 20:7-11), and especially the grumbling and disobedience of the people (Num 21:5-6; 16:14, 49). The basic cause of idolatry by Israel was seen as disloyalty to Yahweh. Paul's concern with the Corinthians is also the possibility of disloyalty and compromise of fellowship with Christ. Like Israel, they could experience the jealousy and hence the wrath of "the Lord" like Israel (1 Cor 10:21-22).

The Fundamental Choice between Knowledge or Love

The key word that divides chapter 8 of 1 Corinthians is γνῶσις: the fact of knowledge (vv 1-3), the content of knowledge

---

[1] Johannes Weiss, *Der erste Korintherbrief völlig neu bearbeitet*, KEK (Göttingen: Vandenhoeck & Ruprecht, 1910), 250; see also Wayne A. Meeks, "'And Rose up to Play': Midrash and Paraenesis in 1 Corinthians 10:1-22," *JSNT* 16 (1982): 64-78.

(vv 4-6), and a lack of knowledge (vv 7-13).¹ Verses 1-6 serve as the partitio of 8:1 – 10:22. A partitio divides the main theme into sub-arguments through the use of general statements and abstract notions. In this partitio, Paul provides two options through general principles that he will develop through deliberative argument to follow: freedom that comes from knowledge or responsibility that comes from love. The first is harmful to the community, and the second builds up the community. The first is discussed in 8:7-12 and the second is developed in 8:13 – 9:27.²

The availability of food sacrificed to idols and the social implications of eating meat influenced the formation of community in the Corinthian church. Two groups developed in the church as a result of eating idol food. The "strong" group were those with whom Paul agrees in principle – that idols are nothing before the one God and one Lord (Deut 6:4; 4:35, 39; Isa 44:8; 45:5) – despite the fact that he disagrees with their practice of this principle because of their abuse of their freedom (ἐξουσία).³ This group is implied in verse 1 with the formula, "we know," which introduces a well-known fact to Paul and the group.⁴ Paul addresses this part of the church because they had the power to change. The statement, "we all possess knowledge," may be ironical because there was in fact another segment of the church that did not have knowledge about idol food. Paul describes this second group in two ways: (1) in the plural, "those who are weak" (1 Cor 8:9, τοῖς ἀσθενέσιν), and (2) in the singular, "the brother for whom Christ died" (8:11). The identity of this latter group is disputed,⁵ but some of the weak may have

---

¹ Adelbert Denaux, "Theology and Christology in 1 Cor 8, 4-6: A Contextual-Redactional Reading," in *The Corinthian Correspondence*, ed. Reimund Bieringer (Leuven: Leuven University, 1996), 596.
² Smit, "1 Cor 8, 1-6: A Rhetorical Partitio," 580, 584.
³ Joël Delobel, "Coherence and Relevance of 1 Cor 8-10," in *The Corinthian Correspondence*, ed. Reimund Bieringer (Leuven: Leuven University, 1996), 178.
⁴ Smit, "1 Cor 8,1-6," 596.
⁵ John C. Hurd argues that the "weak" are hypothetical and indefinite (*The Origin of I Corinthians* [New York: Seabury, 1965], 125). However, they are more than hypothetical literary figures for Paul's argument. There is the very real

been Gentiles who formerly worshiped idols and who still had some form of emotional or psychological attachment to them.¹ The weak are passive victims in this chapter because they lack ἐξουσία due to their weak conscience. However, they are active participants in idol worship in chapter 10 because of the temptation to associate idol food with the worship of idols (10:6-13).

The critical issue in this chapter is the violation of the conscience of the weak believers. The word "conscience" (συνείδησις) occurs eight times in 1 Corinthians 8 and 10.² The compound word combines the verb οἶδα ("to know") and the preposition σύν ("with"), and it has a literal meaning of knowing something in agreement with another. Someone or something sets the standard by which decisions are made for how a person acts.³ The conscience is the self-awareness that determines this action. ⁴ This awareness can lead to developing convictions about moral behavior.⁵ Paul is concerned that the knowledge of some members

---

possibility of sin for violating their consciences (8:12). Yet, they do escape classification. Hans Conzelmann writes, "The 'weak' are neither Jewish Christians, nor any closed group at all. They do not represent a position. They are simply 'weak'" (*1 Corinthians: A Commentary on the First Epistle to the Corinthians*, trans. James W. Leitch, Hermeneia [Philadelphia: Fortress, 1975], 147).

¹ Barrett, *First Corinthians*, 194-95; Willis, *Idol Meat*, 91-95. James D. G. Dunn gives the other possibility that the weak were Jewish. He writes, "For the fear of idolatry as a Jewish concern was primarily the fear of contamination, and eating was strictly governed by taboos against unclean food; idol meat entering the body through the mouth could render spiritually unclean. Hence in 8:7 the fear of defilement, in 10:6-8 the association between idolatry, eating and drinking, and sexual immorality, and in 10:14-22 the abhorrence of any thought of partnership with idols and demons through eating and drinking" (*1 Corinthians* [Sheffield: Sheffield Academic, 1995], 66).

² 1 Cor 8:7, 10, 12; 10:25; 27, 28, 29 (twice); cf. Rom 2:15; 9:1; 13:5; 2 Cor 1:12; 4:2; 5:11; 1 Tim 1:5, 19; 3:9; 4:2; 2 Tim 1:3; Titus 1:15.

³ Victor P. Furnish, *Theology and Ethics in Paul* (Nashville: Abingdon, 1968), 229.

⁴ Christian Maurer, "Σύνοιδα," *TDNT* 8:914.

⁵ For further discussion, see C. A. Pierce, *Conscience in the New Testament* (London: SCM, 1955); Robert Jewett, *Paul's Anthropological Terms*, AGJU 10 (Leiden: Brill, 1971), 402-46; and Maurer, "Σύνοιδα," *TDNT* 8:898-919.

of the church is creating a different awareness of idols that the "weak" are unable to process in their minds. The strong know that idols are nothing, but the weak still attach meaning and importance to them, and they could be drawn back into idolatry. Although Paul agrees with the strong in principle, he still sees an evil power behind the worship of idols that can deceive people if they put value in them. Those who are "weak" in conscience are not able to distinguish the false nature of idols and the demonic power that lies behind their worship (1 Cor 10:20).

Paul realizes that knowledge is both the problem and solution for the Corinthians. The frequent use of the word γνῶσις in these chapters suggests that it may have been a favorite concept for the Corinthians.[1] Conzelmann comments that Paul "takes the 'knowledge' to which the Corinthians appeal and probes its foundations."[2] Basically, Paul redefines knowledge in 1 Cor 8:1– 11:1. Knowledge appears to be the basis for the strong Corinthians' ethical freedom, but at a cost of violating the conscience of the weak. Paul provides an alternative through the use of anaphora and chiasm in verses 1-3:

    A Knowledge puffs up, but
       love builds up (v 1).
        B If anyone thinks he knows something,
           he does not yet know as he should know (v 2).
    A' If anyone loves God,
       this one is known by God (v 3).

"A" gives the basic problem with the Corinthian strong: they boasted in their knowledge and overlooked the better alternative of love. "B" reveals the futility of this position because the type of knowledge they had was not true knowledge but was inferior to the better knowledge given in "A'." For Paul, knowledge consists of being known by God in a relationship of love. Paul in effect grounds the ethic of believers in love rather than knowledge and

---

[1] Gordon D. Fee, *The First Epistle to the Corinthians*, NICNT (Grand Rapids: Eerdmans, 1987), 365-66.
[2] Conzelmann, *1 Corinthians*, 138.

redefines knowledge. Denaux comments, "Knowledge in itself is not a bad thing. But when knowledge about God is not informed by love for God, it leads to pride (φυσιοῖ)."[1] Paul accepts the basic premise of those in position of strength but not the logical conclusion. A different type of logic must be used, and this logic is the new life in Christ Jesus displayed on the cross.

The wrong kind of knowledge is the problem for the strong Corinthians. In verses 4–6, Paul gives the basic theological principle and content of the knowledge described in verse 3. The strong Corinthians and he share the same conviction that there is only one God and one Lord; all other "gods" or "lords" exist only as creations of human imagination. This knowledge freed the strong from any influence of polytheism and provided them freedom to eat food that came through the temple system. Paul's attitude was that "the gods become gods by being believed in, and faith in the one God and the one Lord creates freedom no longer to recognize these powers."[2]

Verse 7 indicates that not all the Corinthians believers shared this liberating knowledge. Since some of them did not have this knowledge, their consciences were still influenced by the inferior knowledge of the culture around them. Their weak self-awareness opened them up to temptation that could potentially lead them back into sin. The strong could be guilty of leading the weak into sin if they violated the conscience of the weak. Smit suggests that this verse serves as the *narratio* or foundation for the argument until 1 Cor 9:27. Verse 8 is the *propositio* or thesis, verses 9–12 are the *refutatio* or antitheses to the thesis, and verse 13 functions as a transition into the *argumentatio* of chapter 9.[3]

The exhortation "look" in verse 9 (βλέπετε) puts the power to change in the hands of the strong because they have knowledge. In verse 10 Paul emphasizes his principle with a rhetorical question

---

[1] Denaux, "Theology and Christology," 598.

[2] Conzelmann, *1 Corinthians*, 145.

[3] Joop F. M. Smit, "The Rhetorical Disposition of First Corinthians 8:7-9:27," *CBQ* 59 (1997): 479–83.

that appeals to the developed conscience of the strong. Verses 11 and 12 gives the negative outcome upon the weak if the strong follow the way of their free knowledge. Paul connects their liberated, self-focused knowledge to faith in Christ. The outcome is the weak brother "for whom Christ died," who could fall back into sin and which could lead to the strong likewise falling into sin. Thus, it is a lose-lose situation if the strong continue on their path of liberation. Paul restates his principle in verse 13 by using double negatives for emphasis and showing the better path to take by his own example: "I will never ever eat meat if it causes my brother to fall." The shift to the first person makes a smooth transition to his personal example in the next chapter. The principle developed in this section guides Paul's rhetoric for the remainder of this section of the letter and is restated in 1 Cor 10:24 to cover any circumstance that violate the ethic of love.

Love that Brings Unity

Paul attempts to help the Corinthians believers live by a different standard from their culture or their old ways of the flesh. He offers to those who may think their knowledge gives them freedom to do as they want a paradigm of submission to the needs of others in the model of the cross of Christ. He challenges the weak to grow to maturity and devotion to the one God and one Lord. His ethic of freedom is conditioned with the responsibility of love. Conzelmann says that this "grace creates freedom."[1] Paul illustrates this love by his willingness to forego his own rights (ἐξουσία) as an apostle in chapter 9. By refusing to patronize the Corinthians for his support, Paul shows his identification with the humiliation of the crucified Christ.[2] As Engberg-Pedersen notes, Paul contends that "the gospel is one of love, of giving up oneself for others and of

---

[1] Conzelmann, *1 Corinthians*, 126.
[2] Richard A. Horsley, "1 Corinthians: A Case Study of Paul's Assembly as an Alternative Society," in *Paul and Empire: Religion and Power in Roman Imperial Society*, ed. Richard A. Horsley (Harrisburg, PA: Trinity Press International, 1997), 250.

willing that and willing it alone. Therefore, 'believing' the gospel ('subscribing' to it) is a matter of living in a certain way."[1]

Paul offers himself as mediator and example of the ethic of Christ. He uses scripture throughout his argument to support his views of morality, but more significantly, he gives himself as a worthy example of what it means to imitate Christ (1 Cor 11:1).[2] Furnish comments that Paul does not single out any specific attributes of the earthly Jesus. "Rather, it seems always to be the humble, giving, obedient love of the crucified and resurrected Lord to which the final appeal is made."[3] This appeal to love forms the foundation of Paul's ethic.

According to Fee, the basis of the Corinthians' behavior is bad theology and their misunderstanding of the ways of God.[4] Paul's basis for correcting the behavior of the Corinthians lies in his understanding of what it means to follow the way of the cross. His ethic is dependent upon the transformation that comes through experiencing God's mystery in Christ. The strong Corinthians misunderstood the eschatological ethic. Fee comments,

> Since salvation is essentially eschatological, always pointing toward its final consummation at the *parousia*, the future is understood to condition everything in the present. This is why ethical life is not optional; life in Christ in the present age is but the life of the future already begun.[5]

Some of the Corinthians had mistakenly used their ἐξουσία to the detriment of the fellowship. They thought their power gave them liberty (ἐλευθερία). Paul knew that the eschatological power of the indwelling Spirit brought liberty (2 Cor 3:17), but he

---

[1] Troels Engberg-Pedersen, "The Gospel and Social Practice According to 1 Corinthians," NTS 33 (1987): 583.

[2] David M. Stanley, "'Become Imitators of Me': The Pauline Conception of Apostolic Tradition," Bib 40 (1959): 874.

[3] Furnish, *Theology and Ethics in Paul*, 223.

[4] Gordon D. Fee, "Toward a Theology of 1 Corinthians," in *Pauline Theology: 1 and 2 Corinthians*, ed. David M. Hay (Minneapolis: Fortress, 1993), 41.

[5] Ibid., 56.

surrendered his freedom to love; his ethic was one of strength through weakness. He qualified his moral freedom by the gospel and by concern for others. He urges the strong Corinthians to join him in this ethic for their own salvation and for the preservation of the church.

Paul's ethic is thoroughly community centered. His desire is for community solidarity. One of the most striking places of conflict between Paul and the Corinthians is over community versus individual concern. Horsley writes, "For the Corinthians, therefore, the eating of idol meat and other matters were issues only in an internal personal sense, for one's individual consciousness, and not in a truly ethical, i.e., relational sense." For Paul, "such issues are ethical, that is, matters of relationships between people, not of one's own inner consciousness."[1] Paul grounds his basis for unity in the community firmly in the fellowship or communion with Christ (1 Cor 10:16-17) and in the common fellowship as the temple of the Holy Spirit (3:16-17; 6:19). The individualism of the strong threatened community. The cross makes fellowship in community possible and demands exclusive loyalty in return.

The church must rise to a higher level than the cultures around it. Fee writes, "Ethics for Paul is ultimately a theological issue pure and simple. Everything has to do with God and with what God is about in Christ and the Spirit. Thus (1) the purpose (or basis) of Christian ethics is the glory of God (10:31); (2) the pattern for such ethics is Christ (11:1); (3) the principle is love, precisely because it alone reflects God's character (8:2-3; 13:1-8); and (4) the power is the Spirit (6:11, 19)."[2]

The primary way that personal holiness becomes community holiness is through love. Love for Paul is the primary evidence of existence in Christ.[3] The so-called strong in the church began with knowledge; Paul began with love. For him, the character

---

[1] Richard A. Horsley, "Consciousness and Freedom Among the Corinthians: 1 Corinthians 8-10," *CBQ* 40 (1978): 589.

[2] Fee, "Toward a Theology of 1 Corinthians," 53.

[3] Love is also the first and foremost fruit of the Spirit in Gal 5:22-23.

of the believer is not based on ἐξουσία or γνῶσις, but on love (1 Cor 13:2; Gal 5:13). His own example in chapter 9 demonstrates that genuine freedom comes in love. Horsley writes, "In his response to the problem posed by the 'freedom of consciousness,' Paul insists on the 'real ethical question' at the interpersonal level. Both the structure and the substance of Paul's response makes the effect of one's behavior on others the criterion of ethics."[1] Unbounded freedom does one of two things: it destroys oneself or destroys community.[2] Paul realized that for the church to exist as community in a hostile environment, it had to create boundaries of purity. But for it to do that, it had to align with his paradigm of sacrificial love that was actually the paradigm of Christ on the cross. Pickett writes, "Ethics is never just a matter of what people do, but a question of the interplay between their identity, attitudes and beliefs, and behaviour."[3]

Conclusion

The primary mark of a community in Christ is its love, the evidence of which can be seen in the willingness of believers to forego their rights for the sake of others. Andreas Lindemann argues that the main problem with the church in Corinth was its relation with unbelievers, in that Paul wants the church to be at peace and not be offensive to the world around it (1 Cor 5:9-13; 10:32). The church needed to be united as family in the everyday situations of life. Paul knew the church could not exist in isolation. Love is what it means to be the church of God.[4] Lindemann's argument needs to be extended to include love within the community. Paul does not want the Corinthians to be indistinguishable from the world but to be clearly set off from the

---

[1] Horsley, "Consciousness and Freedom," 586.

[2] See W. Foerster, " Ἐξουσία," *TDNT* 2:570.

[3] R. Pickett, *The Cross in Corinth. The Social Significance of the Death of Jesus*, JSNTSup 143 (Sheffield: Sheffield Academic, 1997), 87.

[4] Andreas Lindemann, "Die paulinische Ekklesiologie angesichts der Lebenswirklichkeit der christlichen Gemeinde in Korinth," in *The Corinthian Correspondence*, ed. Reimund Bieringer (Leuven: Leuven University, 1996), 63-86.

world. But in their pursuit of holiness, they should not allow γνῶσις or ἐξουσία to take precedence over love. Paul's ethic is based in the gospel and the concept of the cross. The paradigm of the divine paradox symbolizes for him the new life that comes in fellowship with Christ. Furnish writes, "Paul's understanding of what love's way involves—the readiness to surrender one's own status and advantage where that will serve the weak and the disadvantaged—is directly related to his understanding of the word of the cross."[1] To understand Paul's spirituality is critical for a full view of this section of the letter. Paul does not deal simply with a few unrelated moral issues. Everything he has written thus far in the letter revolves around his understanding of the divine mystery and the experience of it. To experience the transforming power of fellowship with Christ involves identification with the paradox of the cross, evidenced by love within the community and conduct fitting for temples of the Holy Spirit. Jerome Murphy-O'Connor's concludes:

> To love and be loved is of the essence of Christianity and is constitutive of the being of the believer. They are bound together by what makes them be what they are.... The independent self, which the world takes for granted as normal, is absorbed into the authenticity of an organic community.... The most fundamental ministry of the church is to be the antithesis of a world which is characterized above all by divisions. Within the framework of hostile blocks (Gal 3:28), individuals are separated from one another by barriers of fear and suspicion (1 Cor 5:10-11; 6:9-10). The role of the church is to liberate the captives by revealing the opportunities of freedom in dependence on others.[2]

May it be so!

---

[1] Victor P. Furnish, "Belonging to Christ: A Paradigm for Ethics in First Corinthians," *Int* (1990): 157.

[2] Jerome Murphy-O'Connor, *Paul: A Critical Life* (New York: Clarendon, 1996), 288.

Translating λόγος as DNA in First Peter 1:22-25[1]

Troy W. Martin

Introduction

Translations of the Greek term λόγος ("logos") into any language are almost always inadequate and frequently misleading. This single term has such a broad and essential significance to the Greek worldview and such wide and varied applications that no single term in any other language apparently has. Attempts to render this term in a modern target language are thus forced to employ several different words. The least adequate translations employ what David Wilmot calls "Password Greek," which assigns particular English words or any other modern language words to a Greek term and then renders this term by the assigned modern word.[2] The Greek term λόγος ("logos") is often rendered this way

---

[1] I am pleased to submit this essay in honor of my friend and colleague Prof. George Lyons. George was the New Testament and Greek Professor at Olivet Nazarene University when I assumed my first full-time teaching position there. He was instrumental in shaping my teaching style and in helping me to develop a rigorous research agenda. I finished my dissertation while at Olivet and planned on revising it substantially before publication. George, however, advised me to submit it for publication immediately and to move on to other publications. I did, and that was some of the best career advice I ever received from anyone. George was a first-rate mentor, not only for me but also for the dozens of students who hung out at his office and who enrolled in his classes. I learned much from him during our short time together at Olivet and still cherish the long conversations we had and the frequent shop-talk that helped me understand my role as a faculty member. I am most grateful to him and submit in his honor this essay with its heavy reliance on the Greek language that he has taught and loved throughout his career.

[2] The late Dr. David Wilmot was my Greek instructor at the University of Chicago, and I am indebted to him for teaching me Classical and Koine Greek. This essay could never have been written without his enormous contribution to my understanding of the Greek language.

and translated as word in many passages where this translation is seriously inadequate.

Wilmot explains that the best translations operate at the level of meaning rather than at the level of the words themselves. These translations analyze the Greek term in its context to determine what particular aspect of the Greek worldview it represents. After determining the meaning, these translations then consider the semantic universe of the target language to see how this language would express such a meaning. Sometimes, the worldview of the target language is so different from that of the source language that no equivalent expression exists, and the translation must resort to paraphrase and description rather than translation. Such is often the case when rendering the term λόγος ("logos"), but sometimes a target language does possess an approximate word or concept for a particular usage of λόγος ("logos") and such is the case in 1 Pet 1:22-25.[1] Examining the grammatical, natal, and scriptural contexts of the usage of λόγος in

---

[1] This essay draws from and relies on several of my publications on First Peter and will form a part of my forthcoming commentary entitled *Apostolic Confirmation and Legitimation in an Early Christian Faith Document: A Commentary on the First Epistle of the Apostle Peter*, NIGTC (Grand Rapids: Eerdmans, forthcoming). See Troy W. Martin, "Dating First Peter to a Hairdo (1 Pet 3:3)," *Early Christianity* 9 (2018): 298–318; idem, "Christ's Healing Sore: A Medical Reading of 1 Petri 2,24," *Vetera Christianorum* 54 (2017): 143–54; idem, "Peter and the Expansion of Early Christianity in the Letters of Acts (15:23–29) and First Peter," in *Delightful Acts: New Essays on Canonical and Non-canonical Acts*, ed. Harold W. Attridge, Dennis R. MacDonald, and Clare K. Rothschild, WUNT 391 (Tübingen: Mohr Siebeck, 2017), 87–99; idem, "Faith: Its Qualities, Attributes, and Legitimization in 1 Peter," *BR* 61 (2016): 46–61; idem, "Emotional Physiology and Consolatory Etiquette: Reading the Present Indicative with Future Meaning in the Eschatological Statement in 1 Pet 1:6," *JBL* 135 (2016): 649–60; idem, "Tasting the Eucharistic Lord as Useable (1 Pet 2:3)," *CBQ* 78 (2016): 515–25; idem, "Christians as Babies: Metaphorical Reality in First Peter," in *Reading 1-2 Peter and Jude: A Resource for Students*, ed. Eric F. Mason and Troy W. Martin, SBL Resources for Biblical Study 77 (Atlanta and Leiden: SBL and Brill, 2014), 99–112; idem, "Roaring Lions among Diaspora Metaphors: First Peter 5:8 in its Metaphorical Context," in *Bedrängnis und Identität: Studien zu Situation, Kommunikation und Theologie des 1. Petrusbriefes*, ed. David du Toit, BZNW 200 (Berlin: Walter de Gruyter, 2013), 167–79.

this passage demonstrates that the most accurate rendering of this term for this passage is DNA.

The Grammatical Context

In 1 Pet 1:23, Peter uses a participial phrase to support his command in verse 22 for his readers to love one another intently. He writes, ἀναγεγεννημένοι οὐκ ἐκ σπορᾶς ἀλλὰ ἀφθάρτου διὰ λόγου ζῶντος θεοῦ καὶ μένοντος ("since you have been generated anew not from a perishable but from an imperishable sowing through the living and enduring λόγος of the living and enduring God").[1] Peter thus supports his exhortation to love intensely by appealing to the notion of everlasting life that results from the new generation of his recipients as siblings of the Father-God. In his account of Peregrinus, Lucian explains the "misguided brotherly" love and concern of Christians for Peregrinus, not only on their belief that they are all siblings but also on their belief that they shall live forever (Peregr. 13). Interestingly, Lucian's outsider critique of Peter's faith tradition names the same two grounds for love that Peter uses to support his exhortation for his recipients to love one another intently as siblings who shall live forever.

Peter explains the source of the new generation of his recipients as οὐκ ἐκ σπορᾶς φθαρῆς ἀλλὰ ἀφθάρτου ("not from a perishable but an imperishable sowing"). Similar to other authors, Peter uses the preposition ἐκ ("from") to designate the source of generation. For example, Aristotle in his discussion of σπέρμα ("semen" or "seed") states that all things in nature arise ἐκ τούτου ("from this;" Gen. an. 1.2 716a). Again, he affirms the common belief that all things are formed and come to be ἐκ σπέρματος ("out of semen;" Gen. an. 1.17 721b). Yet again, he describes semen as the sort of thing ἐξ οὗ ("from which") natural things are formed (Gen. an. 1.18 724a). Thus, Peter uses the usual preposition ἐκ ("from") to indicate the seed as the source of generation, but he does not use the

---

[1] I shall defer to the claim made in the letter and refer to the author as *Peter* even though I realize that this authorial attestation is problematic, sharply disputed, and generally understood as pseudepigraphic.

word σπέρμα ("semen") that is common in these discussions, but instead he uses the genitive form of the word σπορά ("sowing").

Commentators note the unusual use of σπορᾶς ("sowing") to mean σπέρμα ("seed") in this verse.[1] Nevertheless, many of them appeal to some type of metonymy to interpret σπορᾶς ("sowing") in 1 Pet 1:23 as equivalent to σπέρμα ("seed"), although some continue to insist these words do not mean exactly the same thing because σπορά ("sowing") emphasizes more the sowing than the seed itself.[2] Peter's metaphor of siblings in a new siblinghood helps explain his choice of σπορᾶς ("sowing") rather than any of the other more usual words for seed that emphasize the substance of the seed itself in the generative process. Instead of the seed, Peter's emphasis is on the father who generates all these siblings, and ancient authors often use the verb σπείρειν ("to sow") in reference to a father's role in the procreative process.[3] Rather than the usual words for seed that would focus on the substance of the reproductive fluid in the act of

---

[1] Indeed, LSJ cites only 1 Pet 1:23 and one other example of this unusual meaning of σπορά (1629), which usually means *sowing*, and the examples offered by BDAG are few and obscure (939). Whether σπορά actually refers to seed in any of these examples is questionable. This word group uses the masculine σπόρος ("seed") rather than the feminine σπορά ("sowing") in reference to seed.

[2] For the equivalence of these terms, see Paul J. Achtemeier, *1 Peter: A Commentary on First Peter*, Hermeneia (Minneapolis: Fortress, 1996), 139. For some difference in the meaning of these terms, see F. J. A. Hort, *The First Epistle of St Peter I.1 – II.17: The Greek Text with Introductory Lecture, Commentary, and Additional Notes* (London: Macmillan, 1898), 81; and J. Ramsey Michaels, *1 Peter*, WBC 49 (Waco, TX: Word, 1988), 76. Philo represents a common distinction of these terms when he uses σποράν ("sowing") in reference to the divine sowing but then switches to σπόρος ("seed") when he discusses each of the seeds that are sown (*Praem.* 2 [10]).

[3] For example, Philo disparages the adulterer who, after he sows his conceived offspring (ἐπίληπτον σποράν σπείρας), departs to leave the unsuspecting husband to raise it as his own (*Decal.* 24 [129]). Analogous to a human father's sowing, furthermore, God's act in procreation is also portrayed as a sowing. Philo calls God the husband and father of the universe who furnishes the sowing (σποράν) and origin of all things (*Det.* 40 [147]). In his argument that the Sabbath day has no human origin, Philo asserts that it has been sown from the Father God alone and that its generation is both without a human sowing (σπορᾶς) and without a human fetation (κυήσεως; *Mos.* 34 [210]).

generation, Peter uses the word σπορᾶς ("sowing") to emphasize the Father God's role in the generation of those whom this letter addresses.

Peter affirms that the new generation of his recipients is a divine sowing whose agency is διὰ λόγου ζῶντος θεοῦ καὶ μένοντος ("through the living and enduring λόγος of the living and enduring God"). The syntax of this prepositional phrase is significant. The object of the preposition διά ("through") is λόγου ("word"), which is limited by the adnominal genitive θεοῦ ("God"). The syntax of the participles ζῶντος ("living") and μένοντος ("enduring") is ambiguous.[1] Some commentators argue that these participles construe with θεοῦ ("God").[2] Their chief argument is that the qualities of living and enduring often characterize God, and that Dan 6:26 LXX has both these participles modifying God. The Vulgate's translation per verbum Dei vivi et permanentis ("through the word of God who lives and endures") inclines Latin commentators also to construe these participles with θεοῦ ("God").[3] Some others, however, nevertheless connect them with λόγου ("word").[4]

---

[1] Achtemeier, *1 Peter*, 139.

[2] H. Grotius, *Annotata ad Actus Apostolicos Epistolas et Apocalypsim, sive Criticorum Sacrorum*, vol. 12 (London: J. Flasher, 1660), 4509; and J. H. A. Hart, "The First Epistle General of Peter," in *The Expositor's Greek Testament* (Grand Rapids: Eerdmans, 1990), 5:53. See also Hort, *First Epistle of St Peter*, 92.

[3] Alexandre Noël, *Commentarius litteralis et moralis in omnes Epistolas Sancti Pauli Apostoli et in VII Epistolas Catholicas* (Paris: T. Bettinelli, 1768), 61; and David Hurst, trans., *The Commentary on the Seven Catholic Epistles of Bede the Venerable*, Cistercian Studies Series 82 (Kalamazoo, MI: Cistercian Publications, 1985), 79. See also Eugene A. LaVerdiere, "A Grammatical Ambiguity in 1 Pet 1:23," *CBQ* 36 (1974): 90.

[4] A. Camerlynck, *Commentarius in Epistolas Catholicas*, 5th ed. (Brugis: Sumptibus Car. Beyaert, 1909), 102; and Urbanus Holzmeister, *Commentarius in Epistulas SS. Petri et Iudae Apostolorum*, Cursus Scripturae Sacrae 3 (Paris: P. Lethielleux, 1937), 230.

Indeed, the majority of all commentators construe these participles with λόγου ("word").[1] LaVerdiere advances the main arguments usually found among these commentaries.[2] First, he sees a connection between σπορᾶς ("seed") and λόγου ("word") as the means of regeneration and argues that just as Peter describes σπορᾶς ("seed") as imperishable so also does he characterize the λόγου ("word") as living and enduring. Second, LaVerdiere argues that the quotation of Isa 40:6–8 LXX, which immediately follows, specifically characterizes the word as enduring. Finally, he proposes that the placement of the participles indicates that they construe with λόγου ("word") and not θεοῦ ("God"). Some commentators push this argument further and state that to modify θεοῦ ("God"), both participles must follow θεοῦ ("God").[3]

Almost all commentators on both sides of this interpretive issue, however, admit that these participles can construe syntactically with either "God" or "word."[4] A few commentators even connect them with both. Aretius discusses their connection with λόγου ("word") and then comments, "But neither is God, who lives and remains in us, excluded."[5] After discussing their

---

[1] Ernst Kühl, *Die Briefe Petri und Judae*, KEK 12, 6th ed. (Göttingen: Vandenhoeck & Ruprecht, 1897), 131–32; Rudolph Knopf, *Die Briefe Petri und Judä*, KEK 12, 7th ed. (Göttingen: Vandenhoeck & Ruprecht, 1912), 81–82; Edward Gordon Selwyn, *The First Epistle of St. Peter: The Greek Text with Introduction, Notes, and Essays* (London: Macmillan, 1946; repr., Grand Rapids: Baker, 1981), 151; Charles Bigg, *A Critical and Exegetical Commentary on the Epistles of St. Peter and St. Jude*, ICC (Edinburgh: T&T Clark, 1987), 123; Peter H. Davids, *The First Epistle of Peter*, NICNT (Grand Rapids: Eerdmans, 1990), 78 n 8; Reinhard Feldmeier, *The First Letter of Peter: A Commentary on the Greek Text* (Waco, TX: Baylor University, 2008), 124; and I. Howard Marshall, *1 Peter*, IVPNTC (Downers Grove, IL: IVP, 2003), 59. See also Achtemeier, *1 Peter*, 139–140.

[2] LaVerdiere, "Grammatical Ambiguity," 91–93.

[3] Kühl, *Briefe Petri und Judae*, 131; Knopf, *Briefe Petri und Judä*, 82; and Selwyn, *First Epistle of St. Peter*, 151.

[4] E.g., see P. N. Trempelas, Υπομνημα εις την προς Εβραιοθς και τας Επτα Καθολικας (Athens: Αδελφοτης Θεολογων Η Ζωη, 1941), 259. See the discussion by LaVerdiere, "Grammatical Ambiguity," 89.

[5] Benedictus Aretius, *In Novum Testamentum Domini Nostri Iesu Christi Commentarii* (Geneva: Petrum et Iacobum, 1618), 858.

connection to God and the word, Beare proposes that these participles "should perhaps be attached to both."[1] The rhetorical figure of hyperbaton and, more precisely, an interchained hyperbaton actually support this inclusive syntactical explanation.[2] Some commentators mention the odd placement of the noun θεοῦ ("God"), but it is not oddly placed. The words λόγου ("word") and θεοῦ ("God") are grammatically linked in a dependent genitive relationship but are separated by the participle ζῶντος ("living"). The participles ζῶντος ("living") and μένοντος ("enduring") are themselves grammatically linked by the coordinating conjunction καί ("and"), but they are separated by the noun θεοῦ ("God"). The hyperbaton or separation of words that grammatically belong together is thus interchained with the purpose of placing each and every word in emphasis, and the participles without any other clear grammatical indication connect with both λόγου ("word") and θεοῦ ("God") with equal emphasis.

The connection of λόγου ("word") with θεοῦ ("God") also supports an inclusive syntax for the participles. Peter's faith tradition eventually develops a very sophisticated Logos Theology, but Petrine commentators are reticent to read this developed theology into Peter's letter. Instead of being the recipient of this sophisticated theology, Peter writes early in the development of Logos Theology when the λόγος ("word") is still the spoken word about Jesus Christ (1 Pet 1:25; 2:8; 3:1; cf. 1 Cor 14:36; 2 Cor 2:17; Col 1:25; 1 Thess 1:6; 2 Thess 3:1) rather than Jesus Christ himself (John 1:1–18).[3] Peter's failure to identify Jesus as the Logos indicates either that he is unaware of this identification or that he consciously rejects it. The former is more likely and demonstrates that Peter is at a more primitive stage of Logos Theology than the author of John's

---

[1] Francis W. Beare, *The First Epistle of Peter: The Greek Text with Introduction and Notes*, 2nd ed. (Oxford: Blackwell, 1970), 86.

[2] Troy W. Martin, *Metaphor and Composition in First Peter*, SBLDS 131 (Atlanta: Scholars, 1992), 173 n 127.

[3] See J. N. D. Kelly, *A Commentary on the Epistles of Peter and Jude*, BNTC (London: Black, 1969; repr., Grand Rapids: Baker, 1981), 80.

Gospel. Rather than reading parts or even the whole of a well-developed Logos Theology into Peter's letter, a more useful approach investigates the natal context and how Peter specifically uses λόγου θεοῦ ("logos of God") in 1 Pet 1:23 as the means of the divine sowing that generates these recipients anew as siblings of one another.

The Natal Context

In 1 Pet 1:23, Peter uses λόγου ("logos") as the object of the preposition διά ("through"). Since this preposition names an instrument or means that functions as an impersonal agent with some aspect of power, the λόγου ("logos") in this verse is the impersonal agent powerful enough to bring about the new generation of Peter's exilic recipients as siblings. Peter's limitation of this term λόγου ("logos") by the adnominal genitive θεοῦ ("God") specifies the λόγου θεοῦ ("logos of God") as the cause of this new generation. Peter does not explain the biological assumptions for his natal use of the term λόγου ("logos") in the context of generation, but fortunately some other ancient authors do.

For example, Aristotle begins his description of the generation of animals with a discussion of λόγος ("logos") in relation to his four causes including material cause, efficient cause, formal cause, and final cause (*Gen. an.* 1.1 715a). According to Aristotle, these four causes can account for everything in this world (*Phys.* 2.3 194b; *An. post.* 2.11 94a). The material cause is the matter out of which anything is made. The formal cause is the plan or pattern according to which something is made, and the efficient cause comprises all the force necessary to shape the matter into the pattern and includes both the artisan and the tools needed for making something. The final cause is the purpose for which something is made. For Aristotle, these four causes explain the existence of everything including animals and humans.

After mentioning the final cause of an animal, Aristotle states that the formal cause is ὁ λόγος τῆς οὐσίας ("the logos of [the animal's] essence;" *Gen. an.* 1.1 715a). He then comments that these two causes, the formal and the final, should almost be considered one and the same. A few lines later, he explicitly says, ὅ τε γὰρ λόγος καὶ τὸ οὗ ἕνεκα ὡς τέλος ταὐτόν ("The logos [of an animal as its formal cause] and the [end] on account of which [the animal exists] as final cause are the same"). Although Aristotle primarily uses λόγος ("logos") to express the formal cause or the form of an animal, he nevertheless also considers this term to encompass the final cause. For Aristotle, form follows function since Nature forms all the parts of animals and even the animal itself according to the end or function in view (*Part. an.* 1.1 639b). Thus, Aristotle uses λόγος in reference to both the formal and final causes. The form of an animal and its purpose for existing are both determined by the λόγος ("logos") of the animal.

In his previous treatise *De partibus animalium*, Aristotle deals with formal and final causes as they relate to animals and to their parts. He makes an important distinction between the final cause in works of art (τέχνη) and in nature (φύσις). He states that in all works of art and the crafts, the final cause resides in the mind or soul of the artisan and not in the object to be produced (*Part. an.* 1.1 639b). The artisan can provide reasons for everything done to accomplish the final end, but the object itself does not contain within itself these reasons or the end toward which it is being fashioned. Only the goal of the final product in the mind of the artisan justifies these reasons.

In contrast, Aristotle explains that the final cause is more beautiful in the works of Nature than in the crafts, because the final cause in the works of Nature resides in the final object or product itself (*Part. an.* 1.1 639b; cf. 2.1 735a). When Nature generates, Nature instills the final cause in the thing or animal itself. When Nature generates a human being, for example, the embryo already has the ἐντελέχεια ("actualization") of a woman or man already within itself as a δύναμις ("potentiality;" *Gen. an.* 2.1 734a).

This distinction between final causes in the crafts and Nature is crucial for understanding what Aristotle means by the λόγος ("logos") of an animal. Aristotle establishes that the formal and final causes in respect to λόγος ("logos") are the same or at least closely related. Furthermore, he establishes that the final cause and the formal causes are present in the animal from the very beginning of Nature's generation of that animal. Thus, λόγος ("logos") must also be present from the very beginning and throughout the life of an animal, and the λόγος ("logos") of an animal is what shapes its form and specifies its function. By his keen perception and sharp analysis, Aristotle comes very close to expressing with the term λόγος ("logos") what thousands of years in the future will be called DNA (deoxyribonucleic acid). Just as the λόγος ("logos") of an animal for Aristotle explains the formation of the parts of that animal and the functions that animal is capable of performing, so also does DNA explain these features in modern scientific theory.

Aristotle's specific remarks about the role of λόγος ("logos") in the generation of animals further strengthens the similarity of his λόγος ("logos") with the modern understanding of DNA. After dealing with formal and final causes in his treatise *De partibus animalium*, Aristotle turns his attention in his treatise *De generatione animalium* to speaking περὶ αἰτίας δὲ τῆς κινούσης ("about the cause or impetus of movement"), which is the motive or efficient cause of animals. Aristotle distinguishes between the λόγος ("logos") or essential natures of males and females in respect to their respective power or capacity (δύναμις; *Gen. an.* 1.2 716a; 4.1 765b). He states that the λόγος ("logos") or essential nature of the male is the capacity to generate in another while the λόγος ("logos") of the female is for generation to occur within herself. He further says that the male provides the motive or efficient cause and the female the material cause (*Gen. an.* 2.4 738b).

The semen of the male contains within itself the λόγος ("logos") of the offspring both in terms of potentiality and actuality. The introduction of male semen into a female thus sets or curdles the material of her menstrual blood, establishes the λόγος ("logos") of both the potential and actual animal, and initiates a movement that impels the embryo to develop its potentiality into the actuality of its complete and mature nature (Aristotle, *Gen. an.* 2.4 739b). In

Aristotle's terms, therefore, male semen provides the formal, efficient, and final causes, while the female blood serves as the material cause.[1]

Earlier in his treatise, Aristotle already connects the λόγος ("logos") with formal and final causes of generation, but he now also connects it with the motive or efficient cause (*Gen. an.* 2.1 732a). He states that the motive cause contributed by male semen produces the λόγος ("logos") of the animal, whose formation, growth, and development is determined by this λόγος ("logos;" *Gen. an.* 2.1 734b; 2.4 740b). The λόγος ("logos") of the generating male is thus replicated in the offspring, which must be identical in kind with its parent (*Gen. an.* 1.1 715a) and even takes after this parent (*Gen. an.* 4.1 766b).

For Aristotle, the ideal generation is for a male to generate another male according to his own λόγος ("logos"), but Aristotle has to account for the generation of females and even birth defects when the offspring differs markedly from its male parent (*Gen. an.* 4.3 767b). He deems all offspring other than male as deficient (ἔλλειψις) because the male semen does not gain full mastery of the female menstrual blood. The least deviation is when a male offspring resembles his mother rather than his father. The generation of a female indicates that the semen gains even less mastery, and the birth of monstrosities (τέρατα) represents a complete lack of control by the semen. Aristotle's λόγος ("logos") theory thus enables him to explain heredity, and except for some details, much of what he says resonates with modern conceptions of DNA. Although not completely equivalent, the modern understanding of DNA at least approximates the essential role of λόγος ("logos") in Aristotle's theory of generation, and DNA is often a better translation of λόγος ("logos") than any other alternative in Aristotle's biological and natal writings, although it is rarely if ever translated that way.[2]

---

[1] Martin, "Christians as Babies," 108.

[2] This translation will appear in Martin, *Apostolic Confirmation* (forthcoming).

Peter's use of λόγου ("DNA") in 1 Pet 1:23 as the agent of new generation thus has more affinity with ancient discussions of generation that it does to later Christian Logos Theology, and translating λόγος as DNA makes this connection more explicitly than rendering λόγου as "word" or "reason" or any of the other renderings found in modern English translations. Peter describes his exilic recipients as ἀναγεγεννημένοι οὐκ ἐκ σπορᾶς ἀλλὰ ἀφθάρτου διὰ λόγου ζῶντος θεοῦ καὶ μένοντος ("having been generated anew not from a perishable but from an imperishable sowing through the living and enduring DNA of the living and enduring God"). He disparages the λόγος ("DNA") they received from their earthly fathers as a perishable sowing in contrast with the living and enduring λόγου ("DNA") they received from their living and enduring heavenly Father. Since offspring are of the same kind as the generating parent, the perishable sowing of their earthly fathers makes these exiles perishable, but the imperishable sowing of their heavenly Father makes them imperishable. The DNA they receive from their heavenly Father carries his essential characteristics of living and enduring and instills similar characteristics in them as well. God generates Peter's exilic recipients anew with God's very own DNA, and that DNA programs them for eternal life, a life that remains and endures.

The Scriptural Context

In 1 Pet 1:24–25, Peter appeals to Isa 40:6–8 LXX to emphasize and support the contrast between the former perishable essence of these exiles and their new imperishable existence. Peter quotes διότι πᾶσα σὰρξ ὡς χόρτος καὶ πᾶσα δόξα αὐτῆς ὡς ἄνθος χόρτου ἐξηράνθη ὁ χόρτος καὶ τὸ ἄνθος ἐξέπεσεν τὸ δὲ ῥῆμα κυρίου μένει εἰς τὸν αἰῶνα ("on account of all flesh is as herbage and all the reputation of flesh is as the blossom of herbage; the herbage dries up and the blossom falls off, but the word of the Lord remains into the age"). Peter introduces this quotation from Isaiah with the conjunction διότι ("on account of"), which indicates a scriptural warrant for Peter's preceding statement. The verbs ἐξηράνθη ("dries up") and ἐξέπεσεν ("falls off") are gnomic aorists that translate in English as presents of general truths.[1] This gnomic statement provides the rationale for the contrast between the perishable and imperishable sowing, and the conjunction is best translated as "on account of." Peter's contrast is valid on account of the truth of this gnomic statement in Peter's quotation of Isa 40:6–8 LXX.

As these exiles listen to Peter's quotation, they probably have no trouble connecting the "all flesh is as grass" and the references to grass drying up and blossoms falling off to the perishable sowing this quotation is meant to illustrate. The last line of the quotation in 1 Pet 1:25, however, does not correspond to the imperishable sowing through the λόγου θεοῦ ("DNA of God") quite as easily. Instead of the λόγου θεοῦ that is used in 1 Pet 1:23 ("DNA" or "word of God"), the quotation has ῥῆμα κυρίου ("word of [the] Lord"). Some commentators see no distinction in the two phrases at all.[2] Others see no distinction between λόγου ("DNA" or "word") and ῥῆμα ("word") but see the shift from θεοῦ ("God") to κυρίου ("Lord") as a Christianizing tendency that identifies the Lord with Jesus Christ.[3] These commentators usually argue that Peter uses ῥῆμα ("word") because it is in his Vorlage.[4] However, Peter's changing θεοῦ ("God") in his Vorlage to κυρίου ("Lord") weakens this argument since he could also have changed ῥῆμα ("word") to λόγου ("DNA" or "word"). Still other commentators see a distinction in both corresponding words in the two phrases, and these exiles certainly hear different words in the quotation that Peter uses in reference to an imperishable sowing through the λόγου θεοῦ ("DNA of God") in 1 Pet 1:23.[5]

---

[1] Bigg, *Epistles of St. Peter and St. Jude*, 123–24. For a description of these types of uses of the aorist tense, see Herbert Weir Smyth, *Greek Grammar* (Cambridge: Harvard University, 1980), §1931 and §1877.
[2] Knopf, *Briefe Petri und Judä*, 83.
[3] Michaels, *1 Peter*, 78–79; Davids, *First Epistle of Peter*, 78–79; and Achtemeier, *1 Peter*, 141.
[4] Davids, *First Epistle of Peter*, 79 n 10; and Achtemeier, *1 Peter*, 142.
[5] Hort, *First Epistle of St Peter*, 96–97.

The basic distinction between λόγος and ῥῆμα is evident in their respective word formations. The word λόγος ("DNA" or "word") is formed on the ablauted nominal stem λογ of the verb λέγειν, which means to arrange in order.[1] In reference to speaking, this verb means to speak by arranging the words in a reasonable or logical order. Thus, λόγος means word, but a word not simply as a sound but rather as the expression of a connected thought that often means thought or reason itself. In contrast, the noun ῥῆμα forms on the same root-stem ρε as the verb ῥέω, which means to say in the sense of a stream or flow of words.[2] This root-stem lengthens the epsilon vowel before the addition of the μα suffix, and this suffix denotes the concrete result of speaking, namely the sounds of the words.[3] Whereas λόγος refers to the connected thought as a whole, ῥῆμα refers to the individual words themselves.[4]

Philo offers an excellent illustration of this difference in respect to the word of God (Leg. 3.61 [176]). He is explaining the passage in Deut 8:3 LXX, which says that a human shall not live by bread alone but παντὶ ῥήματι ("by every word") that proceeds διὰ στόματος θεοῦ ("through the mouth of God"). Philo then explains the phrase παντὶ ῥήματι ("by every word") as meaning that the human shall be fed διὰ παντὸς λόγου ("through the whole word") as well as διὰ μέρους αὐτοῦ ("through each part of it") that proceeds from the mouth of God. Philo interprets the mouth as σύμβολον τοῦ λόγου ("the symbol of [God's] thought") and says that the individual ῥῆμα ("word") is just a part of it. Philo thus uses λόγος in reference to the whole mind of God, but he uses ῥῆμα as an individual spoken word expressing only part of that whole.

A similar distinction makes sense of Peter's shift from λόγου θεοῦ ("DNA of God") in 1 Pet 1:23 to ῥῆμα κυρίου ("word of [the] Lord") in the quotation in 1 Pet 1:25. The λόγου θεοῦ ("DNA of

---

[1] The Greek verb λέγω means "I arrange or place in order" and is thus an appropriate name for the popular children's toy called Lego Blocks.
[2] See Smyth, *Grammar*, §193.
[3] Ibid., §834h; §841.2.
[4] Hort, *First Epistle of St Peter*, 97.

God") includes the whole character and essential nature of God, while the ῥῆμα κυρίου ("word of [the] Lord") refers to the specific expression of that character in the proclamation about Jesus Christ. Some commentators understand κυρίου ("Lord") as a subjective genitive referring to Jesus's own preaching.[1] However, others take it as an objective genitive as the message about Jesus.[2] The objective genitive finds support in the numerous descriptions of Jesus and his work in this letter (1 Pet 1:3, 18–21; 2:4, 21–24; 3:18, 22; 4:1) with only a single mention of his preaching to the spirits in prison (1 Pet 3:19) and no quotation of any saying of Jesus.[3] The quotation from Isaiah, therefore, permits Peter to transition from a focus on the whole living and enduring character and DNA of God to the particular enduring communication of God's character in the message about Jesus Christ in the proclamation of the gospel.[4]

In 1 Pet 1:25b, Peter concludes his quotation by specifically applying this quotation to his exilic recipients when he says, τοῦτο δέ ἐστιν τὸ ῥῆμα τὸ εὐαγγελισθὲν εἰς ὑμᾶς ("Now, this is the word that was evangelized in you"). Schutter suggests that τοῦτο δέ ἐστιν ("Now this is") "is formulated after the fashion of demonstrative pesher interpretation," but this formula is so common in Greek to introduce a definition or an explanation that any connection with practices at Qumran is unnecessary.[5] Often in nominal sentences, the pronoun is attracted to the gender of the substantive, "but the unattracted neuter is common, especially in definitions where the

---

[1] Michaels, *1 Peter*, 79; and Mark Dubis, *I Peter: A Handbook on the Greek Text*, BHGNT (Waco, TX: Baylor University, 2010), 40–41.

[2] William L. Schutter, *Hermeneutic and Composition in 1 Peter*, WUNT 2.30 (Tübingen: Mohr Siebeck, 1989), 126; and John H. Elliott, *1 Peter: A New Translation with Introduction and Commentary*, AB 37B (New York: Doubleday, 2000), 391.

[3] See Achtemeier, *1 Peter*, 142.

[4] See Hort, *First Epistle of St Peter*, 97; and Beare, *First Epistle of Peter*, 86.

[5] Schutter, *Hermeneutic*, 127. For this usage of τοῦτο δέ ἐστιν ("Now this is"), see Demosthenes, *Mid.* 153 = *Oratio* 21.153; Philo, *Leg.*, 3.57; and Plutarch, *Cupid. divit.* 1 = *Mor.* 523d).

pronoun is the predicate" and the definition then follows.[1] This usage is so frequent for definitions that the compound word τουτέστι ("this is") sometimes occurs.[2] Peter now identifies the word about the Lord Jesus Christ in the Isaiah quotation to the evangelization of the recipients of his letter. In 1 Pet 1:11-12, Peter has already mentioned those who evangelized these exiles and announced to them the message of the prophets about the sufferings and subsequent high honor of Jesus Christ.

In that earlier mention of evangelization, Peter uses the dative ὑμῖν ("to you") and the accusative ὑμᾶς ("you") to refer to his exilic recipients, but he uses a prepositional phrase εἰς ὑμᾶς ("in you") in 1 Pet 1:25. Commentators note that this prepositional phrase to designate these exiles as the target of evangelization is unusual; some think it is equivalent to the dative, while others think it is not but emphasizes the destination of the evangelization.[3] Still others think its position at the very end of the sentence gives it a significance to mean "for your benefit."[4] This unusual usage certainly fits Peter's explanation of these recipients' being generated anew through the DNA of God in the particular proclamation about Jesus Christ "in them." As the word about Jesus Christ entered "into you" (εἰς ὑμᾶς), Peter writes to them, you were generated anew and received the very DNA of God that makes you both alive and enduring.

Peter's quotation of Isa 40:6-8 LXX as well as his application of this gnomic saying to these exiles supports his exhortation for them to love one another intensely as siblings. The perishable sowing of their earthly fathers produces flesh that dies. The imperishable sowing of their Father God produces offspring that

---

[1] Smyth, *Grammar*, §1239a. For examples of the neuter in definitions, see Euripides, *Bacch.* 305; Plato, *Resp.* 4 432b; and Demosthenes, *Fals. leg.* 82 = *Oratio* 19.82.

[2] E.g., see Diogenes Laertius, *Vitae philosophorum* 5.32.

[3] Michaels notes that this prepositional phrase is unusual (*1 Peter*, 79). Bigg thinks it is equivalent to the dative (*Epistles of St. Peter and St. Jude*, 124). Hort interprets it as emphasizing the destination (*First Epistle of St Peter*, 96).

[4] Achtemeier, *1 Peter*, 142.

remain εἰς τὸν αἰῶνα ("into the age [to come]). Their relationship with their biological siblings is limited to the span of this life. Their sibling relationship with one another in their new faith tradition, however, is forever. Thus, their siblinghood is more real, genuine, and lasting than any siblinghood based on physical descent. Whatever claims biological siblings have on one another are even greater for those siblings generated through the living and enduring DNA of the living and enduring God. On the basis of their eternal siblinghood, Peter urges these exiles to love one another intensely.[1]

Conclusion

Translating specific terms from ancient languages is perhaps one of the most challenging tasks facing any interpreter, and a complicated term such as λόγος that is embedded so firmly in an ancient worldview poses particular problems. Translating this term as DNA in 1 Pet 1:23 rather than as word helps explain the syntactical relationship of this term not only to θεοῦ ("God") but also to the participles ζῶντος ("living") and μένοντος ("enduring"). Rendering λόγος in 1 Pet 1:23 as DNA also communicates the function of this term in ancient natal contexts and discussions far better than does the English term word and can account for the shift from λόγου θεοῦ ("DNA of God") in 1 Pet 1:23 to ῥῆμα κυρίου ("word of the Lord") in the Isaian quotation in 1 Pet 1:24. Most importantly, translating λόγου θεοῦ as "DNA of God" exposes the flow of thought as Peter contrasts his recipients' perishable life from the DNA received from their human parents with the eternal life from their being generated anew by the living-and-enduring DNA of their Father God. Sharing this eternal DNA enables these siblings to enjoy a relationship that lasts forever, and Peter appropriately exhorts them to love one another intently, even more intently than they love their own biological and perishable siblings. The term λόγος in 1 Pet 1:23, therefore, is most accurately rendered as DNA.

---

[1] Martin, *Metaphor and Composition*, 173–74.

LISTENING AGAIN TO THE APOCALYPSE

The Remedy for Vengeance

Blood in the Apocalypse

Carol J. Rotz

Are you washed in the blood of the Lamb?[1]

This hymnic question gripped and confused me when we used to sing this and other hymns about Jesus's blood. The wording and melody may be outdated, but the content is biblical. In the book of Revelation, Christ's blood cleanses (Rev 7:14) and empowers (12:11) people. But these are not the only references. The Apocalypse is full of blood: innocent blood (the Lamb's blood as well as the blood of God's holy people, the prophets, those who bore testimony to Jesus, and God's servants) and cosmic blood (a blood-red moon, hail and fire mixed with blood, and springs, rivers and seas of blood).

Blood seems to be ubiquitous in the Apocalypse, yet blood (αἷμα) is specifically mentioned only eighteen times in the entire book. The bloodletting is progressive. At first only one-third of the earth and sea (Rev 8:7-8) is affected. But later the whole water supply is turned to blood (16:3-4). There are, of course, many other instances of violence in Revelation. Wars and plagues fill the pages to overflowing with visions of suffering and death. For example, the riders of four horses bring disasters to the earth (6:1ff), locust-horses torment and sting like scorpions (9:10, 19), and seven angels pour bowls of God's wrath on the earth (chs 16–17). Blood is a part of this larger complex of plagues and upheavals, but it conveys a

---

[1] Elisha A. Hoffman, "Are You Washed in the Blood?" (1878), in *Worship in Song* (Kansas City, MO: Lillenas, 1972), 250. For other information regarding this hymn, see the Hymnary.org website, specifically https://hymnary.org/text/have_you_been_to_jesus_for_the_cleansing.

range of visceral and emotional meaning that other violent images do not.

The evocative language of the book of Revelation seeks to elicit responses of repentance, worship, and witness. And blood graphically portrays the terrors of the book's symbolic world. The horrific scene of blood flowing out of a winepress and "rising as high as the horses' bridles for a distance of 1,600 stadia" (Rev 14:20) is iconic.[1] This overabundance of blood creates a dramatic image with intertwining literal and symbolic historical allusions and metaphorical meaning. It is only one part of a very complex literary and theological book, yet this bloody scene is widely misunderstood. It often becomes the basis of false assumptions about divine interaction with and purposes for God's good creation.

The term "blood" (αἷμα) has a variety of metaphorical uses in the Bible. Understood as the material of conception, children carry the life-bearing blood of both parents, and their blood symbolizes life. To shed blood is to destroy the bearer of life and therefore life itself. The old covenant's sacrificial system is built on this principle. When an animal is sacrificed, its blood as the bearer of life becomes a means of expiation (see Lev 17:11). The prohibition of eating the blood of animals stems from this idea of the sanctity of life-giving blood.

Blood also has polluting power. In the Levitical system the shedding of blood pollutes the land (Num 35:33; Ps 106:38). In the new covenant, however, Jesus's blood cleanses. The saints wash their garments in Jesus's blood so that they are white, pure, and able to be in God's presence (Rev 7:14). This paradox is held in tension throughout Revelation where, as in the rest of the New Testament, the primary reference to blood is to the blood of Christ. On one level, it refers quite literally to Christ's blood in the context of the Jewish Bible's sacrificial motifs. The old covenant of Sinai was sealed and inaugurated by blood (Exod 24:8; Heb 9:18–22), and the new covenant was established and set in force by the blood of Jesus. The language surrounding Jesus's words at the Last Supper in the

---

[1] All biblical references are from the New International Version (2011).

Synoptic Gospels refers to this new covenant (Mt 26:28; Mk 14:24; Lk 22:20) and assures the validity of the new divine order. Jesus spoke of freely shedding his own blood and of its redemptive significance.

Beyond the literal reference to Christ's shed blood is the symbolic reference to life violently taken from him. In Revelation there are twenty-eight references to Jesus as the Lamb, which are coupled with the idea of the violent slaughter of an innocent victim (Rev 5:6, 9, 12; 13:8). Because Jesus's life blood was shed in this manner, he alone is worthy (5:5-14). Like the "cross," the "blood of Christ" is a graphic expression of his death in its soteriological significance. His shed blood signifies the death of the one whose death brings life to all who will accept his sacrifice.

This paradoxical metaphor of blood has not been appreciated for its multi-faceted symbolization of death and life in Revelation. Few have studied its significance. A notable exception is Paul Decock, to whom we are indebted for his careful syntactical work on each occurrence of the term "blood" in Revelation.[1] Although this work need not be redone, his theological perspective drives his eschatological conclusions in unnecessary ways that are in opposition to the Christian gospel. It is therefore necessary to rethink his intertextual associations as well as his division and description of the types of blood references. Doing so will center Revelation's blood motif in Christ's self-giving blood that needs no other work to bring salvation to God's good creation. A narrow focus on Jesus's blood as atonement is not sufficient. In Israel sacrificial blood served both an atoning and bonding function. Christ's sacrifice and ours as his followers are joyful gifts to God.

Decock's argument hinges on his classification of the blood passages in the book of Revelation. He divides the references into three categories: (1) the blood of Christ as saving power (Rev 1:5; 5:9; 7:14; 12:11); (2) the blood of the martyrs as a cry for vengeance

---

[1] Paul B. Decock, "The Symbol of Blood in the Apocalypse of John," *Neot* 38, no. 2 (2004): 157-82; and idem, "Violence in the Apocalypse of John," *AcT*, suppl. 11 (2008): 1-19.

(6:10; 16:6 [2x]; 17:6 [2x]; 18:24; 19:2); and (3) divine vengeance to cleanse the earth (6:12; 8:7, 8; 11:6; 14:20; 16:3, 4, 6).

His first category rightly includes the following passages that clearly show the universal, saving, cleansing, strengthening, and sustaining power of Jesus's blood. However, as I shall show, Decock's list is incomplete and, as a result, the power of Jesus's blood is overshadowed by a further need for bloodshed. Decock's category of Christ's saving blood appropriately includes the following four references:

> ... and from Jesus Christ, who is the faithful witness, the firstborn from the dead, and the ruler of the kings of the earth. To him who loves us and has freed us from our sins by his **blood**. (Rev 1:5)[1]
>
> And they sang a new song, saying: "You are worthy to take the scroll and to open its seals, because you were slain, and with your **blood** you purchased for God persons from every tribe and language and people and nation." (5:9)
>
> I answered, "Sir, you know." And he said, "These are they who have come out of the great tribulation; they have washed their robes and made them white in the **blood** of the Lamb." (7:14)
>
> They triumphed over him [Satan] by the **blood** of the Lamb and by the word of their testimony; they did not love their lives so much as to shrink from death. (12:11)[2]

These references to Christ's blood highlight its beneficial effects for those who follow him. The cleansing and liberating results of Christ's shed blood include its rescuing (1:6), purchasing (5:9), cleansing (7:14), and empowering (12:11) efficacy. In Revelation the blood of Jesus becomes a paradoxical symbol of love. It speaks of slaughter and sacrifice, but it also symbolizes rescue or ransom, and expresses God's concern and care for creation. It is

---

[1] All emphases on **blood** are mine.
[2] Decock thinks this fourfold mention of Jesus's blood indicates its worldwide effect ("The Symbol of Blood in the Apocalypse of John," 161), but as we shall see, the list is incomplete.

both the means of purification and the victorious power over the enemy.

The second category, the blood of the saints, captures the extent to which God's people have suffered because of their testimony. In Revelation the primary meaning of the Greek term μάρτυς is witness, but because such faithful witness often led to death, the word eventually took on the meaning of death by martyrdom. In this category of references to blood, Satanic bloodthirst is held in tension with the need to avenge the suffering of the saints. Yet Rev 19:2 makes it clear that only God can render true judgment. Consider the following five verses about the blood of the saints:

> They called out in a loud voice, "How long, Sovereign Lord, holy and true, until you judge the inhabitants of the earth and avenge our blood?" (6:10)
> ... for they have shed the blood of your holy people and your prophets, and you have given them blood to drink as they deserve. (16:6)
> I saw that the woman was drunk with the blood of God's holy people, the blood of those who bore testimony to Jesus. When I saw her, I was greatly astonished. (17:6)
> In her was found the blood of prophets and of God's holy people, of all who have been slaughtered on the earth. (18:24)
> For true and just are his judgments. He has condemned the great prostitute who corrupted the earth by her adulteries. He has avenged on her the blood of his servants. (19:2)

Decock's second category appropriately includes the blood of Christians at the hand of their historical and metaphorical enemies, represented in the world of Revelation as Babylon/ Rome.[1] The theme of this group of references is the just punishment of the

---

[1] The metaphor of political giants oppressing others was well known. Unfortunately, it aptly applies to a succession of "Babylons" throughout history.

saints' enemies for the bloodshed they have inflicted on the righteous. It is a cry for vengeance, one that we might also voice in similar circumstances. It depicts the elegance of the lex talionis rule that just punishment shows relationship, portion, and similarity to the crime: an "eye for an eye." The appropriate fate of God's enemies is paradoxically and dramatically captured in such statements as that of the angel in charge of the waters: God made those who had shed the saints' blood drink blood as they deserved (Rev 16:5-6). The drinking of blood is symbolic for death and the punishment may mean that they drink each other's blood, referring to the oppressors fighting among themselves.

Unfortunately, Decock's understanding goes another less helpful direction. According to his work, shedding the blood of the saints is an evil that undermines creation. God manages that pollution until the end when God will punish the evil and unrepentant and, as a result, cleanse the land. Decock's logic then leads to the third category of blood, which he labels "divine vengeance." He understands the verses within this category as a picture of a bloodbath that will cleanse the earth of the pollution brought to it by the shedding of innocent blood. In this scenario God's patience runs out, and divine punishment rights the wrongs of the present world. Just as innocent blood polluted the earth, the blood of those who caused it must cleanse it. The following seven verses speak of God's just punishment:

> I watched as he opened the sixth seal. There was a great earthquake. The sun turned black like sackcloth made of goat hair, the whole moon turned blood red. (Rev 6:12)
>
> The first angel sounded his trumpet, and there came hail and fire mixed with blood, and it was hurled down on the earth. A third of the earth was burned up, a third of the trees were burned up, and all the green grass was burned up. (8:7)
>
> The second angel sounded his trumpet, and something like a huge mountain, all ablaze, was thrown into the sea. A third of the sea turned into blood. (8:8)

> They were trampled in the winepress outside the city, and blood flowed out of the press, rising as high as the horses' bridles for a distance of 1,600 stadia. (14:20)[1]
>
> The second angel poured out his bowl on the sea, and it turned into blood like that of a dead person, and every living thing in the sea died. (16:3)
>
> He is dressed in a robe dipped in blood, and his name is the Word of God. (19:13)[2]

According to Decock, divine vengeance is associated with day of the Lord when God conquers the source of idolatry in a bloody military victory. The enemies have spilled the blood of the saints, and their just punishment (lex talionis) is their own blood flowing from the winepress (Rev 19:15; 14:19-20). Their murderous bloodshed of the innocent has poisoned the sea and the rivers, and purification must therefore come from their own blood. These dark passages are difficult, but Decock's conclusion—that divine vengeance is necessary—negates the miracle of grace.

Decock acknowledges the saving power of Christ's death on the cross, which is represented in Revelation by the Lamb's shed blood. He sees the beauty of this terrible symbol but fails to acknowledge its finality. In his mind two additional stages are required for final victory over Satan. First, the Lamb's blood empowers the saints so that they can persevere in their witness to the Lamb, sometimes to the point of death. This is an important theme, but Decock limits the effectiveness of the blood of Christ to the current time. There must be an additional step: the blood of God's enemies must purify the earth so that heaven can come down. He cites Num 35:33 to show that the cleansing is necessary. His controlling metaphor is "holy war," which he sees as necessary to end the dragon's rule and restore the earth to its purity. According to this view, Christ (depicted as Lion; Rev 5:5) and his

---

[1] But see my comments on this verse below.

[2] I will argue that this verse is misplaced and does not belong in this category.

followers must wage and win a holy war (19:11). Only then can heaven descend.

War is a dominant theme in Revelation,[1] and war would have been all too familiar to the first-century Christians who lived with the imminent threat of invading armies as well as the constant reality of an occupying Roman army. They may have suffered persecution under Rome's rule and would have welcomed divine intervention to make everything right.[2] From beginning to end, John's rhetoric creates tension and makes its readers ill at ease. However, in the drama of Revelation's story as well as in Christian theology, a cleansing holy war is not necessary. The cry for

---

[1] See especially Richard Bauckham, "The Book of Revelation as a Christian War Scroll," *Neot* 22, no. 1 (1988): 17-40.

[2] In the third century, Tertullian, Origen, and Eusebius described the persecution of Christians under Domitian. This traditional view continued into the twentieth century; see, e.g., Henry B. Swete, *The Apocalypse of St. John: The Greek Text with Introduction, Notes, and Indices* (New York: Macmillan, 1909); G. B. Caird, *A Commentary on the Revelation of St. John the Divine*, BNTC (London: Black, 1966); J. Massyngberde Ford, *Revelation: Introduction, Translation, and Commentary*, AB 38 (Garden City, NY: Doubleday, 1975); and Colin J. Hemer, *The Letters to the Seven Churches of Asia in Their Local Setting*, Biblical Resource Series (Sheffield: JSOT, 1986. Revisionist interpretations refer to "perceived persecution"; see Adela Yarbro Collins, *The Combat Myth in the Book of Revelation*, HDR 9 (Missoula, MT: Scholars, 1976); and Leonard L. Thompson, *The Book of Revelation: Apocalypse and Empire* (New York: Oxford University, 1990). Others look to the imperial cult as a political-economic cause of suffering for the early Christians; see Elisabeth Schüssler Fiorenza, *Revelation: Vision of a Just World*, Proclamation Commentaries (Minneapolis: Fortress, 1991); and Steven J. Friesen, *Twice Neokoros: Ephesus, Asia, and the Cult of the Flavian Imperial Family*, RGRW 116 (Leiden: Brill, 1993). Alan S. Bandy calls for a return to the classic view based on Roman jurisprudence; see his "Persecution and the Purpose of Revelation with Reference to Roman Jurisprudence," *BBR* 23.3 (2013): 377-98. L. Michael White provides an accessible review of the various positions in his article, "Understanding the Book of Revelation," which is part of PBS's FrontLine series (https://www.pbs.org/wgbh/pages/frontline/shows/apocalypse/revelation/white.html). The extent and manner of persecution are debated, but there was another side to the tensions between Christians and Rome. The allure of Roman power, wealth, and culture was strong, and the church was in danger of compromise so that it could enjoy Rome's benefits.

vengeance from beneath the altar is real but does not require equally terrible retributive bloodshed on the persecutors. The blood of the Lamb extends grace to all, and the witness/martyrdom of the saints will make the good news of Christ's sacrifice known. The believers as the ἐκκλησία are the called-out-ones who extend God's grace to everyone, giving all an opportunity to repent and return to their Creator. They follow the conquering Christ wearing fine linen—dressed for a banquet, not for war. And Christ conquers not by shedding his enemies' blood but by offering his own shed blood.

War references begin in chapter 12 (vv 7, 17) where the war in heaven between Michael and the dragon and ends with a defeated dragon angrily and defensively waging war on Jesus's followers. After this ignominious defeat in heaven, the followers of the seven-headed beast ask a ridiculous, rhetorical question, "Who can make war against [the beast]?" (Rev 13:4). As the war in heaven demonstrates (12:7-9), this representative of the dragon is no match for an angel, let alone the Lamb. And yet the beast is given power for a short time not only to make war against God's people but to conquer them (13:7). The battle against evil is real, but no evil power can defeat those who have God's seal (7:2-4; 9:4). Faithful witness to the Lamb may result in martyrdom, but a place in the New Jerusalem is guaranteed. In the plot of Revelation, the end is delayed multiple times, but there will be an end to evil.

John symbolizes evil in the figure of this dragon that is the "ancient serpent, called the devil, or Satan" (Rev 12:9; cf. 20:2). These terms are rich with allusions and associations both to the Old Testament and Greek mythology. This chief opponent in John's visions obstructs God's design and makes war with angels and humans; the dragon slanders the saints and deceives the world. The dragon is joined by a beast from the sea (13:1-3), whose number is 666 (13:16-18), and has been misleadingly popularized as the "antichrist."[1] Another beast comes up from the land and is known

---

[1] Note that the term "antichrist" does not appear in Revelation. First John explains that the antichrist is anyone who denies that Jesus is the Christ and that many antichrists have already come (1 John 2:18, 22; 4:3).

as "the false prophet" (13:11–15). These three form an unholy trinity that tries to seize God's power and influence over humanity. This false god is already conquered, and its end is the lake of fire along with Death and Hades (the personification of death). This death of death and evil makes way for the restoration of God's plan for humanity. It does not require, as Decock imagines, God's cleansing earth with the blood of the obdurate sinners.

Christ's life, death, and resurrection form the apex of history. The blood of Christ makes possible the denouement or the coming of the kingdom that was inaugurated by his presence in and present to the world. In Revelation the various pictures of what will happen in human history are the inevitable result of sin or repentance. The visions are possible outcomes based on the choices humans make. Destruction is the inevitable result of a life of sin that is not washed in the blood of Christ. But victory is assured to those who listen to what the Spirit says and persevere (Rev 2–3).

The outworking of God's great plan of salvation includes warnings in the form of plagues as well as glimpses of heaven. There is no need for further action by God or the saints to bring the kingdom to earth. The delay is not so that the last elements of the salvation plan can be implemented. Rather, it is a gracious provision of time for people to repent, for more to become citizens of the kingdom.

The crucial difference in Decock's interpretation of blood in Revelation and one that centers on Christ's once-and-for-all, sufficient sacrificial death is the placement of the reference to blood in Rev 19:13. There, the blood on Christ's robe is not from the saints or his enemies. In the supreme example of self-giving love, it is Christ's own blood. This contrasts sharply with Decock's understanding that this is part of a further necessary bloodletting of "divine vengeance" against those who spilled the blood of the saints. Decock acknowledges that the blood on the robe of the Word of God is interpreted by many scholars as the blood of Christ.[1] One

---

[1] For example, Decock cites David E. Aune, *Revelation*, WBC 52 (Waco, TX: Word, 1997–98); Loren L. Johns, *The Lamb of God Christology in the Apocalypse of John*,

could easily add others in support of that reading.[1] Of course, other scholars also agree with Decock.[2] Yet the importance of this difference cannot be ignored. Understanding the blood on Christ's robe as his own reshapes the perception of blood throughout the book of Revelation. It moves Rev 19:13 from the third category of blood passages—which focus on "divine vengeance"—to the first category of blood passages, which focus on the life-giving blood of Jesus. Thus, it requires a different label for the third category of blood usages since the controlling metaphor becomes Christ's sacrificial blood rather than "holy war." "Divine vengeance" is not necessary or adequate in describing those passages and God's final answer to evil.

The term "blood" occurs first in the book's letter opening, where it is part of a doxology in praise of Christ "who loves us and has freed us from our sins by his blood" (Rev 1:5). The symbol of blood continues throughout the book until God's enemies are destroyed in chapter 19 where it is part of the description of Christ whose robe is dipped in his own blood. These occurrences of Christ's blood, in typical Semitic fashion, form an *inclusio* setting the theological framework from which to understand all of the occurrences of the blood symbol in the book.

Christ's blood initiates the major action of the drama. The first two passages that mention his saving blood (Rev 1:5; 5:9) set the drama in motion and preview its conclusion. Before the recounting of the visions of the end, we as readers are informed that Jesus's blood frees the saints and wins complete victory. Only Christ is worthy to reveal God's plan for the triumph of the faithful and the destruction of evil. He is worthy because he was

---

WUNT 167 (Tübingen: Mohr Siebeck, 2003); and Edmondo Lupieri, *L'Apocalisse di Giovanni* (Milano: Arnoldo Mondadori [Scrittori Greci e Latini], 1999).

[1] For example, see M. Eugene Boring, *Revelation*, IBC (Louisville, KY: John Knox, 1989), 194–99; and Robert W. Wall, *Revelation*, NIBCNT 18 (Peabody, MA: Hendrickson, 1991), 230–31.

[2] Robert H. Mounce, *The Book of Revelation*, rev. ed., NICNT (Grand Rapids: Eerdmans, 1998), 353–54; and G. K. Beale, *The Book of Revelation: A Commentary on the Greek Text*, NIGTC (Grand Rapids: Eerdmans, 1999), 957–60.

slaughtered and his blood restores to God a people who will serve God and reign on earth (5:9-10). The end is never in question, and Jesus's blood infuses all of the remaining blood imagery with the overarching reality of his ultimate life-giving blood. Revelation's story reveals that judgment will come, but Jesus's blood demonstrates the radical nature of the new covenant. Sinners do not have to shed their own blood for their sins, and God does not have to cleanse the land by slaughtering the enemy.

Decock sees God's vengeance as a necessary concluding act to cleanse the earth, but Christ's salvific blood is all that is necessary to liberate all of creation. Throughout Revelation everyone is invited, even cajoled, frightened, and threatened to persuade them to forsake the dragon and accept God as their Lord. The entreaties, examples, and plagues provide opportunities for repentance and a change of allegiance. Unfortunately, they rarely work. For example, when a third of humankind is killed after the sixth trumpet, those who survive refuse to repent and continue to worship demons and idols (Rev 9:20-21; see also 7:4; 12:13-17; 16:9, 11; 14:18-20). Yet the survivors of a great earthquake give glory to God. The dire warnings give way to a scene of myriads from every tribe and nation worshipping God (5:11; 7:9; 14:3). In the end, kings and nations have been won over (21:24, 26). Decock agrees that the plagues are gracious displays of God's patience and mercy, but only until divine patience ends and God's vengeance destroys those who do not repent.

These questions arise: Why is Christ's blood not sufficient? Why must God's vengeance be carried out on those who refuse to believe in order to cleanse the earth? Is it the blood of these enemies that is both destructive and purifying, symbolic of both life and death? Is it necessary that God fulfill the wish of those who have suffered so that justice can be done? Will this vengeful bloodletting cleanse the earth so that heaven can come to earth? Is God a god of vengeance?

The Apocalypse, as a letter to the Church,[1] calls the saints to follow the Lamb as faithful witnesses, even to their death, in imitation of Christ. This is what will draw the nations to God and to the salvation that is provided through Christ's sacrificial victory. The power to change lives is Christ's sharp two-edged sword that projects from his mouth (Rev 1:6; 2:12, 16; 19:15, 21). Those who follow the Lamb overcome because of his sacrifice and "the word of their testimony" (12:11) even when it means physical death (6:9; 20:4). In the passages where the verbs "conquer" or "overcome" are used, Satan and the evil powers conquer by killing (11:7; 13:7), but Christ and his followers paradoxically overcome by dying (2:7, 11, 17, 26; 3:5, 12, 21; 5:5; 12:11; 15:2). This radical picture undermines conventional understandings of power and judgment. Following the Lamb means demonstrating and embodying his kind of self-sacrificing power. It challenges the need for vengeance while it judges those who reject God. The final judgment assumes that the suffering witness of Jesus and his church has brought people to repentance and worship of the true God.

The final battle surprisingly follows the same theme. Only the Lamb can wage war with justice (Rev 19:11) because he not only knows the beginning and the end but has experienced human life and can discern peoples' thoughts and motives. Jesus and his army are arrayed to battle the beast along with the kings and their assembled armies (19:11–14), but the war does not happen. The beast and the false prophet are captured and thrown into the fiery lake (19:19). The beast's armies are ironically slain not by literal swords that result in the spilling of their blood, but by a figurative sword through the words from Jesus as the Word of God (19:13, 15, 21; see 1:16; 2:16). The kings and their armies are defeated by their own choice of lord, with the terrible result of being cut off from the One who hopes and seeks to save them.

---

[1] Revelation begins (Rev 1:4-9) with a letter opening typical of the epistolary style of the first century. The author and recipients are identified and the salutation takes the form of a blessing.

It is not necessary for God to slay the forces of evil. Their choice of lord cuts themselves off from the grace of God. The nature of evil destroys itself. Although not couched in terms of bloodshed, the fall of Babylon demonstrates the inevitable result of sin and evil. In the metaphorical world of the book of Revelation, the beast with ten horns hates the prostitute Babylon, who in the first century represents Rome. The evil triumvirate will "bring her to ruin and leave her naked …eat her flesh and burn her with fire" (Rev 17:16).

Does the fate of the two beasts and the birds' banquet of the armies (Rev 19:21) satisfy the retaliation that the martyrs requested, who cried out for God to make things right (6:9–11)? Their cry for God to avenge (6:10) was a call for justice by those who had been wronged. It implies retribution for unjustified injury through the dispensation of rightly deserved punishment. God is the only one who is qualified to do so (see Deut 32:35, 41; Rom 12:19). If God is holy and just, God cannot allow sin and rebellion to go unpunished. But God is loving and does not wish that any should perish (2 Pet 3:9). The shedding of innocent blood does not pollute the land, but it requires the death of the ones who shed it (see Num 35:33). In the old covenant, bloodshed in sacrifice restored relationship with God through fulfillment of the law and needed to be repeated. Jesus's blood seals the new covenant and provides eternally saving and purifying power for those who will follow him.

The metaphor of shed blood refers to the old covenant and the slaughter of the lamb, but the greater reality is that he freely gave his blood because of his love for all of creation. The book of Revelation begins with a doxology ascribing "glory and power for ever and ever" because Jesus Christ "loves us and has freed us from our sins by his blood." More than that he "has made us to be a kingdom and priests to serve his God and Father" (Rev 1:5b).

This service to God rather than vengeance is the thrust of Revelation's second category of the blood of the saints. The petition of these saints is a cry for justice from those who are unable to help themselves, but it is also a rhetorical device to call the church to be the church. It is a call for Christ's followers to be Christians, little

Christs, who follow him unconditionally. Their faithful witness to Jesus, the faithful and true witness (Rev 1:5; 3:14), will do what the plagues cannot accomplish. Christ rides into battle clothed in a robe dipped in his own blood (19:13), and his armies wear fine linen that is white and clean (19:14) because they have washed those linens in Christ's blood (7:14). The cleansing of the land and its people comes not from the vengeful shedding of the blood of God's enemies but from Christ's own sacrificial blood. Thus, this gracious provision transcends the law. All persons can wash their garments in the blood as a metaphorical cleansing ritual. Yet it surpasses mere cultic cleansing. It is a true cleansing from sin, a changing of allegiance. It surpasses lex talionis. The new covenant does not require an eye for an eye because Christ's blood has more than countered the pollution of all other bloodshed. The Creator of the universe gave himself as a lamb to the slaughter so that all who wish can be cleansed and enter the kingdom.

Christ is the Lion leading his people to battle, but the Lion is also the Lamb (Rev 5:5-6). The title, Lion of the tribe of Judah (5:5; Gen 49:9), is coupled with Isaiah's root/branch imagery (Isa 11:1, 10). Jesus as the Root of David (Rev 5:5; 22:16) recalls Isaiah's rich metaphor and emphasizes Jesus's royal descent.[1] As the Lion of the tribe of Judah, Jesus fulfills the Jewish expectation of a warrior Messiah who would conquer the nations and rule as king, judge the righteous, and reign in peace. The good news is that the risen Christ has already triumphed, not by coercion but ironically through his own blood as the sacrificial Lamb. His sacrifice accomplishes the victory in the holy war.

The holy war motif is outbalanced by God's care, righteous judgments, and hatred of sin in the book of Revelation. The visions of plagues and scenes of suffering and death throughout the book portray the seriousness of sin. They call the church to repent and to

---

[1] See also the branch metaphor in Zech 3:8; 6:12. Isaiah 11:1 promises a branch out of the roots of Jesse, King David's father. Jeremiah (23:5; 33:15) speaks of a Davidic branch of righteousness, who will be king and Savior. Zechariah (3:8; 6:12) calls him a servant whose name is Branch.

fulfill our calling as faithful witness to those who have not yet responded to God's great promises. They powerfully urge us to be a missional church that beckons people to leave the deceptive, evil world and enter into safety within the walls of the New Jerusalem. Chapter 21 describes the consummation of the kingdom of God when it comes to earth, with its gates that welcome all who will to enter.

But what about the iconic scene of the blood flowing from the winepress (Rev 14:20)? How can we reconcile this scene with a grace-full God? How does this overabundance of blood fit in the categories of blood in Revelation? What is its significance? Decock understands it to be the final act of God's righteous vengeance bringing the appropriate punishment to those who have rejected grace. It therefore purifies the land polluted by the shedding of the innocent blood of the saints. On the surface, this may seem to be true. The prodigious flow of wine-blood from the grape press seems to serve as a hyperbolic image of terrible judgment. God cannot tolerate sin, and the scene reveals the horrible consequences of evil and the finally impenitent.

It is true: God cannot tolerate sin. Throughout the book of Revelation, the blood passages show the seriousness of sin and evil. The vision of the winepress is yet another precautionary scene showing the terrible consequences of sin. In this picture of judgment, the promise of salvation through Christ's blood is evident. It is located outside the city of Jerusalem, just as Jesus was crucified outside the gate (see Heb 13:12). The literal distance of the blood flow of 1,600 stadia equals about 180 miles, approximately the length of Palestine. Everyone will be judged. In historical context, this hyperbolic metaphor is fulfilled by the siege of Jerusalem in 70 C.E. and the subsequent decades until Constantine. The number 1,600 is also a numeric symbol. As the square (an intensification) of four (the number of the earth, see Rev 7:1; 20:8) multiplied by the square of ten (the number for completeness), it represents the entire earth. Futurists fear the fulfillment of a world-wide blood bath in the future. Yet its meaning is greater than any possible historical scenario.

References to Christ's blood frame all of the blood passages of Revelation and therefore influence their meaning. His self-sacrifice is more powerful than any attack by the enemy and is the power to be emulated by his followers. In contrast, evil craves the blood of the innocent, yet the inevitable consequence of sin is death. Evil collapses upon itself and is dealt with by a word from the rider of the white horse. Jesus's robe is stained with his own blood, representing the awful price of salvation. The risen Christ leads his army into a battle that does not play out as we would expect. Christ is the only one who can judge justly, and his shed blood purifies. The martyrs' cry for vengeance does not require more bloodshed. Rather, God's reply to the call for vengeance is Christ's own blood and a call to all people, tribes, and nations to turn from sin to grace.

The scenes of battle, bloodshed, and judgment are replaced by a vision of a new heaven and a new earth. The blood of sinners need not flow from the vine press. The visions are not so much sequential as alternative. Each person has a choice to make: continue to sin and identify with the vision of death represented by the horrible flow of blood or turn to God and enjoy a bride-like relationship with God where there is no more death, mourning, crying, or pain. The people of God following Jesus on the white horse are dressed for the wedding feast in their white garments, and all can wash their robes in Christ's blood to join the celebration.

This promise is verified by God's declaration, "I am making everything new!" (Rev 21:5). The prophetic present of the verb (ποιῶ) highlights the certainty of a future new creation grounded in the ongoing work of the Father and Spirit as well as the saving shed blood of the Lamb. The speaker, the Alpha and Omega (see also 1:8), guarantees truthfulness, trustworthiness, faithfulness, and power to complete what has been set in motion. God's speech continues with a statement like that of Jesus on the cross (John 19:30): "It is done" (Rev 21:5). No other sacrifice or provision must be put in place. Nothing more than the blood of the Lamb is necessary. The saints wait for the end, defying the evil triumvirate as faithful witnesses and as priests who draw people to life in the presence of God asking, "Are you washed in the blood of the Lamb?"

Divine Judgment and the Missio Dei in the Book of Revelation[1]

Dean Flemming

Friedrich Nietzsche labeled John's Apocalypse as "that most obscene of all the written outbursts, which has revenge on its conscience."[2] More recently, John Dominic Crossan claimed that Revelation turns "the nonviolent resistance of the slaughtered Jesus into the violent warfare of the slaughtering Jesus."[3] Are such readings brutally honest assessments of Revelation's vengeful character or simply "fake news"? More specifically for this study, are John's visions of judgment in Revelation so violent and vindictive that they remain hopelessly incompatible with the loving, life-giving mission of God?

This essay contends that Revelation's judgment scenes do not resist or cancel out the gracious mission of God and the Lamb. On the contrary, Revelation portrays judgment as an integral dimension of that divine mission. A full treatment of Revelation's visions of judgment runs well beyond the scope of this essay. Consequently, I will try to show the link between judgment and the *missio Dei* in the Apocalypse by focusing on three texts: Rev 11:11-13; 14:6-20; and 15:1-4. In each case, the themes of God's mission and judgment intertwine. I will conclude with some biblical

---

[1] It is a privilege to dedicate this essay to George Lyons, whom I have known as an editor, a New Testament colleague, and a friend of many years. His careful scholarship and passion for Scripture have inspired and challenged my own ministry of the Word.

[2] Frederick Nietzsche, *The Genealogy of Morals*, trans. Horace B. Samuel (New York: Boni and Liveright, 1913; repr., Whithorn, IRE: Anados, 2017), 27.

[3] John Dominic Crossan, *God and Empire: Jesus against Rome, Then and Now* (San Francisco: HarperSanFrancisco, 2007), 224.

theological reflections on the role of divine judgment in the divine mission in Revelation.

Judgment and Costly Witness (Rev 11:11–13)

Revelation 11:3–13 stands out as a crucial text for understanding the shape of God's mission in Revelation. John's vision of the two witnesses especially spotlights the role of God's people in the coming of God's kingdom and eternal rule (see Rev 11:15). Although the two witnesses evoke the ministry of Old Testament prophetic figures like Moses and Elijah (11:6), above all they symbolize the church as a whole in its role of witness bearing.[1]

In this passage, John takes great pains to narrate the church's mission in ways that recall the story of Jesus, the "faithful witness" (Rev 1:5; cf. 3:14; 19:11). Like Jesus in his earthly ministry, the two witnesses display miraculous power and uncommon authority in their prophetic testimony (11:4–6).[2] The consuming fire issuing from their mouths stands for the word of God (11:5). It reminds John's audience of the triumphant sword of the word that proceeds from the mouth of Christ (19:13, 15; cf. 1:16; 2:16; 19:21). What is more, even as Jesus was shamed and slain at the hands of his enemies, so God's faithful witnesses are killed by the beast, in the city "where also their Lord was crucified," and publicly humiliated by the peoples of the earth (11:7–10).

The vision reaches a climax in verses 11–13. Here the witnesses follow the pattern of Jesus's resurrection and ascension. After "three and a half days" of humiliation, God breathes new life into the witnesses (Rev 11:11; cf. Ezek 37:1–10) and calls them to heaven (11:12). Unlike the story of Jesus, however, the fate of the witnesses remains on display for all the world to see. John goes out of his way to spotlight the public character of these events. First,

---

[1] John makes this connection clear when he identifies the witnesses as lampstands (Rev 11:4), a symbol that earlier in Revelation represents the seven churches (1:12, 20).

[2] See Joseph P. Mangina, *Revelation*, BTCB (Grand Rapids: Brazos, 2010), 138.

people of every tribe, language, and nation gaze on the slain bodies of God's prophets and throw a city-wide party to celebrate their demise (11:9-10). Then the inhabitants of the earth "observe" (θεωρέω) both their resurrection and their exaltation by God (11:11, 12). Lest anyone on earth miss the point, a thunderous voice from heaven issues a global bulletin, announcing the witnesses' ascension to heaven (11:12).

Simultaneous with this public vindication of God's witnesses ("at that moment"), an act of divine judgment—a "great earthquake"—afflicts the earth-dwellers. One in ten inhabitants of the great city perish. But the remnant—the vast majority of those on earth—not only demonstrates fear (ἔμφοβος), but they give "glory to the God of heaven" (Rev 11:13). What should we make of the earthquake survivors' response? Some interpreters deny that John's language in Rev 11:13 suggests true conversion.[1] "Fear," it is argued, represents simply a response of terror, and "giving God glory" a case of "judgment doxology," in which unbelievers are forced, against their wills, to acknowledge God's heavenly sovereignty.[2] For this reading, the witnesses' primary ministry in Rev 11 entails pronouncing judgment upon the nations, not seeking their repentance.[3]

Viewed on the wider canvas of Revelation, however, the final words of verse 13 strongly indicate the conversion of people from all nations to God. Although fear, at times, can spring from the prospect of judgment (Rev 18:10, 15), elsewhere it signifies genuine reverence for God (11:18; 14:7; 15:4; 19:5). In Rev 11:13, both of these manifestations of fear commingle in the earth-dwellers—terror at

---

[1] E.g., G. K. Beale, *The Book of Revelation: A Commentary on the Greek Text*, NIGTC (Grand Rapids: Eerdmans, 1999), 603-7; Eckhard J. Schnabel, "John and the Future of the Nations," *BBR* 12 (2002): 247-57; and Gordon D. Fee, *Revelation*, NCC (Eugene, OR: Cascade, 2011), 155.

[2] Schnabel, "John and the Future of the Nations," 254. Cf. Fee, *Revelation*, 155: "[I]n giving 'glory to the God of heaven' they are acknowledging God's divine majesty and power; but that falls several leagues short of offering themselves to the living—and only—God as obedient servants."

[3] Beale, *Book of Revelation*, 600.

the devastation of the earthquake and a positive turning to God.[1] Moreover, the language of "giving glory to God" functions in the Apocalypse almost as shorthand for genuine repentance and conversion on the part of the nations (see 14:6-7; 15:4; 21:26). Indeed, the same combination of "fearing" and "glorifying" God appears in both passages later explored in this essay (14:7; 15:4), and in both cases, these notions are inseparable from the worship of the one true God.

How, then, should we understand the relationship between judgment and mission in Rev 11:13? The sequence of events in verse 13 displays an explicit connection between God's judgment in the earthquake and the repentance and conversion of the survivors.[2] However—and this is a crucial point—nowhere in Revelation does judgment alone lead to repentance. On the contrary, when unbelievers encounter the naked plagues of God's wrath, they do not "repent and give [God] glory" (Rev 16:9, cf. 16:11). They do not forsake their evil deeds or their idolatrous worship (9:20, 21). Rather, what seems to make all the difference here in 11:3-13 is the faithful, costly testimony of the two witnesses, who represent the church. That witness takes the form of both prophetic word and poured-out life.

John spotlights the critical role of God's witnesses in God's mission in a number of ways, not least by their wardrobe selection. They enter the scene dressed in sackcloth, signaling repentance and

---

[1] Note the implied contrast between the multinational spectators who are smitten with "great fear" (φόβος μέγας) at God's raising of his faithful witnesses in Rev 11:11 and the fear that accompanies their repentance and conversion in 11:13.

[2] Felise Tavo makes the stimulating suggestion that the primary function of the earthquake in Rev 11:13, rather than judgment, is to reinforce the patterning of the story of the two witnesses after the story of Jesus. Even as a "great earthquake" (Matt 28:2; 27:51) signals the death and resurrection of Jesus, so an earthquake heralds the vindication of the two witnesses. *Woman, Mother and Bride: An Exegetical Investigation into the 'Ecclesial' Notions of the Apocalypse,"* BTS 3 (Leuven: Peters, 2007), 215. This is a plausible canonical connection. However, the function of earthquakes elsewhere in Revelation is to effect judgment (Rev 6:12; 8:5; 16:18). This suggests that above all the "great earthquake" in 11:13 is intended to bring about a partial judgment, ultimately leading to repentance.

mourning (Rev 11:3). It follows, then, that the fiery words that pour from their mouths call beast-worshipers to turn from their idolatrous ways (11:5). Above all, by their faithful witness, even to the point of death, and their public vindication by God, their lives broadcast the story of the crucified and risen Lamb. As Joseph P. Mangina elegantly comments, "[T]he apostolic preaching must be performed in the key of the cross, so that there is a real congruity between the message and the messenger."[1] This sacrificial, Lamb-like witness draws people from the world's nations into the sphere of worshiping God (11:13).[2] In this way, the church fulfills its role as a community of priests, who mediate God's presence to the world's nations (1:6; 5:10; cf. Exod 19:5-6).

In Rev 11:13, then, judgment in the form of the great earthquake functions primarily for the purpose of warning, rather than punishment. The earthquake, in conjunction with the witness, death, and vindication of the community, carries a stunning effect. According to John's "theological mathematics," only one tenth of humanity perishes in the earthquake, meaning that nine tenths repent and give glory to God! This constitutes a "merciful reversal" of the prophetic pattern, in which a remnant of one tenth are spared and the rest fall under God's judgment (Isa 6:13; Amos 5:3).[3] Likewise, whereas during the ministry of Elijah God preserves a remnant of 7000 worshipers, who do not bow to Baal (1 Kgs 19:18), in Revelation precisely the opposite happens: only 7000 perish and the vast majority of earth-dwellers worship the true God (Rev 11:13). These converts represent people from every tribe, language, and nation (11:9). John's vision of an immense multitude from all nations turning to God, in response to the church's faithful witness,

---

[1] Mangina, *Revelation*, 141.

[2] As Andy Johnson notes, Revelation's pattern of God's people fulfilling their missional vocation through suffering and death "is precisely the opposite of the logic of a 'secret rapture' theology," in which God saves his people "by whisking them out of a rebellious world so that he can then extinguish all the rebels" (*Holiness and the* Missio Dei [Eugene, OR: Cascade, 2016], 165).

[3] Ibid., 165; cf. Richard Bauckham, *The Theology of the Book of Revelation* (Cambridge: Cambridge University), 86-87.

shows that the overarching purpose of judgment in this context is not retribution, but repentance and salvation.

Judgment and the Eternal Gospel (Rev 14:6–20)

Nowhere does the connection between mission and judgment in Revelation display itself more clearly than in Rev 14:6–20. The passage lies within one of Revelation's interludes (Rev 14:1–20), just prior to the unleashing of seven bowls of judgments (15:1 – 16:21). Rev 14:6 kicks off a series of five visions, beginning with three shouting angels (14:6–11) and concluding with two images of end-time harvest (14:14–20).

First, an angel soars in mid-heaven with, literally, "an eternal gospel to gospel" (εὐαγγέλιον αἰώνιον εὐαγγελίσαι, "an eternal gospel to proclaim;" Rev 14:6 NRSV).[1] In contrast with the vision in Rev 14:1-5, which pictures the redeemed from humankind worshiping the Lamb, this gospel proclamation targets unbelievers, the "earth-dwellers" (14:6). What is more, the good news issues a universal appeal: it calls people from "every nation and tribe and language and people" (cf. 11:9; 13:7-8) to fear and glorify God, as well as to worship the Creator of all things (14:7).

Once again, some interpreters play down the missional implications of the passage. For example, G. K. Beale argues that, in the context of verses 8-11, this "gospel" is primarily a message of wrath, not grace.[2] For Beale, the angel's exhortation to fear and worship God cannot signal an opportunity to repent in order to avoid judgment, since the time for repentance is past. Instead, it calls for "a coerced acknowledgment of God's sovereignty."[3]
Sovereignty, yes—coercion, no. It's true that Revelation's εὐαγγέλιον ("gospel") includes the following declarations: (a) God has liberated creation from all the evil powers that dominate it; (b) God has established his eternal reign over the world (Rev 11:15-18;

---

[1] This is the only occurrence of the noun εὐαγγέλιον within the entire Johannine corpus.
[2] Beale, *Book of Revelation*, 748–49.
[3] Ibid., 751–53.

cf. Isa 40:9-10; 52:7; Nah 1:15); and (c) all nations must acknowledge this (Rev 15:3-4). But these hardly demand a forced confession in Rev 14:6-7. Would John, for example, later spotlight the beast-worshipers' refusal to "repent and give God glory" (16:9) if they had no opportunity whatever to do so? To shut off any hope of a positive turning to God among the nations effectively turns the angel's hope-laden announcement of good news into a damning pronouncement of bad news.

John's language tells a different story, one that reveals God's desire for people from every tribe, tongue, and nation to respond to the gracious gospel of God's salvation.[1] The combination of "fearing God," "giving God glory," and "worshiping" the Creator (Rev 14:7) represents an appeal to genuine repentance and conversion (11:13; 15:4; cf. 16:9; 19:5, 7). The angel's call to worship in verse 7 reflects a wider "worship war" in Revelation, which pits the worship of the maker of heaven and earth against the idolatrous worship of the beast (14:9, 11; cf. 5:9-14; 9:20; 13:4, 12, 15; 16:2; 19:20; 20:4).[2] In the first five verses of chapter fourteen, John pictures the redeemed from the earth singing a new song of praise before the throne of God and the Lamb. Now beast-worshipers from every nation are urged to switch sides and join the company of those who worship

---

[1] Richard Bauckham makes a strong case that the language of proclaiming "an eternal gospel" in Rev 14:6 echoes Psalm 96:2 (95:2 LXX): "Tell [the good news εὐαγγελίζεσθε LXX) of his salvation from day to day," particularly since the Psalmist goes on to urge the "nations" and "all peoples" to give God glory (96:3; cf. 96:8-9, in which the calls to "ascribe to the Lord glory" and "tremble before him" reflect language similar to Rev 14:7). *The Climax of Prophecy: Studies in the Book of Revelation* (London: T&T Clark, 2000), 286-89.

[2] For John and his readers, such good news stands in barefaced contrast with Rome's "gospel," which is bound up with the birth, rule, or victories on the emperor. See, e.g., the well-known Priene inscription, which celebrates the birth of Caesar Augustus as "the beginning of good tidings [εὐαγγέλια] to the world," cited in J. Nelson Kraybill, *Apocalypse and Allegiance: Worship, Politics, and Devotion in the Book of Revelation* (Grand Rapids: Brazos, 2010), 57. What is more, John's *eternal* gospel reflects God's eternal character and reign, in contrast with the transient rule of powers like Babylon or Rome, which was exalted as the "eternal city" (Craig R. Koester, *Revelation*, AYB 38A (New Haven: Yale University, 2014), 612.

the Creator of all things (14:6–7). The Creator hasn't given up on the creation.[1]

In Rev 14:6–7, God's judgment plays a key role in God's mission. The angel's message includes a specific motivation for the earth-dwellers to abandon their idolatrous ways and give God glory: "because the hour of his judgment has come" (14:7 ESV). This announcement, on the one hand, leaves no doubt about the certainty of God's ultimate judgment of the wicked. There is good reason for beast-worshipers to fear God. On the other hand, this judgment pronouncement does not represent a fait accompli, which simply describes the fate of unbelievers from all nations. In this setting, the reminder of God's final judgment functions primarily as a call to receive the good news of God's salvation. John essentially confronts the earth's inhabitants with two stark alternatives: either repent and worship the Creator, or persist in your stubborn attachment to a lifestyle that glorifies the beast.

Rhetorically, the alternatives between worshiping God and facing God's judgment operate on multiple levels. First, as we have noted, they bear witness to God's gracious offer of hope to his rebellious creatures in all nations, along with the alternative possibility of ultimate judgment for those who stubbornly refuse to repent (Rev 16:9, 11). Second, Rev 14:6–7 appeals to John's Christian readers in the churches in Asia. How they hear that message depends on their spiritual condition. For some, like the faithful oppressed in Smyrna and Philadelphia (Rev 2:8–11; 3:7–13), the angelic announcement comes as a call to reverence and worship God, along with the assurance that the righteous Creator will also serve as judge and will ultimately rid God's creation of evil (14:12–13). For others, however, like the arrogant and self-satisfied Christians in Laodicea (3:14–22), the command to "fear God" (14:7) carries a stern warning. For them, the angel's message delivers a jolt, like an electric shock. They must repent and change their lifestyle, or face God's judgment.

---

[1] Craig R. Koester, *Revelation and the End of All Things* (Grand Rapids: Eerdmans, 2001), 138.

Third, for John's audience, the angel's words function as a summons to mission. As the church father Primasius noted centuries ago, the announcement of the gospel in the context of God's eschatological judgment spotlights the urgency of the church's mission to all peoples and nations (Matt 24:14).[1] At the same time, it is noteworthy that John enumerates four familiar categories of unbelievers who receive the invitation to fear and glorify God: "every nation and tribe and language and people" (Rev 14:6; cf. 10:11; 11:9; 13:7). These are the very demographics that, elsewhere in Revelation, constitute the redeemed who stand before God's throne in jubilant worship (5:9; 7:9). The repetition of the same formula in Rev 14 gives John's audience hope that God's universal saving mission, and the church's participation in it, will bear abundant fruit.[2]

The choice between glorifying God and persisting in their allegiance to the beast in Rev 14:6-7 plays out in the rest of the chapter. The second and third angelic messages (Rev 14:8-11) picture the consequences of refusing to repent. In 14:8, the announcement of Babylon's doom for its corrupting of all nations foreshadows a story of judgment on wicked Babylon and its collaborators that unfolds in chapters 16–18. The third angel bellows the grimmest message of all (14:9-11). Those who spurn the first angel's call to worship the Creator and persist in the idolatrous worship of the beast—highlighted at both the beginning and end of the passage (14:9, 11)—face gruesome, unrelenting judgment. They have stubbornly refused the salvation purchased by the Lamb at great cost (5:9-10), and now the Lamb is present among them, allowing their rejection to take its course (14:10).

Finally, John offers his audience two parallel and contrasting visions of reaping (Rev 14:14-20). In the first, "one like the Son of Man" descends, sickle in hand, to reap the grain harvest of the earth

---

[1] Primasius, *Commentary on the Apocalypse*. 14.7, cited in William C. Weinrich, ed., *Revelation*, ACCSNT (Downers Grove, IL: IVP Academic, 2005), 224.

[2] John Christopher Thomas and Frank D. Macchia, *Revelation*, THNTC (Grand Rapids: Eerdmans, 2016), 257.

(14:14-16). In the second, an angel, also bearing a sickle, garners a harvest of grapes and tosses them into the wine press of God's wrath (14:17-20). Virtually all commentators agree that this second vision—of the gathering of grapes—symbolizes God's end-time judgment. But what about the prior vision of the grain harvest? Many interpreters take this harvest as a symbol of the same act of judgment.[1] Perhaps the strongest argument in favor of this reading is that both images draw from Joel 3:13, which only pictures divine judgment:

> Put in the sickle,
>   for the harvest is ripe.
> Go in, tread,
>   for the wine press is full.
> The vats overflow,
>   for their wickedness is great.[2]

It is true that the image of the harvest, whether grain, grape, or olive, takes us onto well-trodden ground as a biblical picture of end-time judgment (e.g., Isa 17:5; 18:4-5; 24:13; 63:1-4; Jer 51:33; Hos 6:11; Joel 3:13; Mic 4:12-13; Matt 13:39-42; Mark 4:29; cf. 4 Ezra 4:28-32; 2 Bar 70:2). Nevertheless, I agree with Richard Bauckham and others that Rev 14:14-16 offers a positive, missional image of God's harvest, in contrast to the gathering for the wine press of God's wrath in 14:17-20.[3] Several factors point to this missional reading.

---

[1] See, e.g., Beale, *Book of Revelation*, 772-74; David E. Aune, *Revelation 6-16*, WBC 52B (Waco, TX: Word, 1998), 801-2, 842-45; Schnabel, "John and the Future of the Nations," 257-62.

[2] Other common arguments for reading both Rev 14:14-16 and 14:17-20 as images of judgment include: (1) heavenly beings act in parallel ways in both passages; (2) the image of the "sharp sickle" (14:14, 17) found in both passages is primarily a negative image of judgment; and (3) the phrase "for the hour to reap has come" refers back to the similar phrase, "for the hour of judgment has come" in 14:7. See Beale, *Book of Revelation*, 774; Aune, *Revelation 6-16*, 802.

[3] Bauckham, *Theology of the Book of Revelation*, 95-98; idem, *Climax of Prophecy*, 289-96; cf. Koester, *Revelation*, 627-29. A third option takes the harvest in 14:14-16 as both a negative and positive image, symbolizing the ingathering of the righteous and the judgment of the wicked. See Primasius, *Commentary on the Apocalypse* 14.15-16, cited in Weinrich, *Revelation*, 233; Mitchell G. Reddish,

First, earlier in the chapter, John pictures the redeemed from the earth as the "first fruits" (Rev 14:4) of a much greater harvest to come, which is now realized in the ripe grain harvest. Second, this harvest is carried out by "one like the Son of Man," a figure already identified as the risen Christ, who stands among the churches (1:12–20). Like his counterpart in Dan 7, this messianic Son of Man comes, not in judgment of the nations, but to gather people from all nations into his universal kingdom. Third, when the harvest image represents judgment in Scripture, it normally involves the activities of threshing and separating the chaff (see Jer 51:33; Mic 4:12-13; Hab 3:12; Matt 3:12; 13:30; Luke 3:17). In contrast, the New Testament pictures the specific action of reaping the grain harvest as a positive image of bringing people into the kingdom (see Matt 9:37-38; 13:30; Mark 4:29; John 4:35-38).

The harvest of grain, then, represents a great ingathering of people for God at the time of Jesus's return, which is the fulfillment of God's missional purpose for the nations. Rhetorically, Rev 14:14–20 confronts readers with a similar choice as in 14:6-13. On the one hand, they can welcome the good news of God's salvation and respond to it by holding fast to the commandments of God and the faith of Jesus (14:12). This will enable them to participate in the eschatological harvest, when the Son of Man gathers his own (14:14-16). On the other hand, they can reject the gospel, stubbornly continue in their idolatrous worship of the beast, and ultimately suffer the fate of those who are trampled in the wine press of God's judgment (14:17-20). The passage pictures the latter fate in graphic and grisly terms. Having drunk the wine of Babylon's immorality, violence, and injustice (14:8), rebellious humanity now becomes the wine, squeezed from the blood-spattered wine press of God's wrath.[1] Their blood rises like a flood to inundate a vast stretch of the

---

Revelation, SHBC (Macon, GA: Smyth and Helwys, 2001), 281; Stephen S. Smalley, *The Revelation to John* (Downers Grove, IL: IVP Academic, 2005), 374. However, both the background of the "Son of Man" figure and the positive role of eschatological grain harvest in Scripture make this unlikely.

[1] Koester, *Revelation*, 630.

earth (14:19-20). Likewise, in 14:9-11, the Lamb apparently watches as impenitent humanity suffers ceaseless torment with fire, sulfur, and smoke.[1]

Are such violent and seemingly vengeful images compatible with the gracious mission of God? First, it is crucial to remember that these are symbols, not descriptions of actual events. We are no more justified in reading these vivid images literally than we are in asserting that Jesus is actually a wooly lamb, or that the woman in Rev 17 literally sits on many waters, a scarlet beast, and seven mountains—all at once! Second, Revelation portrays this punishment as an outworking of God's justice. For example, those who drink of the wine of Babylon's passion (θυμός) and participate in her sins (Rev 14:8) must also drink the wine of God's passion and share Babylon's judgment (14:10).[2] Third, John deploys such deliberately hyperbolic, rhetorical language for a purpose.

Above all, it sends a warning bulletin to his audience, particularly the complacent in the Asian churches. John's gruesome images of judgment confront readers with both the genuine danger of persisting in their idolatrous lifestyle and the opportunity to repent and avoid God's righteous judgment.

Judgments and the Worship of the Nations (Rev 15:2-4)

John's vision of a heavenly victory celebration in Rev 15:2-4 represents a third crucial link between judgment and the *missio Dei*. Strategically positioned between the announcement of the final set of judgments in Revelation (Rev 15:1) and the unleashing of the seven bowls of God's wrath (15:5—16:21), this brief vision provides an important context for the judgments that follow. The vision of God's people standing beside the sea of glass with harps in hand and singing a song of praise to God and the Lamb recalls earlier worship scenes in Revelation (4:6; 5:8-9; 14:2-3). Here the

---

[1] Such images are apparently borrowed from the OT story of God's judgment on Sodom and Gomorrah (Gen 19:24, 28; Deut 29:23; cf. Luke 17:29). See Richard Bauckham, "Judgment in the Book of Revelation," *ExAud* 20 (2004): 19.

[2] Bauckham, "Judgment in the Book of Revelation," 20.

worshipers represent "those who have conquered the beast and its image" (15:2). Although outward appearances might indicate that the beast has triumphed by killing God's faithful (11:7; 13:7), in truth the Lamb-followers have defeated the beast. They have done so, not by wielding the beastly weapons of power and violence, but through the blood of the slaughtered Lamb and their own costly witness, even to the point of death (12:11; cf. 5:5–6).

Echoing the exodus, these overcomers sing the song of Moses and the Lamb (Rev 15:3). Even as Israel, delivered from the clutches of Pharaoh, sang their praises to God along the shores of the Red Sea (Exod 15), now the redeemed sing a new song beside the fiery sea.[1] But this hymn transposes the original song of Moses into a new key. Instead of focusing on Israel's deliverance through God's crushing of the pagan nations, the lyrics of Revelation's song tell the story of the nations coming to worship their true king.[2] Crucially, the song of Moses is also the song of the Lamb. The hymn qualifies as the Lamb's song, not only because God's people have conquered the evil powers through the Lamb's blood (Rev 12:11),[3] but also because, in a new exodus event, the slaughtered Lamb has redeemed people for God from every tribe, language, and nation (5:9; 14:4).

John develops the song's missional theme by interpreting the original song of Moses with a "patchwork quilt of OT phrases"[4] (e.g., Deut 32:4; Pss 86:8–10; 98:1–2; 111:2; 139:14; 145:17; Jer 10:6–7). As in our previous texts, we encounter the language of the nations "fearing" and "glorifying" God (Rev 15:4; cf. 11:13; 14:7) and "worshiping" him (15:4; cf. 14:7). The rhetorical question, "Lord,

---

[1] It is likely that the sea "mixed with fire" (μεμιγμένην πυρί, Rev 15:2) symbolizes God's judgment that is about to be unleashed on the world (cf. 8:8–9; 14:10; 19:20; 20:10). Here, "the faithful stand beyond the fiery sea of judgment," which will descend upon the beast and its unrepentant allies (Koester, *Revelation*, 631).

[2] Bauckham, *Theology of the Book of Revelation*, 101.

[3] So ibid., 99; Koester, *Revelation and the End of All Things*, 142.

[4] Ben Witherington III, *Revelation*, NCBC (Cambridge: Cambridge University, 2003), 206.

who will not fear and glorify your name?" (15:4) demands the immediate response, "No one, surely!" But the fuller answer comes later in the verse: "All nations will come and worship before you." The worship of all peoples, then, shows the goal of God's mission. In the wider context of Revelation, this universal worship represents a positive response to the proclamation of the eternal gospel (14:6) and the suffering witness of the redeemed (11:3-13). Here the worship of those who have courageously conquered the beast seeks to draw others from all nations to join them in the act of worshiping God and the Lamb (15:3-4; cf. 14:1-7).

Once again, however, divine judgment plays a crucial role in fulfilling God's missional purpose for the nations. The song by the glassy sea closes by affirming: "All nations will come and worship before you, for your judgments [δικαιώματα] have been revealed" (Rev 15:4, italics added). As in 14:7, God's righteous judgment functions as a reason and motivation (ὅτι) for the nations turning to God. Here God's δικαιώματα probably include both his righteous saving acts on behalf of God's people (cf. "your deeds," ἔργα σου, 15:3) and God's just judgments against the ungodly (cf. Rom 1:32; 5:16), which surround this passage.[1] As Thomas and Macchia note, "God's acts of judgment are not random acts but are indeed righteous acts designed to encourage true worship, even among those who rebelliously worship the dragon, the beast, and the image of the beast."[2] The song's lyrics assume that, when the rebellious nations truly recognize the greatness of God's deeds, the truth of God's ways, the holiness of God's character, and the justice of God's judgments, they will be magnetically attracted to join the chorus of worshipers who sing the song. This notion echoes the ringing Old Testament hope that when the nations witness God's mighty acts of blessing, judgment, and restoration, both in relation to Israel and the whole of creation, they will be drawn to know and worship

---

[1] Koester, *Revelation*, 633. Bauckham (*Climax of Prophecy*, 304) argues that the language of God's justice being revealed in Rev 15:4 echoes Ps 98:2, which affirms that "God has revealed his righteousness in the sight of the nations" (ESV).

[2] Thomas and Macchia, *Revelation*, 274.

Israel's God (e.g., 1 Kgs 8:41–43; Pss 47:1–2; 66:3–4; 67:1–3; 86:8–10; 96:1–13; 98:1–9; 138:4–5; Ezek 36:20–23).[1]

What is more, the striking picture of all nations coming to worship God (Rev 15:4) builds on the most sweeping hopes of the prophets, who foresee an end-time, worldwide pilgrimage of the nations to Jerusalem (Isa 2:2–4; 60:1–9; 66:20–23; Zech 8:22). This breathtaking vision of "all nations" worshiping their King (Rev 15:3, 4) foreshadows the culmination of God's mission in the new Jerusalem, where John pictures two things: (1) all nations walk by the light of God and the Lamb, and (2) the kings of the earth bringing their glory (worship) into it (21:24). The city's gates remain perpetually open and face every direction, welcoming people from all points on the compass (21:13, 25). Indeed, God's missional purpose in the new creation is no less than "the healing of the nations" (22:2).[2]

Does the "all" in "all nations" (Rev 15:4) signify that every person in every nation will be converted in the end? That is not the case from John's perspective. The warnings of judgment that surround this passage and continue even into his description of the new Jerusalem (21:8, 27; 22:15) underscore that John is no universalist. Nevertheless, the conviction that people from all nations will enter the sphere of divine worship in the end would bring enormous hope and encouragement to John's audience. Because they have overcome the beast through the blood of the Lamb and their own suffering testimony (15:2; cf. 12:11), and because their worship bears witness to the power, holiness, and justice of their God (15:3-4), they hold the assurance that their costly witness will bear abundant fruit in the end.

---

[1] On the development of this theme in the OT, see Christopher J. H. Wright, *The Mission of God: Unlocking the Bible's Grand Narrative* (Downers Grove, IL: IVP Academic, 2006), 467–89.

[2] The fulfillment of John's vision of global worship in Rev 15:3–4 in the new Jerusalem makes it highly unlikely that the nations' "worship" in 15:4 consists of a forced subjugation to God's sovereignty, as argued by Schnabel, "John and the Future of the Nations," 262–65.

Revelation's hope-full vision continues to offer the same encouragement to Christian communities today, which feel the scorpion sting of persecution or labor in the deserts of spiritual apathy. Having done ministry in Western Europe for over a decade, I know what it is to cling to such a hope. Revelation assures God's people that, despite present circumstances, their faithful witness will not be in vain and that it will contribute to the nations turning to God, as God's universal mission reaches its goal.

Reflections on Judgment and Mission

What can we conclude about the interaction between God's judgment and God's mission in Revelation? Building on the evidence that has been considered from the passages studied in this essay, I close with a number of biblical-theological reflections on the role of judgment in the fulfillment of the *missio Dei*.

First, judgment and mission in Revelation are not independent, but interdependent. In each of the three passages we examined, judgment plays a critical role in realizing God's missional purpose for humanity and the whole creation. In chapters 14 and 15, John makes divine judgment an explicit motivation for repentance and conversion, while in chapter 11, the warning earthquake that accompanies the earth-dwellers' change of heart strongly implies such a connection. In a sense, judgment is the flip-side of God's salvation. God's righteous judgments on evil in all its forms are essential for "the kingdom of the world" to "become the kingdom of our Lord and of his Messiah" (Rev 11:15). God's undaunted faithfulness to his creation requires a divine war against the powers that seek to destroy the earth. God's righteous judgments testify that nothing will be allowed to derail God's missional purpose to liberate, redeem, and restore the world.[1]

Second, judgment does not oppose God's redemptive love, but functions as a dimension of that love. In the Apocalypse, God's love is not flabby, and his grace isn't cheap. Rather, God's love

---

[1] Dean Flemming, "Revelation and the *Missio Dei*: Toward a Missional Reading of the Apocalypse," *JTI* 6 (2012): 166.

remains a holy love that conquers evil through righteous and merciful judgments. John reveals God's love as "an all-powerful redemptive force that casts a dark shadow of judgment over those who continue to oppose its liberating work in the world."[1] Yet, even in judgment, divine love triumphs over evil through the spilled blood of the Lamb (Rev 5:6; 12:11; 15:2). Victory comes through vulnerable, self-giving love, not through violence.

Third, judgment is not an end in itself, but is primarily a means to an end.[2] In each text we considered, the goal of divine judgment is to lead people from all nations to fear, glorify, and worship the Creator of all things. More broadly, Revelation's final word comes, not with the wine press of God's wrath (Rev 14:17-20) or the lake of fire (20:7-15), but with the new heaven and the new earth (chs 21–22). Beyond the eradication of evil lies the new Jerusalem, where a holy people from every tongue, tribe, and nation will dwell in the presence of a holy God (21:3). God's loving mission culminates in the "healing of the nations" (22:2), a comprehensive restoration that touches every dimension of human need. Further, the *missio Dei* in Revelation embraces the restoring of the whole creation. God is in the business of making "all things new" (21:5).

Fourth, it follows, then, that the overarching purpose of judgment is not revenge or retribution, but repentance and restoration. Revelation makes this purpose explicit in the messages to the seven churches in chapters 2 and 3, where the call to repent and the warning of judgment go hand in hand (Rev 2:5; 16, 21-22; 3:3, 16, 19). But the link between judgment and repentance also emerges implicitly. We find it in the chilling observations that sinful humanity did not repent in the face of God's judgments (9:20-21; 16:9, 11). But it appears in the picture of God's two witnesses clothed in sackcloth (11:3). And it emerges in the unspoken call to repent in the admonition, "Fear God and give him glory," in light of

---

[1] Thomas and Macchia, *Revelation*, 411.

[2] See Michael J. Gorman, *Reading Revelation Responsibly: Uncivil Worship and Witness: Following the Lamb into the New Creation* (Eugene, OR: Cascade, 20011), 138, 153-54.

the hour of judgment (14:7). Moreover, the very structure of Revelation's judgment visions, which are strung out over three sets of seven plagues, with growing intensity (chs 6, 8–9, 15–16), suggests that time yet remains for humans to heed their message, repent, and glorify God.[1] God's judgments arise, not from vindictiveness, but out of God's missional purpose to bring about the worship, wholeness, and salvation of all people in all nations.

Fifth, the conversion of the nations does not come through judgment alone, but through the suffering witness of the church. We have noted that, whenever the earth-dwellers encounter God's judgments alone, whether cosmic or historical, those unbelievers patently refuse to repent of their idolatrous ways and their evil deeds (Rev 9:20-21; 16:9, 11, 21). Our three passages demonstrate that only the costly witness of the followers of the slain Lamb can spark a change of heart. In chapter 11, the prophetic word and poured-out lives of God's witnesses precede God's warning judgment; in 14:6-7, judgment operates in conjunction with the proclamation of the gospel and the call to give God glory; in chapter 15, the worship of the community, as it bears witness to the saving acts of God, above all through the slaughtered and risen Lamb, combines with God's righteous judgments to lead the nations to repent. For Christian communities today, the story of the slaughtered Lamb remains not only the source of our salvation, but the pattern of our life and mission in the world.

Sixth, God's judgment does not represent divine vengeance, but God's holiness and justice. The coming of God's kingdom in its fullness requires the destruction of evil. Consequently, judgment and punishment become unfortunate, but necessary dimensions of God's redeeming mission. God, in God's loving sovereignty over God's creation, refuses "to allow human beings to go on indefinitely treating others as less than the images of God they are and thereby become more and more beastly and dehumanized themselves."[2] Throughout the three judgment cycles in Revelation, God allows

---

[1] Bauckham, "Judgment in the Book of Revelation," 7.
[2] Johnson, *Holiness and the* Missio Dei, 160.

humans to experience the disastrous consequences of their rebellious and idolatrous lifestyles. In other words, they experience the chaos, injustice, violence, and death that result from lives that refuse to give glory to God, with the hope that they might awaken out of their stupor and turn to their Creator (Rev 9:20-21; 16:9, 11). Such a perspective could almost serve as a commentary on Paul's indictment of unbelievers in Rom 1:18-32.

Ultimately, however, those who persist in spurning the mercy of their Creator must fall under the shadow of judgment. Revelation portrays God's judgment as an outworking of God's truth and justice (Rev 19:2; cf. 11:16-18; 15:3-4; 16:5-7). Those who seek the destruction of the earth will be destroyed (11:18). Those who drink of the wine of Babylon's passion, participating in her sins, must in turn drink the wine of God's passion, sharing Babylon's judgment (14:8, 10).[1] God will not allow the martyrs' cries for vindication forever to go unheeded (6:9-11). As Bauckham frames it, "When the truth is finally established and all illusion dispelled, those who persist to the end in refusing the truth must perish with the lies they will not relinquish."[2]

Seventh, Revelation does not try to resolve the tension between judgment and mission, but allows it to stand. On the one hand, a strain courses through the Apocalypse that pictures the world's nations in rebellion against God and as the object of divine wrath. The nations rage against God (Rev 11:18), worship the dragon and the beast (13:4, 7-8, 12), succumb to Satan's deceptions (20:3, 7, 10), and doggedly refuse to repent (9:20-21; 16:9, 11). Even as Revelation draws near to its end, an angel's exhortation makes it sound as though the time for turning to God is past: "Let the evildoer still do evil, and the filthy still be filthy" (22:11a; cf. 21:8, 27; 22:15).

On the other hand, each of the three passages we examined gives considerable hope that the faithful testimony of God's witnesses will result in an abundant harvest. Revelation pictures a

---

[1] Bauckham, "Judgment in the Book of Revelation," 20.
[2] Ibid., 8.

vast multitude of people from all tribes and nations glorifying God (Rev 11:13) and celebrates "all nations" being drawn into the worship of God (15:3-4). In chapter 14, the redeemed followers of the Lamb become the first fruits of a far greater harvest of salvation to come (14:4, 14-16). Such passages foreshadow a greater fulfillment in the new Jerusalem, where surprising characters suddenly show up on the streets of the holy city. The rebellious nations, which previously had been judged by God (11:18; 16:19; 19:15) and consumed by heavenly fire (20:7-15) now walk by the light of God's glory in the eternal city (21:23-24). Even more astounding, the kings of the earth, until now uniformly pictured as God's doomed enemies (6:15; 17:2, 18; 18:3, 9; 19:19), glorify God in the new Jerusalem (21:24).[1]

As frustrating as it might seem to modern readers, John makes no attempt to reconcile these two streams. As Craig Koester wisely notes, "The tension between sweeping visions of judgments and unqualified visions of hope cannot be resolved in a simple logical fashion. Revelation places both types of visions before the readers in order to alienate them from the powers of destruction while drawing them to God, where life is found."[2]

Eighth, the visions of judgment in Revelation are targeted in the first place, not to unbelievers, but to the church. Churches, both those of the first century and the twenty-first century, must hear and receive these visions according to their spiritual condition and need. For some, they bring assurance that a holy and loving God will overcome all injustice, violence, and evil in the end, that nothing will be permitted to foil his purpose to heal the nations. For other Christian communities, those same visions sound an alarm bell (see Rev 2:5, 16, 21-22; 3:3, 19; 9:20-21; 16:9, 11). They warn Christians who are in danger of compromising with the beastly powers that the path ahead leads to destruction. There are both a harvest and a wine press (14:14-20), and Revelation calls for "the endurance of the saints" (14:12).

---

[1] Flemming, "Revelation and the *Missio Dei*," 168.
[2] Koester, *Revelation*, 636.

At the same time, Revelation casts a vision that reaches beyond God's righteous judgment to a vast multinational harvest. This vision issues a call to mission, energizing God's people to mediate God's sweeping work of restoration in the world. It beckons the church to engage in prophetic and costly witness, as it speaks the "eternal gospel," embodies the life of the slaughtered Lamb, and gets caught up in God's purpose to create an unfathomable community of worship from every people and nation.

Contributors

DAVID A. ACKERMAN (PhD, Iliff School of Theology/University of Denver) is currently Field Education Coordinator, Philippines/Micronesia Church of the Nazarene and lead pastor of Guam First Church of the Nazarene. Previously, he served as a pastor for over fifteen years and Professor of New Testament at Asia-Pacific Nazarene Theological Seminary (Taytay, Philippines). Dr. Ackerman is the author of several books: *The Emmaus Model: Discipleship, Theological Education, and Transformation* (with Bruce G. Allder; Global Nazarene Publications, 2019), *Transformation in Christ: Paul's Experience of the Divine Mystery* (Pickwick, 2019), *1 and 2 Timothy, Titus: A Commentary in the Wesleyan Tradition* (Beacon Hill, 2016), and *Lo, I tell You a Mystery: Cross, Resurrection, and Paraenesis in the Rhetoric of 1 Corinthians* (Pickwick, 2006).

KENT E. BROWER (PhD, University of Manchester) is currently Senior Research Fellow and Senior Lecturer in Biblical Studies at Nazarene Theological College (Manchester, UK), where he has served for over three decades. In addition to numerous articles, Dr. Brower is the author of *Mark: A Commentary in the Wesleyan Tradition* (Beacon Hill, 2012), *Living as God's Holy People: Holiness and Community in Paul* (Paternoster, 2010), and *Holiness in the Gospels* (Beacon Hill, 2005). He served as co-editor and contributor for *Holiness and Ecclesiology in the New Testament* (Eerdmans, 2007) and *"The Reader Must Understand": Eschatology in Bible and Theology* (IVP, 2000; repr., Wipf and Stock, 2013), as well as a section editor for the New Beacon Bible Commentary series and an editor for *Global Dictionary of Wesleyan Theology* (Beacon Hill, 2013).

DEAN FLEMMING (PhD, University of Aberdeen) is currently Professor of New Testament and Missions at Mid-America

Nazarene University (Olathe, KS), where he has taught since 2011. He previously spent 24 years as a missionary educator in Asia and Europe. In addition to a number of articles, Dr. Flemming is an award-winning author of several books, including *Why Mission?* within the Reframing New Testament Theology series (Abingdon, 2015); *Recovering the Full Mission of God: A Biblical Perspective on Being, Doing and Telling* (IVP Academic, 2013); *Philippians: A Commentary in the Wesleyan Tradition* (Beacon Hill, 2009), which received the 2012 Smith-Wynkoop Book Award from the Wesleyan Theological Society; and *Contextualization in the New Testament: Patterns for Theology and Mission* (IVP Academic, 2005), which won a 2006 *Christianity Today* Book Award.

Andy Johnson (PhD, Luther Seminary) is currently Professor of New Testament at Nazarene Theological Seminary (Kansas City, MO), where he has taught since 2002. Prior to his present position, he held faculty positions at Eastern Nazarene College (Quincy, MA) and Trevecca Nazarene University (Nashville, TN). Dr. Johnson is the author of two books: *1 and 2 Thessalonians* in the Two Horizons New Testament Commentary (Eerdmans, 2016) and *Holiness and the Missio Dei* (Cascade, 2016). He co-edited (with Kent E. Brower) and contributor for *Holiness and Ecclesiology in the New Testament* (Eerdmans, 2007).

PAMELA K. LIEW (BA, Olivet Nazarene University) is a freelance artist whose work includes photography, poetry, book cover designs, and other creative projects.

TAT-SIONG BENNY LIEW (PhD, Vanderbilt University) is currently the Class of 1956 Professor in New Testament Studies at the College of the Holy Cross (Worcester, MA). Prior to his appointment at Holy Cross, Dr. Liew held faculty positions at the Pacific School of Religion (Berkeley, CA) and Chicago Theological Seminary

(Chicago, IL). He is the author of *Politics of Parousia: Reading Mark Inter(con)textually* (Brill, 1999) and *What is Asian American Biblical Hermeneutics? Reading the New Testament* (University of Hawaii, 2007). He is also the editor of the important series, T&T Clark's Study Guides to the New Testament.

KARA LYONS-PARDUE (PhD, Princeton Theological Seminary) is currently Professor of New Testament in the School of Theology and Ministry, Point Loma Nazarene University (San Diego, CA), where she has taught since 2011. She also serves as co-director of the university's Women's Studies Program. Dr. Lyons-Pardue is the author of *Gospel Women and the Long Ending of Mark* (T&T Clark, 2020) and "Commentary on Philemon" in *Ephesians, Colossians, and Philemon: A Commentary in the Wesleyan Tradition* (Beacon Hill, 2019), as well as co-editor and contributor for the book, *Following Jesus: Prophet, Priest, King* (The Foundry Publishing, 2018).

TROY W. MARTIN (PhD, University of Chicago) is currently Professor of Religious Studies at St. Xavier University (Chicago, IL), where he has taught for nearly three decades. Prior to his present position, he was on the faculty at Olivet Nazarene University (Bourbonnais, IL). A prolific writer and contributor to scholarly journals, Dr. Martin is the author of two books: *By Philosophy and Empty Deceit: Colossians as Response to a Cynic Critique* (Sheffield Academic, 1996) and *Metaphor and Composition in 1 Peter* (Scholars, 1992). He has also served as co-editor (with Eric F. Mason) and contributor for *Reading 1-2 Peter and Jude: A Resource for Students* (Society of Biblical Literature, 2014).

THOMAS E. PHILLIPS (PhD, Southern Methodist University) is currently Dean of Library and Professor of Theological Bibliography and New Testament at Claremont School of Theology (Claremont, CA). He has held faculty positions previously at Eastern Nazarene College (Quincy, MA), Colorado Christian University (Lakewood, CO), and Point Loma Nazarene University (San Diego, CA). In addition to many articles, Dr. Phillips is the author of three books: *Paul, His Letters, and Acts* (Baker Academic, 2010), *Acts within Diverse Frames of Reference* (Mercer University, 2009), and *Reading Issues of Wealth and Poverty in Luke-Acts* (Mellen, 2000). He has also served as editor and contributor for *Contemporary Studies in Acts* (Mercer University, 2009) and *Acts and Ethics* (Sheffield Phoenix, 2005), as well as co-editor/contributor for several other works in New Testament and Acts studies.

CAROL J. ROTZ (DLitt et Phil, University of Johannesburg) is retired Professor of Biblical Studies and former Chair of the Department of Religion at Northwest Nazarene University (Nampa, ID), where she was on the faculty for seven years. She continues to teach online courses for the university. Prior to her appointment to the NNU faculty, Dr. Rotz and her husband Jim served with distinction as missionary educators for the Church of the Nazarene for 20 years. She is the author of *Revelation: A Commentary in the Wesleyan Tradition* (Beacon Hill, 2012).

RICHARD P. THOMPSON (PhD, Southern Methodist University) is currently Professor of New Testament and Chair of the Department of Philosophy and Religion, within the College of Theology and Christian Ministries at Northwest Nazarene University (Nampa, ID), where he has taught for thirteen years. Prior to his present appointment, he held faculty positions at Olivet Nazarene University (Bourbonnais, IL) and Spring Arbor University (Spring Arbor, MI). In addition to a number of articles and essays, Dr. Thompson is the author of three books, including *Acts: A Commentary in the Wesleyan Tradition* (Beacon Hill, 2015) and *Keeping the Church in Its Place: The Church as Narrative Character in Acts* (T&T Clark, 2006). He has also served as co-editor and contributor for several other books, including *Reading the Bible in Wesleyan Ways: Some Constructive Proposals* (with Barry L. Callen; Beacon Hill, 2004), and *Literary Studies in Luke-Acts: Essays in Honor of Joseph B. Tyson* (with Thomas E. Phillips; Mercer University, 1998).

Bibliography

Achtemeier, Paul J. *1 Peter: A Commentary on First Peter*. Hermeneia. Minneapolis: Fortress, 1996.

Aretius, Benedictus. *In Novum Testamentum Domini Nostri Iesu Christi Commentarii*. Geneva: Petrum et Iacobum, 1618.

Aune, David E. *Revelation*. 2 vols. WBC 52. Waco, TX: Word, 1997–98.

Bandy, Alan S. "Persecution and the Purpose of Revelation with Reference to Roman Jurisprudence." *Bulletin for Biblical Research* 23.3 (2013): 377-98.

Barrett, C. K. "Things Sacrificed to Idols." In *Essays on Paul*, 40–59. Philadelphia: Fortress, 1982.

Batson, C. Daniel. *The Altruism Question: Toward a Social-Psychological Answer*. Hillsdale, NJ: Lawrence Erlbaum Associates, 1991.

Bauckham, Richard. "The Book of Revelation as a Christian War Scroll." *Neotestamentica* 22.1 (1988): 17-40.

———. *The Climax of Prophecy: Studies in the Book of Revelation*. London: T&T Clark, 2000.

———. *Jesus and the Eyewitnesses*. Grand Rapids: Eerdmans, 2006.

———. "Judgment in the Book of Revelation." *Ex Auditu* 20 (2004): 1-24.

———. *The Theology of Revelation*. New Testament Theology Cambridge: Cambridge University, 1993.

Beale, G. K. *The Book of Revelation: A Commentary on the Greek Text*. NIGTC. Grand Rapids: Eerdmans, 1999.

Beale, G. K. and Mitchell Kim. *God Dwells Among Us: Expanding Eden to the Ends of the Earth*. Downers Grove, IL: IVP, 2014.

———. *The Temple and the Church's Mission: A Biblical Theology of the Dwelling Place of God*. NSBT 17. Downers Grove, IL: IVP, 2004.

Beare, Francis W. *The First Epistle of Peter: The Greek Text with Introduction and Notes*. 2nd ed. Oxford: Blackwell, 1970.

Bede the Venerable. *The Commentary on the Seven Catholic Epistles of Bede the Venerable*. Trans. Hurst, David. Cistercian Studies Series 82. Kalamazoo, MI: Cistercian Publications, 1985.

Betsworth, Sharon. *The Reign of God is Such as These: A Socio-Literary*

Analysis of the Daughters in the Gospel of Mark. LNTS 422. New York: T&T Clark, 2010.

Betz, Hans Dieter. *A Commentary on the Sermon on the Mount*. Hermeneia. Minneapolis: Fortress, 1995.

Bigg, Charles. *A Critical and Exegetical Commentary on the Epistles of St. Peter and St. Jude*. ICC. Edinburgh: T&T Clark, 1987.

Black, Matthew. *An Aramaic Approach to the Gospels and Acts*. 3rd ed. Oxford: Clarendon, 1967.

Bonhoeffer, Dietrich. *The Cost of Discipleship*. Trans. Reginald H. Fuller. London: SCM, 1959.

Bookides, N. and J. E. Fischer. "The Sanctuary of Demeter and Core." *Hesperia* 41 (1972): 283–331.

Bookides, N. and R. S. Stroud. *Demeter and Persephone in Ancient Corinth* Princeton: ASCSA, 1987.

Boring, Eugene. "The Gospel of Matthew: Introduction, Commentary, and Reflections." In *New Interpreter's Bible*. Nashville: Abingdon, 2015.

Boring, M. Eugene. *Revelation*. IBC. Louisville, KY: John Knox, 1989.

Brodie, Thomas L. "The Systematic Use of the Pentateuch in 1 Corinthians." In *The Corinthian Correspondence*, 441-57. Ed. Reimund Bieringer. Leuven: Leuven University, 1996.

Brower, Kent R. "Elijah in the Markan Passion Narrative." *JSNT* 18 (1983): 85–101.

_____. "Let the Reader Understand: Temple and Eschatology in Mark." In *The Reader Must Understand: Eschatology in Bible and Theology*, 119-43. Ed. Kent E. Brower and Mark Elliott. Leicester: IVP Apollos, 1997.

_____. *Holiness in the Gospels*. Kansas City, MO: Beacon Hill, 2007.

_____. *Mark: A Commentary in the Wesleyan Tradition*. Kansas City, MO: Beacon Hill, 2012.

_____. "'You Wonder Where the Spirit Went:' The Spirit and the Resurrection of the Son in Matthew and John." *Journal of Theological Interpretation* 12 (2018): 58–75.

Brown, Jeannine. "Creation's Renewal in the Gospel of John." *Catholic Bibical Quarterly* 72 (2010): 275–90.

Brown, Raymond E. *The Death of the Messiah: From Gethsemane to the Grave: A Commentary on the Passion Narratives in the Four Gospels*. 2 vols. ABRL. New York: Doubleday, 1994.

Bruce, F. F. *Paul: Apostle of the Heart Set Free*. Grand Rapids: Eerdmans, 1977.

Bruner, Frederick D. *Matthew: A Commentary*.Dallas, TX: Word, 1990.
Caird, G. B. *A Commentary on the Revelation of St. John the Divine*. BNTC. London: Black, 1966.
Camerlynck, A. *Commentarius in Epistolas Catholicas*. 5th ed. Brugis: Sumptibus Car. Beyaert, 1909.
Campbell, Leroy A. *Mithraic Iconography and Ideology*. EPRO 11. Leiden: Brill, 1968.
Chilton, Bruce. *God in Strength: Jesus' Announcement of the Kingdom*. SNTSU B.1. Freistadt: F. Plöchl, 1979.
Collins, Adela Yarbro. *The Combat Myth in the Book of Revelation*. HDR 9. Missoula, MT: Scholars, 1976.
Coloe, M. L. "Theological Reflexions on Creation in the Gospel of John." *Pacifica* 24 (2011): 1-12.
Conzelmann, Hans. *1 Corinthians: A Commentary on the First Epistle to the Corinthians*. Trans. James W. Leitch. Hermeneia. Philadelphia: Fortress, 1975.
Crossan, John Dominic. *God and Empire: Jesus against Rome, Then and Now*. San Francisco: HarperSanFrancisco, 2007.
Crowe, Brandon C. *The Last Adam: A Theology of the Obedient Life of Jesus in the Gospels*. Grand Rapids: Baker Academic, 2017.
D'Ambrosio, Joseph G. "Love During Divorce: Development of the Sorokin Pyscho-Social Love Inventory (SPSLI)." PhD Dissertation. University of Louisville, 2012.
Davids, Peter H. *The First Epistle of Peter*. NICNT. Grand Rapids: Eerdmans, 1990.
Davies, William D. and Dale C. Allison. *A Critical and Exegetical Commentary on the Gospel according to Saint Matthew*. 3 vols. ICC. Edinburgh: T&T Clark, 1988.
Dawkins, Richard. *The Selfish Gene*. 4th ed. Oxford Landmark Science. New York: Oxford University, 2016.
Decock, Paul B. "The Symbol of Blood in the Apocalypse of John." *Neotestamentica* 38.2 (2004): 157-82.
_____. "Violence in the Apocalypse of John." *Acta Theologica*, suppl. 11 (2008): 1-19.
Denaux, Adelbert. "Theology and Christology in 1 Cor 8, 4-6: A Contextual-Redactional Reading." In *The Corinthian Correspondence*. Ed. Reimund Bieringer. Leuven: Leuven University, 1996.
Delobel, Joël. "Coherence and Relevance of 1 Cor 8-10." In *The Corinthian*

Correspondence. Ed. Reimund Bieringer. Leuven: Leuven University, 1996.

Donahue, John R. *The Gospel of Mark*. SP 2. Collegeville, MN: Liturgical, 2002.

Dubis, Mark. *1 Peter: A Handbook on the Greek Text*. BHGNT. Waco, TX: Baylor University, 2010.

Dunn, James D. G. *1 Corinthians*. Sheffield: Sheffield Academic, 1995.

_____. *The Theology of Paul the Apostle*. Grand Rapids: Eerdmans, 1998.

Elliott, John H. *1 Peter: A New Translation with Introduction and Commentary*. AB 37B. New York: Doubleday, 2000.

Engberg-Pedersen, Troels. "The Gospel and Social Practice According to 1 Corinthians." *New Testament Studies* 33 (1987): 557-84.

Ermakov, Arseny. "The Holy One of God in Markan Narrative." *Horizons in Biblical Theology* 36 (2014): 177-201.

Evans, Craig. *Mark 8:27–16:24*. WBC 34B. Waco: Word, 2001.

Fee, Gordon D. *The First Epistle to the Corinthians*. NICNT. Grand Rapids: Eerdmans, 1987.

_____. *Revelation*. NCC. Eugene, OR: Cascade, 2011.

_____. "Toward a Theology of 1 Corinthians." In *Pauline Theology: 1 and 2 Corinthians*. Ed. David M. Hay. Minneapolis: Fortress, 1993.

Feldmeier, Reinhard. *The First Letter of Peter: A Commentary on the Greek Text*. Waco, TX: Baylor University, 2008.

Fiorenza, Elisabeth Schüssler. *Revelation: Vision of a Just World*. Proclamation Commentaries. Minneapolis: Fortress, 1991.

Flemming, Dean. "'On Earth as It Is in Heaven': Holiness and the People of God in Revelation." In *Holiness and Ecclesiology in the New Testament*), 343-62. Ed. Kent E. Brower and Andy Johnson. Grand Rapids: Eerdmans, 2007.

Flemming, Dean. "Revelation and the *Missio Dei*: Toward a Missional Reading of the Apocalypse." *Journal of Theological Interpretation* 6 (2012): 161-68.

Flescher, Andrew Michael and Daniel L. Worthen. *The Altruistic Species: Scientific, Philosophical, and Religious Perspectives of Human Benevolence*. Philadelphia: Templeton Foundation, 2007.

Fletcher-Louis, C. H. T. "The Destruction of the Temple and the Relativization of the Old Covenant: Mark 13:31 and Matthew 5:18." In *Eschatology in Bible and Theology*. Ed. Kent E. Brower and Mark W. Elliott. Downers Grove, IL: IVP, 1997.

Ford, J. Massyngberde. *Revelation: Introduction, Translation, and Commentary*. AB 38. Garden City, NY: Doubleday, 1975.
Fowl, Stephen E. *Ephesians: A Commentary*. Louisville: Westminster John Knox, 2012.
France, R. T. *The Gospel of Mark*. NIGTC. Carlisle: Paternoster, 2002.
―――. *The Gospel of Matthew*. NICNT. Grand Rapids: Eerdmans, 2007.
Fretheim, Terence E. *Creation Untamed: The Bible, God, and Natural Disasters. Theological Explorations for the Church Catholic*. Grand Rapids: Baker Academic, 2010.
Friesen, Steven J. *Twice Neokoros: Ephesus, Asia, and the Cult of the Flavian Imperial Family*. RGRW 116. Leiden: Brill, 1993.
Fuller, Reginald H. *The Foundations of New Testament Christology*. London: Lutterworth, 1965.
Furnish, Victor P. "Belonging to Christ: A Paradigm for Ethics in First Corinthians." *Interpretation* (1990): 145-57.
―――. *The Love Command in the New Testament*. Nashville: Abingdon, 1972.
―――. *Theology and Ethics in Paul*. Nashville: Abingdon, 1968.
Gamel, Brian K. *Mark 15:39 as a Markan Theology of Revelation: The Centurion's Confession as Apocalyptic Unveiling*. LNTS 574. London: Bloomsbury T&T Clark, 2017.
Garland, David E. *Reading Matthew: A Literary and Theological Commentary on the First Gospel*. New York: Crossroad, 1993.
Garnsey, Peter. "Mass Diet and Nutrition in the City of Rome." In *Hourir la plebe*, 67-101. Ed. A. Giovanni. Basel: Herder, 1991.
Glancy, Jennifer A. *Slavery in Early Christianity*. Minneapolis: Fortress, 2006.
Gnilka, Joachim. *Das Matthäusevangelium*. 2 vols. HThKAT. Freiburg: Herder, 1986-88.
Gooch, Peter D. *Dangerous Food: 1 Corinthians 8-10 in Its Context*. SCJ 5. Waterloo, ON: W. Laurier University, 1993.
Gorman, Michael J. "'Although/Because He Was in the Form of God': The Theological Significance of Paul's Master Story," *Journal of Theological Interpretation* 1 (2007): 147-69.
―――. *Cruciformity: Paul's Narrative Spirituality of the Cross*. Grand Rapids: Eerdmans, 2001.
―――. *Reading Revelation Responsibly: Uncivil Worship and Witness: Following the Lamb into the New Creation*. Eugene, OR: Cascade, 2010.

Grotius, H. *Annotata ad Actus Apostolicos Epistolas et Apocalypsim, sive Criticorum Sacrorum.* vol. 12. London: J. Flasher, 1660.

Grundmann, Walter. *Das Evangelium nach Matthäus.* THKNT 1. Berlin: Evangelische Verlagsanstalt, 1968.

Gundry, Robert H. *Matthew.* Grand Rapids: Eerdmans, 1982.

Hagner, Donald A. *Matthew.* 2 vols. WBC. Dallas, TX: Word, 1993.

_____. "The *Sitz im Leben* of the Gospel of Matthew." In *Treasures New and Old: Recent Contributions to Matthean Studies,* 27-68. Ed. David R. Bauer and Mark Allan Powell. JBL Symposium Series. Atlanta: Scholars, 1996.

Hallett, Garth L. *Christian Neighbor-Love: An Assessment of Six Rival Versions.* Washington, DC: Georgetown University, 1989.

Harrington, Daniel J. *The Gospel of Matthew.* Sacra Pagina. Collegeville, MN: Liturgical, 1991.

Harrington, Hannah K. *Holiness: Rabbinic Judaism and the Graeco-Roman World.* New York: Routledge, 2001.

Hart, J. H. A. "The First Epistle General of Peter." In *The Expositor's Greek Testament.* Grand Rapids: Eerdmans, 1990.

Hatina, Thomas R. *In Search of a Context: The Function of Scripture in Mark's Narrative.* JSNTSup 232. Sheffield: Sheffield Academic, 2002.

Hays, Richard B. *Echoes of Scripture in the Gospels.* Waco, TX: Baylor University, 2016.

_____. *Reading Backwards.* Waco, TX: Baylor University, 2014.

Head, Peter M. "A Text-Critical Study of Mark 1:1: The Beginning of the Gospel of Jesus Christ." *NTS* 37 (1991): 621–29.

Hemer, Colin J. *The Letters to the Seven Churches of Asia in Their Local Setting.* Biblical Resource Series. Sheffield: JSOT, 1986.

Hill, David. *The Gospel of Matthew.* NCB. Grand Rapids: Eerdmans, 1972.

Hochholzer, Martin. *Feindes- und Bruderliebe im Widerstriet? Eine vergleichende Studie zur synoptischen und johanneischen Ausprägung des Liebesgebots.* Frankfurt am Main: Peter Lang, 2007.

Hoffman, Elisha A. "Are You Washed in the Blood?" (1878). In *Worship in Song.* Kansas City, MO: Lillenas, 1972.

Holzmeister, Urbanus. *Commentarius in Epistulas SS. Petri et Iudae Apostolorum.* Cursus Scripturae Sacrae 3. Paris: P. Lethielleux, 1937.

Hooker, Morna D. *A Commentary on the Gospel according to St Mark.* London: A. & C. Black, 1991.

Horsley, Richard A. "1 Corinthians: A Case Study of Paul's Assembly as an Alternative Society." In *Paul and Empire: Religion and Power in Roman Imperial Society*. Ed. Richard A. Horsley. Harrisburg, PA: Trinity Press International, 1997.

―――――. "Consciousness and Freedom Among the Corinthians: 1 Corinthians 8-10." *CBQ* 40 (1978): 574-89.

Hoskyns, E. C. *The Fourth Gospel*. London: Faber & Faber, 1940.

Hort, F. J. A. *The First Epistle of St Peter I.1 – II.17: The Greek Text with Introductory Lecture, Commentary, and Additional Notes*. London: Macmillan, 1898.

Hurd, John C. *The Origin of I Corinthians*. New York: Seabury, 1965.

Jackson, Howard M. "The Death of Jesus in Mark and the Miracle from the Cross." *New Testament Studies* 33 (1987): 16-37.

Jeremias, Joachim. *The Parables of Jesus*. Trans. S. H. Hooke. Rev. ed. New York: Charles Scribner's Sons, 1963.

Jewett, Robert. *Paul's Anthropological Terms*. AGJU 10. Leiden: Brill, 1971.

Johns, Loren L. *The Lamb of God Christology in the Apocalypse of John*. WUNT. 167. Tübingen: Mohr Siebeck, 2003.

Johnson, Andy. *Holiness and the* Missio Dei. Eugene, OR: Cascade, 2016.

―――――. "Missional from First to Last: Paul's Letters and the *Missio Dei*." In Missio Dei: *A Wesleyan Understanding*, 67-74. Ed. Keith Schwanz and Joseph Coleson. Kansas City, MO: Beacon Hill, 2011

―――――. "The 'New Creation,' the Crucified and Risen Christ, and the Temple: A Pauline Audience for Mark," *Journal of Theological Interpretation* 1 (2007): 171-91.

Johnston, Barry V. *Pitirim A. Sorokin: An Intellectual Biography*. Lawrence: University of Kansas, 1996.

Kelhoffer, James A. "A Tale of Two Markan Characterizations: The Exemplary Woman Who Anointed Jesus's Body for Burial (14:3-9) and the Silent Trio Who Fled the Empty Tomb (16:1-8)." In *Women and Gender in Ancient Religions: Interdisciplinary Approaches*, 85-98. Ed. Stephen P. Ahearne-Kroll et al. WUNT 263. Tübingen: Mohr Siebeck, 2010.

Kelly, J. N. D. *A Commentary on the Epistles of Peter and Jude*. BNTC. London: Black, 1969; Repr., Grand Rapids: Baker, 1981.

Kerr, Alan. *The Temple of Jesus' Body: The Temple Theme in the Gospel of John*. LNTS 220. Sheffield: Sheffield Academic, 2002.

Kinukawa, Hisako. *Women and Jesus in Mark? A Japanese Feminist Perspective*. Maryknoll, NY: Orbis, 1994.

Knopf, Rudolph. *Die Briefe Petri und Judä*. KEK 12. 7th ed. Göttingen: Vandenhoeck & Ruprecht, 1912.

Koester, Craig R. *Revelation*. AYB 38A. New Haven: Yale University, 2014.

_____. *Revelation and the End of All Things*. Grand Rapids: Eerdmans, 2001.

Kraybill, J. Nelson. *Apocalypse and Allegiance: Worship, Politics, and Devotion in the Book of Revelation*. Grand Rapids: Brazos, 2010.

Kühl, Ernst. *Die Briefe Petri und Judae*. KEK 12. 6th ed. Göttingen: Vandenhoeck & Ruprecht, 1897.

LaVerdiere, Eugene A. "A Grammatical Ambiguity in 1 Pet 1:23." *Catholica Biblical Quarterly* 36 (1974): 89-94.

Lee, Dorothy. *Transfiguration*. New Century Theology. London: Continuum, 2004.

Levenson, Jon. *Sinai and Zion: An Entry into the Jewish Bible*. Minneapolis: Winston, 1985.

Levison, John R. *Filled with the Spirit*. Grand Rapids: Eerdmans, 2009.

Lewis, Sinclair. *Elmer Gantry*. New York: Harcourt, Brace and Co, 1927; Repr., New York: Dell Publishing, 1954.

Lindemann, Andreas. "Die paulinische Ekklesiologie angesichts der Lebenswirklichkeit der christlichen Gemeinde in Korinth." In *The Corinthian Correspondence*, 63–86. Ed. Reimund Bieringer. Leuven: Leuven University, 1996.

Litwa, M. D. "Behold Adam: A Reading of John 19:5." *Horizons in Biblical Theology* 32 (2010): 130–35.

Lupieri, Edmondo. *L'Apocalisse di Giovanni*. Milano: Arnoldo Mondadori [Scrittori Greci e Latini], 1999.

Luz, Ulrich. *Matthew 1-7: A Continental Commentary*. Trans. Wilhelm C. Linss (Minneapolis: Fortress, 1989.

_____. *Matthew 1 – 7*. Hermeneia. Minneapolis: Fortress, 2007.

Lyons, George. "Church and Holiness in Ephesians." In *Holiness and Ecclesiology in the New Testament*, 238-56. Ed. Kent Brower and Andy Johnson. Grand Rapids: Eerdmans, 2007.

Lyons-Pardue, Kara J. "A Syrophoenician Becomes a Canaanite: Jesus Exegetes the Canaanite Woman in Matthew." *Journal of Theological Interpretation* 13. 2 (Nov. 2019): 235–50.

Mangina, Joseph P. *Revelation*. BTCB. Grand Rapids: Brazos, 2010.

Marcus, Joel. *Mark 1 – 8: A New Translation with Introduction and Commentary*. AB 27. New York: Doubleday, 2000.

Marcus, Joel. *Mark 8 – 16: A New Translation with Introduction and Commentary*. AB 27A. New Haven: Yale University, 2009.

Marshall, I. Howard. *1 Peter*. IVPNTC. Downers Grove, IL: IVP, 2003.

_____. "Son of God or Servant of Yahweh? – A Reconsideration of Mark 1:11." In *Jesus the Saviour: Studies in New Testament Theology*, 326-36. Leicester: IVP, 1990.

Martin, Dale B. *The Corinthian Body*. New Haven: Yale University, 1995.

Martin, Ralph P. *Mark: Evangelist and Theologian*. Exeter: Paternoster, 1972.

Martin, Troy W. *Apostolic Confirmation and Legitimation in an Early Christian Faith Document: A Commentary on the First Epistle of the Apostle Peter*. NIGTC. Grand Rapids: Eerdmans, forthcoming.

_____. "Christians as Babies: Metaphorical Reality in First Peter." In *Reading 1–2 Peter and Jude: A Resource for Students*, 99-112. Ed. Eric F. Mason and Troy W. Martin, 99-112. SBL Resources for Biblical Study 77. Atlanta and Leiden: SBL and Brill, 2014.

_____. "Dating First Peter to a Hairdo (1 Pet 3:3)." *Early Christianity* 9 (2018): 298–318.

_____. "Emotional Physiology and Consolatory Etiquette: Reading the Present Indicative with Future Meaning in the Eschatological Statement in 1 Pet 1:6." *Journal of Biblical Literature* 135 (2016): 649–60.

_____. "Faith: Its Qualities, Attributes, and Legitimization in 1 Peter." *Biblical Research* 61 (2016): 46–61.

_____. *Metaphor and Composition in First Peter*. SBLDS 131. Atlanta: Scholars, 1992.

_____. "Peter and the Expansion of Early Christianity in the Letters of Acts (15:23–29) and First Peter." In *Delightful Acts: New Essays on Canonical and Non-canonical Acts*, 87-99. Ed. Harold W. Attridge, Dennis R. MacDonald, and Clare K. Rothschild. WUNT 391. Tübingen: Mohr Siebeck, 2017.

_____. "Roaring Lions among Diaspora Metaphors: First Peter 5:8 in its Metaphorical Context." In *Bedrängnis und Identität: Studien zu Situation, Kommunikation und Theologie des 1. Petrusbriefes*, 167-79. Ed. David du Toit, BZNW 200. Berlin: Walter de Gruyter, 2013.

_____. "Tasting the Eucharistic Lord as Useable (1 Pet 2:3)." *CBQ* 78 (2016): 515–25.

Marxsen, Willi. *Mark the Evangelist: Studies on the Redaction History of the Gospel*. Trans. James Boyce et al. Nashville: Abingdon, 1969.

Meeks, Wayne A. "'And Rose up to Play': Midrash and Paraenesis in 1

Corinthians 10:1-22." *Journal for the Study of the New Testament* 16 (1982): 64-78.
Meyer, Ben F. *The Aims of Jesus*. London: SCM, 1979.
Michaels, J. Ramsey. *1 Peter*, WBC 49. Waco, TX: Word, 1988.
Middleton, J. Richard. *New Heaven and a New Earth: Reclaiming Biblical Eschatology*. Grand Rapids: Baker Academic, 2014.
Miller, Susan. *Women in Mark's Gospel*. JSNTSup 259. New York: T&T Clark, 2004.
Mitchell, Joan L. *Beyond Fear and Silence: A Feminist-Literary Approach to the Gospel of Mark*. New York: Continuum, 2001.
Moore, Anthony. *Signs of Salvation: The Theme of Creation in John's Gospel*. Cambridge: James Clark, 2013.
Moss, Candida. "The Man with the Flow of Power: Porous Bodies in Mark 5:25-34." *JBL* 129 (2010): 509-17.
Mounce, Robert H. *The Book of Revelation*. Rev. ed. NICNT. Grand Rapids: Eerdmans, 1998.
_____. *Matthew*. Good News Commentary. San Francisco: Harper and Row, 1985.
Murphy-O'Connor, Jerome. *Paul: A Critical Life*. New York: Clarendon, 1996.
Nagel, Thomas. *The Possibility of Altruism*. Oxford: Clarendon, 1970.
Nauck, Wolfgang. "Salt as a Metaphor in Instructions for Discipleship." *Studia Theologica* 6 (1952): 165-78.
Nietzsche, Frederick. *The Genealogy of Morals*. Trans. Horace B. Samuel. New York: Boni and Liveright, 1913; Repr., Whithorn, IRE: Anados, 2017.
Noël, Alexandre. *Commentarius litteralis et moralis in omnes Epistolas Sancti Pauli Apostoli et in VII Epistolas Catholicas*. Paris: T. Bettinelli, 1768.
Nolland, John. *The Gospel of Matthew: A Commentary on the Greek Text*. NIGTC. Grand Rapids: Eerdmans, 2005.
Oakes, Peter. "Revelation 17.1-19.10: A Prophetic Vision of the Destruction of Rome." In *The Future of Rome: Roman, Greek, Jewish and Christian Perspectives*. Ed. Jonathan Price and Katell Berthelot. Cambridge: Cambridge University, forthcoming.
Oord, Thomas Jay. *Defining Love: A Philosophical, Scientific, and Theological Engagement*. Grand Rapids: Baker Academic, 2010.
_____. *Science of Love*. Philadelphia: Templeton Foundation, 2004.
Osborne, Grant R. *Matthew*. ZECNT. Grand Rapids: Zondervan, 2010.

Overman, J. Andrew. *Matthew's Gospel and Formative Judaism: The Social World of the Matthean Community*. Minneapolis: Fortress, 1990.

Patte, Daniel. *The Gospel According to Matthew: A Structural Commentary on Matthew's Faith*. Philadelphia: Fortress, 1987.

Perrin, Nicholas. *Jesus the Temple*. Grand Rapids: Baker Academic, 2010.

Phillips, Thomas E. *Paul, His Letters, and Acts*. Library of Pauline Studies. Peabody, MA: Hendrickson, 2009; Grand Rapids: Baker Academic, 2010.

————. "Subtlety as a Literary Technique in Luke's Characterization of Jews and Judaism." In *Literary Studies in Luke-Acts*, 313-26. Ed. Richard P. Thompson and Thomas E. Phillips. Macon, GA: Mercer University, 1998.

Pickett, R. *The Cross in Corinth. The Social Significance of the Death of Jesus*. JSNTSup 143. Sheffield: Sheffield Academic, 1997.

Pierce, C. A. *Conscience in the New Testament*. London: SCM, 1955.

Plummer, Alfred. *An Exegetical Commentary on the Gospel According to St. Matthew*. Grand Rapids: Baker, 1982.

Post, Stephen G. *Unlimited Love: Altruism, Compassion, and Service*. Philadelphia: Templeton Foundation, 2003.

Reddish, Mitchell G. *Revelation*. SHBC. Macon, GA: Smyth and Helwys, 2001.

Ridley, Matt. *The Origins of Virtue: Human Instincts and the Evolution of Cooperation*. New York: Viking, 1996.

Ringe, Sharon H. "A Gentile Woman's Story, Revisited: Rereading Mark 7.24-31." In *A Feminist Companion to Mark*, ed. Amy-Jill Levine. Cleveland, OH: Pilgrim, 2001.

Robertson, A. T. *A Grammar of the Greek New Testament in the Light of Historical Research*. Nashville: Broadman, 1934.

Rudman, D. "The Crucifixion as *Chaoskampf*: A New Reading of the Passion Narrative in the Synoptic Gospels." *Biblica* 84 (2003): 102-07.

Saldarini, Anthony J. "The Gospel of Matthew and Jewish-Christian Conflict." In *Social History of the Matthean Community*, 38-61. Ed. David L. Balch. Minneapolis: Fortress, 1991.

Schnabel, Eckhard J. "John and the Future of the Nations." *Bulletin of Biblical Research* 12 (2002): 247-57.

Schutter, William L. *Hermeneutic and Composition in 1 Peter*. WUNT 2.30. Tübingen: Mohr Siebeck, 1989.

Schweizer, Eduard. *The Good News according to Matthew*. Trans. David E.

Green. Atlanta: John Knox, 1975.

Selwyn, Edward Gordon. *The First Epistle of St. Peter: The Greek Text with Introduction, Notes, and Essays*. London: Macmillan, 1946; Repr., Grand Rapids: Baker, 1981.

Siliezar, Carlos Raúl Sosa. *Creation Imagery in the Gospel of John*. LNTS 546. London/New York: Bloomsbury/T&T Clark, 2015.

Smalley, Stephen S. *The Revelation to John*. Downers Grove, IL: IVP Academic, 2005.

Smit, Joop F. M. "1 Cor 8, 1–6: A Rhetorical *Partitio*." In *The Corinthian Correspondence*. Ed. Reimund Bieringer. Leuven: Leuven University, 1996.

———. "The Rhetorical Disposition of First Corinthians 8:7-9:27." *CBQ* 59 (1997): 479–83.

Smyth, Herbert Weir. *Greek Grammar*. Cambridge: Harvard University, 1984.

Snow, Robert S. *Daniel's Son of Man in Mark*. Eugene, OR: Pickwick, 2016.

Sober, Elliot and David Sloan Wilson. *Unto Others: The Evolution and Psychology of Unselfish Behavior*. Cambridge: Harvard University, 1998.

Sorokin, Pitirim. *A Long Journey*. New Haven: College & University Press, 1963.

———. *The Ways and Power of Love: Types, Factors, and Techniques of Moral Transformation*. Boston: Beacon, 1954; Repr., Philadelphia: John Templeton Foundation, 2002.

Spencer, F. Scott. *Dancing Girls, Loose Ladies, and Women of the Cloth: The Women in Jesus' Life*. New York: Continuum, 2004.

Stanley, David M. "'Become Imitators of Me:' The Pauline Conception of Apostolic Tradition." *Biblica* 40 (1959): 859-77.

Suggit, John. "Jesus the Gardener: The Atonement in the Fourth Gospel as Re-creation." *Neotestamentica* 33 (1999): 161-68.

Sutherland, A. *The Origin and Growth of the Moral Instinct*. New York: Longmans, Green, & Co., 1998.

Swete, Henry B. *The Apocalypse of St. John: The Greek Text with Introduction, Notes, and Indices*. New York: Macmillan, 1909.

Tavo, Felise. *Woman, Mother and Bride: An Exegetical Investigation into the 'Ecclesial' Notions of the Apocalypse*." BTS 3. Leuven: Peters, 2007.

Theissen, Gerd. *The Social Setting of Pauline Christianity: Essays on Corinth*. Trans. and ed. by John H. Schütz. Philadelphia: Fortress, 1982.

Thomas, John Christopher and Frank D. Macchia. *Revelation*. THNTC. Grand Rapids: Eerdmans, 2016.
Thompson, James W. *The Church according to Paul: Rediscovering the Community Conformed to Christ*. Grand Rapids: Baker Academic, 2014.
Thompson, Leonard L. *The Book of Revelation: Apocalypse and Empire*. New York: Oxford University, 1990.
Tomson, Peter. *Paul and the Jewish Law: Halakha in the Letters of the Apostle to the Gentiles*. Van Gorcum: Assen/Maastricht; Minneapolis: Fortress, 1990.
Toolan, David. *At Home in the Cosmos*. Maryknoll, NY: Orbis, 2001.
Trempelas, P. N. Υπομνημα εις την προς Εβραιοθς και τας Επτα Καθολικας. Athens: Αδελφοτης Θεολογων Η Ζωη, 1941.
Trible, Phyllis. *Texts of Terror: Literary-Feminist Readings of Biblical Narratives*. Philadelphia: Fortress, 1984.
Turner, David L. *Matthew*. BECNT. Grand Rapids: Baker Academic, 2008.
Ulansey, David. "The Heavenly Veil Torn: Mark's Cosmic *Inclusio*." *Journal of Biblical Literature* 110 (1991): 123–25.
Wall, Robert W. *Revelation*. NIBCNT 18. Peabody, MA: Hendrickson, 1991.
Weinrich, William C. *Revelation*. ACCSNT. Downers Grove, IL: IVP Academic, 2005.
Weiss, Johannes. *Der erste Korintherbrief völlig neu bearbeitet*, KEK. Göttingen: Vandenhoeck & Ruprecht, 1910.
White, L. Michael. "Crisis Management and Boundary Maintenance: The Social Location of the Matthean Community." In *Social History of the Matthean Community*, 211–47. Ed. David L. Balch. Minneapolis: Fortress, 1991.
Willis, Wendell. *Idol Meat in Corinth: The Pauline Argument in 1 Corinthians 8 and 10*. SBLDS 68. Chico, CA: Scholars, 1985.
Witherington III, Ben. *Revelation*. NCBC. Cambridge: Cambridge University, 2003.
Wright, Christopher J. H. *The Mission of God: Unlocking the Bible's Grand Narrative*. Downers Grove, IL: IVP Academic, 2006.
Wright, N. T. *Paul and the Faithfulness of God*. Christian Origins and the Question of God 4. Minneapolis: Fortress, 2013.
_____. "Yet the Sun Will Rise Again: Reflections on the Exile and Restoration in Second Temple Judaism, Jesus, Paul, and the Church Today." In *Exile: A Conversation with N. T. Wright*. Ed. James M. Scott. Downers Grove, IL: IVP Academic, 2017.

Yarbro Collins, Adela. *Mark,* Hermeneia. Minneapolis: Fortress, 2007.
Zaidman, L. Bruit and P. Schmitt Pantel, *La religion grecque dans la cité grecque à l'époque Classique.* Paris: A. Colin, 1991.

Authors

Achtemeier, P. J.	138, 139, 140, 147, 149, 150
Ahearne-Kroll, S. P.	46
Allison, D. C.	5, 6, 7, 10, 11
Aretius, B.	140
Attridge, H. W.	136
Aune, D. E.	165, 182
Balch, D. L.	23
Bandy, A. S.	162
Barrett, C. K.	118, 125
Batson, C. D.	97, 99
Bauckham, R.	25, 35, 162, 179, 182, 184, 185, 186, 190, 191
Bauer, D. R.	23
Beale, G. K.	74, 76, 79, 165, 175, 178, 182
Beare, F. W.	141, 149
Berman, S. A.	68
Berthelot, K.	35
Bertram, G.	7, 15, 20
Betsworth, S.	46, 50, 52, 53, 55, 57, 58
Betz, H. D.	4, 9, 12–13, 15, 18, 19, 20
Bieringer, R.	121, 122, 124, 131
Bigg, C.	140, 147, 150
Black, M.	7, 8, 14
Blass, F.	11, 13, 16, 20, 79
Bonhoeffer, D.	37
Bookides, N.	120
Boring, M. E.	4, 5, 7, 9, 12, 165
Boyce, J.	28
Brodie, T. L.	122
Brower, K. E.	25, 26, 29, 32, 35, 37, 38, 40, 41, 42, 76, 78, 92
Brown, J.	81, 84
Brown, R. E.	82–83, 84
Bruce, F. F.	92
Bruner, F. D.	4, 5, 8, 9, 20
Caird, G. B.	162
Camerlynck, A.	139

Campbell, L. A.	76
Chilton, B.	26
Coloe, M. L.	83
Coleson, J.	88
Collins, A. Y.	31, 34, 39, 162
Conzelmann, H.	125, 126, 127, 128
Crossan, J. D.	173
Crowe, B. C.	74, 81
D'Ambrosio	99
Davids, P. H.	140, 147
Davies, W. D.	5, 6, 7, 10, 11
Dawkins, R.	96–97
Debrunner, A.	11, 13, 16, 20, 79
Decock, P.	157–58, 159–60, 161–62, 164–65, 166, 170
Delobel, J.	124
Denaux, A.	124, 127
Donahue, J. R.	35
du Toit, D.	136
Dubis, M.	149
Dunn, J. D. G.	87, 88, 125
Elliott, J. H.	149
Elliott, M. W.	76, 78
Engberg-Pedersen, T.	128–29
Ermakov, A.	32
Evans, C.	40
Fee, G. D.	126, 129, 175
Feldmeier, R.	140
Fischer, J. E.	120
Flemming, D.	35, 188, 192
Flescher, A. M.	98
Fletcher-Louis, C. H. T.	76
Foerster, W.	131
Ford, J. M.	162
Fowl, S.	92, 93
France, R. T.	22, 26
Fretheim, T. E.	75
Friesen, S. J.	162
Fuller, R. H.	37, 43
Funk, R. W.	11, 13, 16, 20
Funk, R. W.	79

Furnish, V. P.	112, 125, 129, 132
Gamel, B. K.	40–41, 42
Garland, D. E.	5, 10, 22
Garnsey, P.	120
Giovanni, A.	120
Glancy, J. A.	67
Gnilka, J.	20, 22
Gooch, P. D.	119, 120, 121
Gorman, M. J.	87, 189
Greig, J. C. G.	54
Grotius, H.	139
Grundmann, W.	6, 19
Gundry, R. H.	7
Hagner, D. A.	4, 5, 8, 18, 20, 23
Hallett, G. L.	114
Hallett, G. L.	99, 101–3, 104, 108
Harrington, D. J.	8, 35, 78
Hart, J. H. A.	139
Hatina, T. R.	28
Hauck, F.	5, 6, 8
Hay, D. M.	129
Hays, R. B.	26, 31
Head, P. M.	26
Hemer, C. J.	162
Hill, D.	6, 9
Hochholzer, M.	109
Hoffman, E. A.	155
Holzmeister, U.	139
Hooke, S. H.	7
Hooker, M. D.	28, 79
Horsley, R. A.	128, 130, 131
Hort, F. J. A.	138, 139, 147, 148, 149, 150
Hoskyns, E. C.	83
Hurd, J. C.	124
Hurst, D.	139
Jackson, H. M.	79
Jeremias, J.	7, 8, 14
Jewett, R.	125
Johns, L. L.	165
Johnson, A.	30–31, 35, 75, 76, 79, 81, 88, 90, 91, 92, 177, 190

Johnston, B. V.	99
Kelhoffer, J. A.	46
Kelly, J. N. D.	141
Kerr, A.	80
Kim, M.	74, 76
Kinukawa, H.	46
Knopf, R.	140, 147
Koester, C. R.	179, 180, 182, 183, 185, 186, 192
Kraybill, J. N.	179
Kühl, E.	140
LaVerdiere, E. A.	139, 140
Lee, D.	38, 39–40
Leitch, J. W.	125
Levenson, J.	76, 81
Levine, A.-J.	57
Levison, J. R.	90
Lewis, S.	96
Lindemann, A.	131–32
Linss, W. C.	7
Litwa, M. D.	84
Lupieri, E.	165
Luz, U.	7, 11, 15, 20
Lyons-Pardue, K. J.	57, 64
Lyons, G.	92
Macchia, F. D.	181, 186, 189
MacDonald, D. R.	136
Malina, B. J.	105
Mangina, J. P.	174, 177
Marcus, J.	33, 42, 46, 54, 55, 60, 61, 105
Marshall, I. H.	31, 140
Martin, D. B.	77
Martin, R. P.	43
Martin, T. W.	136, 141, 145, 151
Marxsen, W.	28
Mason, E. F.	136
Maurer, C.	125
Meeks, W. A.	123
Meyer, B. F.	30
Michaels, J. R.	138, 147, 149, 150
Middleton, J. R.	74, 75, 84

Miller, S.	46
Mitchell, J. L.	46
Moore, A.	82, 83
Moss, C.	56
Mounce, R. H.	8, 9, 165
Murphy-O'Connor, J.	132-33
Nagel, T.	98, 99
Nauck, W.	6-7, 8, 14
Nietzsche, F.	173
Noël, A.	139
Nolland, J.	7, 12, 14, 20, 22
Oakes, P.	35
Oord, T. J.	98, 99
Osborne, G. R.	19
Overman, J. A.	23
Pantel, P. S.	119
Patte, D.	6, 8
Perrin, N.	74, 77, 80
Phillips, T. E.	95, 106
Pickett, R.	131
Pierce, C. A.	125
Plummer, A.	9, 10, 20, 22
Post, S. G.	99
Powell, M. A.	23
Price, J.	35
Reddish, M. G.	182-83
Ridley, M.	97, 99
Ringe, S. H.	57, 58
Roberts, J. J. M.	76
Robertson, A. T.	16
Rothschild, C. K.	136
Rudman, D.	79
Saldarini, A. J.	23
Schnabel, E. J.	175, 182
Schüssler Fiorenza, E.	162
Schutter, W. L.	149
Schütz, J. H.	121
Schwanz, K.	88

Schweizer, E.	5, 9–10, 20, 22
Scott, J. M.	29
Seeseman, H.	20
Selwyn, E. G.	140
Siliezar, C. R. S.	81, 82, 83, 85
Smalley, S. S.	183
Smit, J. F. M.	121, 124, 127
Smyth, H. W.	11, 13, 14, 16, 147, 148, 150
Snow, R. S.	27
Sober, M.	97–98, 99
Sorokin, P.	98–101, 104, 113–14
Spencer, F. S.	46, 51, 55–56, 62
Stanley, D. M.	129
Stroud, R. S.	120
Suggit, J.	82, 83
Sutherland, A.	99
Swete, H. B.	162
Tavo, F.	176
Theissen, G.	121
Thomas, J. C.	181, 186, 189
Thompson, J. W.	88, 90, 93
Thompson, L. L.	162
Thompson, R. P.	106
Tomson, P.	120–21
Toolan, D.	77
Trempelas, P. N.	140
Trible, P	45
Ulansey, D.	79
Wall, R. W.	165
Weinrich, W. C.	181, 182
Weiss, J.	123
White, L. M.	23, 162
White, L. M.	162
Willis, W.	119, 120, 121, 125
Wilmot, D.	135, 136
Wilson, D. S.	97–98, 99
Witherington, B.	185
Worthen, D. L.	98
Wrede, W.	54
Wright, C. J. H.	187

Wright, N. T.   28–29, 91, 92
Wyatt, N.   84

Zaidman, L. B.   119

Biblical and Apocryphal References

Old Testament/Hebrew Bible
Genesis

1	75, 85
1 – 3	81, 82, 85
1:1	25
1:2	84
1:2–5	84–85
1:5	85
1:26	84
1:27	83
1:28	75
1:31	75
2	75, 82, 83
2:7	75, 81, 83, 84, 85
2:8	82, 83
2:9	83
2:15	75
2:17	84
3:19	84
3:22–24	84
16:1–16	45
19:24	184
19:28	184
21:9–21	45
22:2	31
49:9	169

Exodus

13:21	123
14:22	123
15	185
16:4–35	123
17:6	123
19:5–6	177
20:4	122
24	33
24:8	156

Exodus (*continued*)
- 32 — 123
- 32:6 — 123
- 34:17 — 122

Leviticus
- 2:13 — 6
- 11:44–45 — 122
- 17:11 — 156
- 19:2 — 122
- 20:7 — 122
- 20:26 — 122
- 21:8 — 122
- 26:1 — 122

Numbers
- 16:14 — 123
- 16:49 — 123
- 18:19 — 5
- 20:7–11 — 123
- 21:5–6 — 123
- 35:33 — 156, 162, 168

Deuteronomy
- 4:24 — 123
- 4:27–28 — 122
- 4:35 — 124
- 4:39 — 124
- 6:4 — 124
- 6:4–5 — 122
- 6:4–9 — 122
- 6:12–15 — 122
- 6:16 — 122
- 7:25 — 122
- 8:3 — 148
- 11:16 — 122
- 16:22 — 122
- 29:23 — 184
- 32:4 — 185
- 32:35 — 168
- 32:41 — 168

Joshua
24:19	123

Judges
11	62
11:1–11	63
11:21–22	63
11:30–31	62
11:32–33	62, 63
11:34	63
11:35	62, 63
11:35	63
11:37	63
11:37–38	63
11:38	63
11:39	63
11:40	68
19	45

2 Samuel
24:10	17

1 Kings
8:41–43	187
14:22	123
16:31	64
17:11–12	65
17:17	65
18:4	64
18:13	64
19:2	64
19:18	177
21:23	64

2 Kings
2:1–12	64
9:10	64

2 Chronicles
13:5	5

Ezra
4:14	5

Esther
	1:10–22	65
	3:1–11	65
	7:1–10	65
	7:2	65

Psalms
	2:7	31
	22:2	40
	47:1–2	187
	66:3–4	187
	67:1–3	187
	81:9	122
	86:8–10	185, 187
	96:1–13	187
	96:2	179
	96:3	179
	96:8–9	179
	98:1–2	185
	98:1–9	187
	98:2	186
	106:38	156
	111:2	185
	118:22	78
	138:4–5	187
	139:14	185
	145:17	185

Ecclesiastes
	2:5	83

Isaiah
	2:2–4	187
	6:13	177
	11:1	169
	11:10	169
	17:5	182
	18:4–5	182
	19:11	17
	24:13	182
	40 – 66	28
	40:3	29

Isaiah (*continued*)
  40:6-8   140, 146-47, 150
  40:9-10   179
  42:1   31
  43:19   26
  44:8   124
  44:25   17
  45:5   124
  52:7   179
  60:1-9   187
  63:1-4   182
  64:1   30
  66:20-23   187

Jeremiah
  10:14   17
  10:6-7   185
  23:5   169
  33:15   169
  51:33   182, 183

Ezekiel
  36   30
  36:20-23   187
  36:35   83
  37:1-10   174
  43:24   6

Daniel
  6:26   139
  7   183

Hoses
  6:11   182

Joel
  3:13   182

Amos
  5:3   177

Micah
  4:12-13   182, 183

Nahum
  1:15   179

Habakkuk
  3:12   183

Zechariah
  3:8   169
  6:12   169
  8:22   187

Malachi
  2:17 – 3:5 28
  3:1   28, 29
  4:5   30

New Testament
Gospel of Matthew
  3:12   183
  5:3–16   22
  5:3–12   21
  5:10–16   22
  5:10–12   4, 21
  5:10   22
  5:11–12   11, 21
  5:11   21
  5:12   12, 21
  5:13–16   4
  5:13–14   13
  5:13   3–24
  5:14–16   21, 22
  5:14   11, 12, 13
  5:16   12
  5:18   12
  5:19   12
  5:42   107
  5:43–48   106
  5:43   109
  6:1   12
  6:2   12
  6:4   107
  6:5   12

Matthew (*continued*)
- 6:6 — 107
- 6:14–16 — 12
- 6:18 — 12, 107
- 6:19–20 — 12
- 6:25–32 — 107
- 6:47 — 107
- 7:9 — 12
- 7:12 — 12
- 9:30 — 54
- 9:37–38 — 183
- 10:37–39 — 107
- 13:5 — 12
- 13:8 — 12
- 13:23 — 12
- 13:30 — 183
- 13:39–42 — 182
- 15:22 — 64
- 15:28 — 58
- 16:24–28 — 107
- 19:19 — 105
- 22:37–39 — 105
- 23:1–36 — 105
- 24:14 — 181
- 25:14–30 — 67
- 25:18 — 12
- 25:25 — 12
- 26:28 — 157
- 27:50 — 79
- 27:51 — 176
- 28:2 — 176
- 28:18 — 12

Gospel of Mark
- 1:1 — 26, 27, 42
- 1:2 — 28
- 1:3 — 28–30
- 1:8 — 30
- 1:9–11 — 79
- 1:10 — 31, 41, 79
- 1:11 — 27, 30–31, 39, 42
- 1:14 — 26
- 1:14–15 — 34

Mark (*continued*)
1:15	26
1:24	31–33, 34, 35, 77, 92
1:26	27, 57
1:29–34	77–78
1:31	53
1:34	57
1:35	54
1:39	57
1:39–44	78
1:40	52
1:44	54
2:1–12	77
2:9	53
2:11–12	53
2:11	53
2:12	54
2:14	54
3:3	53
3:11	27, 33, 35, 57
3:13–15	27, 33–36
3:13	33
3:15	34
3:19–21	34
3:21	54
3:28	53
3:31–35	33–36, 40
3:31	34
3:33	34
3:34	34, 37
3:35	34, 43
4:29	182, 183
4:37–41	36
4:41	35
5 – 7	46
5	50, 52, 57
5:7	27, 35
5:9	35
5:10	52
5:11	35–36
5:12	52
5:13	57
5:17	52

Mark (*continued*)

5:18–20	52
5:18	52
5:19	36, 52
5:21–43	46, 47
5:21–24	64
5:21	36
5:22–23	52, 57
5:22	63
5:23	47–48, 56, 63, 78
5:24	52
5:25–26	51
5:25	55
5:26	55
5:27–28	51, 55
5:28	78
5:29	56
5:30–31	55
5:30	51, 56
5:32	56
5:33	55, 56
5:34	48, 55, 58, 78
5:35–38	64
5:35	48, 52
5:36	38
5:38–39	52
5:39–40	53
5:40–43	56
5:41–42	60, 61
5:41	48, 53
5:42	48, 54, 55
5:43	54
6:7–13	36, 37, 43
6:13	57
6:14	51, 52
6:14–29	46, 48–49, 62
6:17–19	59
6:17–29	51, 59
6:19	51
6:20	51
6:21–26	65
6:22–23	60
6:22	48, 51, 59–60, 63

Mark (*continued*)

6:23	60, 65
6:23	65
6:24	51, 60
6:25	60
6:26	51, 66
6:28	49, 60, 61
6:29	60
6:30	36
6:30–31	43
6:30–32	37
6:51	54
6:56	52
7	50, 56
7:1–5	52
7:19	59
7:24–30	46, 49–50
7:24	51, 54
7:25	49, 57
7:26	49–50, 57
7:27	57
7:28	58
7:29	50, 58
7:30	58
7:32	52
7:36	54
8:11	38
8:12	38, 53
8:13–21	38
8:22	52
8:27–30	43
8:28	38
8:29	27
8:29	27
8:30	54
8:31–33	37, 39
8:31	27, 54
8:34 – 10:52	37
8:34 – 9:1	107
8:34–38	27, 36–38
8:34	37
8:35	37
9:1	53

Mark (continued)

9:2-9	33
9:4	33
9:7	27, 33, 38–40, 42
9:13	53
9:9–10	54
9:14–29	34
9:25	57
9:31	54
9:38–40	34
9:41	53
9:50	4, 6, 10–11, 13
10:1	54
10:2–12	52
10:13–14	34
10:15	53
10:17–22	105
10:29	53
10:34	54
11:12–21	78
11:23	53
11:24	53
11:33	53
12:1–9	78
12:10	78
12:18–27	52
12:28	106
12:31	105
12:33	105
12:35	27
12:43	53
13:2	78
13:21	27
13:30	53
13:32	27
13:37	53
14:1–2	52
14:9	53
14:18	53
14:24	157
14:25	53
14:28	53
14:33	38

Mark (*continued*)
14:53	52
14:55–65	52
14:56–59	78
14:61	27, 42
15:24	42
15:29–32	42
15:29	78
15:32	27
15:33–39	78
15:33	40
15:34	27, 42
15:37–39	79
15:37	27, 40, 79
15:38	79
15:39	27, 40–42
15:41	34
16:6	53
16:7	53
16:8	54
16:9	54

Gospel of Luke
3:17	183
6:27–36	106
6:30	107
6:32	107
6:35	107
8:56	54
9:23–27	107
9:51–56	106
10:25	106
10:29	106
12:22–30	107
14:25–27	107
14:34–35	4, 10–11, 17
14:34	13, 14
17:29	184
17:33	107
18:18–23	105
22:20	157
23:47	40

Gospel of John
- 1:1–18   141
- 1:14   31, 80
- 1:14   31
- 1:51   81
- 2:19–21   80
- 2:19   80
- 2:21   80
- 3:34   86
- 4:35–38   183
- 6:63   84
- 6:69   32, 81, 92
- 13:34   108
- 13:35   108
- 14:26   82
- 15:12–13   108
- 15:13   108
- 17:9   108
- 17:18   85–86
- 18:1   81
- 18:26   82
- 19:30   79, 171
- 19:41   82, 83, 84
- 19:5   83
- 20:1   81, 85
- 20:15   82
- 20:17   82, 86
- 20:19   81, 85
- 20:22   81, 82, 85–86
- 20:27   86

Acts of the Apostles
- 1:9–11   82
- 9:4–5   87
- 15:20   118
- 15:29   118
- 18   119
- 18:1–17   119
- 21:25   118

Romans
- 1:18–32   191
- 1:18–21   17
- 1:22   17
- 1:32   186
- 2:15   125
- 5:12–21   91
- 5:16   186
- 8:11   90
- 9 – 11   111
- 9:1   125
- 9:21   118
- 12:10   109
- 12:19   168
- 12:4–5   73, 87
- 13:1   118
- 13:3   118
- 13:5   125
- 13:8   110
- 13:9   110
- 13:10   110
- 14:15   110

1 Corinthians
- 1 – 4   117
- 1:18 – 2:5   117
- 1:20   17
- 2:6–16   117
- 2:16   118
- 3:1–3   117
- 3:3   118
- 3:9–17   93
- 3:16–17   73, 90, 130
- 4:17   117
- 5 – 11   117
- 5:1 – 11:1   117
- 5   90
- 5:9–13   131
- 5:10–11   119, 132
- 6:9–10   123, 132
- 6:9   119
- 6:11   130
- 6:12–20   89

1 Corinthians (*continued*)

6:12	117
6:15	73, 87, 89
6:18	89, 90, 118
6:19	73, 89, 90, 130
7:1	119
7:37	118
8:1 – 11:1	126
8 – 10	117, 118
8:1 – 10:22	124
8	123, 125
8:1	119, 124, 126
8:1–6	124
8:1–3	123, 126
8:2–3	130
8:2	126
8:3	126, 127
8:4–6	122, 124, 127
8:7	125, 127
8:7–12	124
8:7–13	124
8:8	127
8:9–12	127
8:9	118, 124, 127
8:10	125, 128
8:11–12	128
8:11	124
8:12	125
8:13 – 9:27	124
8:13	119, 127, 128
9	127, 128, 131
9:27	127
10	125
10:1–13	122, 123
10:6–13	125
10:6–8	125
10:7	123
10:14–22	125
10:14	118, 123
10:15–17	123
10:16–17	130
10:17	73, 87
10:20	126

1 Corinthians (*continued*)

10:21–22	123
10:22	123
10:23	117
10:24	128
10:25	125
10:27	125
10:28	125
10:29	125
10:31	130
10:32	131
11:1	117, 129, 130
11:25	122
12 – 14	110
12 – 13	118
12:12	89
12:12–27	73, 87, 89
12:3	122
13	110
13:1–8	130
13:2	131
13:3	110
14:36	141
15:28	75
15:45	86, 91
15:50	123
16:24	109

2 Corinthians

1:12	125
2:4	109
2:8	109
2:17	141
3:17	130
4:2	125
4:4	81, 89
5:11	125
5:17	73, 91, 92
5:19	43
6:16	73, 90
8:7–8	109
8:24	109
11:7–11	111

2 Corinthians (*continued*)
- 11:9 — 111
- 11:11 — 109
- 12:15 — 109, 111

Galatians
- 3:28 — 132
- 4:15 — 111
- 5:13–14 — 110
- 5:13 — 110, 131
- 5:14 — 110
- 5:22–23 — 131
- 6:15 — 73, 91, 92

Ephesians
- 1:10 — 93
- 1:15 — 111
- 1:22–23 — 73, 87, 92
- 2:10 — 92
- 2:15 — 73, 91, 92
- 2:16 — 73, 87
- 2:19–22 — 73, 90
- 2:21–22 — 93
- 4:2 — 111
- 4:4 — 73, 87
- 4:12–16 — 73, 87
- 4:15–16 — 92, 111
- 4:22–24 — 73, 91
- 4:24 — 92, 118
- 5:2 — 111, 118
- 5:23 — 92
- 5:25 — 111
- 5:28 — 111
- 5:33 — 111
- 6:5–9 — 67

Philippians
- 1:16 — 109
- 2:6–11 — 88
- 2:25–30 — 111
- 4:1 — 109
- 4:15–17 — 111

Colossians
- 1:4 — 111
- 1:16 — 118
- 1:18 — 73, 87
- 1:25 — 141
- 2:2 — 111
- 2:10 — 118
- 2:15 — 118
- 3:9–11 — 73, 91
- 3:14 — 111
- 3:15 — 73, 87
- 3:19 — 111

1 Thessalonians
- 1:6 — 141
- 2:8 — 109
- 3:6 — 109
- 3:12 — 110
- 4:9–10 — 109
- 5:13 — 109

2 Thessalonians
- 1:13 — 112
- 3:1 — 141
- 3:9 — 118

1 Timothy
- 1:5 — 112, 125
- 1:19 — 125
- 3:9 — 125
- 4:2 — 125

2 Timothy
- 1:3 — 125
- 4:10 — 112

Titus
- 1:15 — 125
- 2:4 — 112
- 3:15 — 112

Philemon
- 5 — 109
- 7 — 109
- 10 — 67
- 12 — 67
- 16–19 — 67

Hebrews
- 6:10 — 112
- 9:18–22 — 156
- 13:12 — 170

James
- 2:1–13 — 112

1 Peter
- 1:3 — 149
- 1:11–12 — 150
- 1:18–21 — 149
- 1:22–25 — 135–51
- 1:22 — 112, 137
- 1:23 — 137–46, 147, 148, 149, 151
- 1:24–25 — 146
- 1:24 — 151
- 1:25 — 141, 147, 148, 150
- 2:4 — 149
- 2:8 — 141
- 2:17 — 112
- 2:21–24 — 149
- 3:1 — 141
- 3:8 — 112
- 3:18 — 149
- 3:19 — 149
- 3:22 — 149
- 4:1 — 149
- 4:18 — 112
- 5:14 — 112

2 Peter
- 3:9 — 168

1 John
- 2:10   108
- 2:15   109
- 3:10   109
- 3:11   108
- 3:16   109
- 3:17–18   109
- 3:23   108
- 4:7   108
- 4:11–12   108
- 4:20   109
- 4:21   108
- 5:2   108

2 John
- 1   108
- 5   108

3 John
- 1   108
- 6   108

Revelation
- 1:4–9   167
- 1:5   158, 165, 168, 169, 174
- 1:6   158, 167, 177
- 1:8   171
- 1:12–20   183
- 1:12   174
- 1:16   167, 174
- 1:20   174
- 2–3   164, 189
- 2:5   189, 192
- 2:7   167
- 2:8–11   180
- 2:11   167
- 2:12   167
- 2:14   118
- 2:16   167, 174, 189, 192
- 2:17   167
- 2:20   118
- 2:21–22   189, 192
- 2:26   167

Revelation (*continued*)

3:3	189, 192
3:5	167
3:7–13	180
3:12	167
3:14–22	180
3:14	169, 174
3:16	189
3:19	189, 192
3:21	167
4:1	38
4:6	184
5:5–14	157
5:5–6	169, 185
5:5	162, 167, 169
5:6	157, 189
5:8–9	184
5:9–14	179
5:9–10	166, 181
5:9	157, 158, 165, 181, 185
5:10	177
5:11	166
5:12	157
6	190
6:1ff	155
6:9–11	168, 191
6:9	167
6:10	158, 159
6:12	158, 160, 176
6:15	192
7:1	170
7:2–4	163
7:4	166
7:9	166, 181
7:14	155, 156, 158, 169
8–9	190
8:5	176
8:7–8	155
8:7	158, 160–61
8:8–9	185
8:8	158, 161
9:4	163
9:10	155

Revelation (*continued*)

9:19	155
9:20–21	166, 189, 190, 191, 192
9:20	176, 179
9:21	176
10:11	181
11	175, 188, 190
11:3–13	174, 176, 186
11:3	177, 189
11:4–6	174
11:4	174
11:5	174, 177
11:6	158, 174
11:7–10	174
11:7	167, 185
11:9–10	175
11:9	177, 178, 181
11:11–13	173, 174–78
11:11	174, 175, 176
11:12	174, 175
11:13	175, 176, 177, 179, 185, 192
11:15–18	178
11:15	174, 188
11:16–18	191
11:18	175, 191, 192
12	163
12:7	163
12:7–9	163
12:9	163
12:11	155, 158, 167, 185, 187, 189
12:13–17	166
12:17	163
13:1–3	163
13:11–15	164
13:12	179, 191
13:15	179
13:16–18	164
13:4	163, 179, 191
13:7–8	178, 191
13:7	163, 167, 181, 185
13:8	157
14 – 15	188
14	181, 192

Revelation (*continued*)
	14:1–20	178
	14:1–7	186
	14:1–5	178, 179
	14:2–3	184
	14:3	166
	14:4	183, 185, 192
	14:6–20	173, 178–84
	14:6–13	183
	14:6–11	178
	14:6–7	176, 179, 180, 181, 190
	14:6	178, 179, 181, 186
	14:7	175, 176, 178, 179, 180, 182, 185, 186, 190
	14:8–11	178, 181
	14:8	181, 183, 184, 191
	14:9–11	181, 184
	14:9	179, 181
	14:10	181, 184, 185, 191
	14:11	179, 181
	14:12–13	180
	14:12	183, 192
	14:14–20	178, 181, 183, 192
	14:14–16	182, 183, 192
	14:14	182
	14:17–20	182, 183, 189
	14:17	182
	14:18–20	166
	14:19–20	161, 184
	14:20	156, 158, 161, 170
	15 – 16	190
	15:1 – 16:21	178
	15	190
	15:1–4	173
	15:1	184
	15:2–4	184–88
	15:2	167, 185, 187, 189
	15:3–4	179, 186, 187, 191, 192
	15:3	185, 186, 187
	15:4	175, 176, 179, 185, 186, 187
	15:5 – 16:21	184
	16 – 18	181
	16 – 17	155
	16:2	179

Revelation (*continued*)

16:3–4	155
16:3	158, 161
16:4	158
16:5–7	191
16:5–6	160
16:6	158, 159
16:9	166, 176, 179, 180, 189, 190, 191, 192
16:11	166, 176, 180, 189, 190, 191, 192
16:18	176
16:19	192
16:21	190
17	184
17:2	192
17:6	158, 159
17:16	168
17:18	192
18:3	192
18:9	192
18:10	175
18:15	175
18:24	158, 159
19	165
19:2	158, 159, 191
19:5	175, 179
19:7	179
19:11–14	167
19:11	162, 167, 174
19:13	161, 164, 165, 167, 169, 174
19:14	169
19:15	161, 167, 174, 192
19:19	192
19:20	179, 185
19:21	167, 168, 174
20:2	163
20:3	191
20:4	167, 179
20:7–15	189, 192
20:7	191
20:8	170
20:10	185, 191
21 – 22	189
21	170

Revelation (*continued*)

21:3	189
21:5	171, 189
21:8	187, 191
21:11	75
21:13	187
21:22	75
21:23–24	192
21:24	166, 187, 192
21:25	187
21:26	166, 176
21:27	187, 191
22:2	187, 189
22:3–5	75
22:11	191
22:15	187, 191
22:16	169

Jewish Apocryphal/Pseudepigraphical Writings

4 Ezra

4:28–32	182

Sirach

23:14	17–18
24:30–31	83

2 Baruch

70:2	182

Ancient Sources

Early Christian Sources
Didache
    6:3   118

Primasius
Commentary on the Apocalypse
    14.7   181
    14.15–16   182

Jewish Sources
Dead Sea Scrolls
    1QS 8:8–14   29
    4Q174   88

Josephus
Jewish Antiquities (Ant.)
    1.1.3–4 §§38, 45, 51   83
    1.1.3 §37   83
    3.6.4 §123   76
    3.7.7 §§180–87   76
    18.136   60
Jewish War (J.W.)
    5.5.5 §§212–14, 219   76

Philo
De decalogo (Decal.) – Decalogue
    24 (129)   138
Quod deterius potiori insidari soleat (Det.) – That the Worse Attacks the Better
    40 (147)   138
Legum allegoriae (Leg.) – Allegorical Interpretation
    3.57   149
    3.61 (176)   148
De vita Mosis (Mos.) – On the Life of Moses
    34 (210)   138
De praemiis et poenis (Praem.) – On Rewards and Punishments
    2 (10)   138

Mishnah
m. Soṭah
    9:15   6

Other Greco-Roman Sources
Aeschylus
Septem contra Thebas (Sept.) – Seven against Thebes
    814   14

Aristotle
Analytica posteriora (An. post.) – Posterior Analytics
    2.11 94a   142
Ethica nicomachea (Eth. nic.) – Nicomachean Ethics
    8.3.8   5–6
De generatione animalium (Gen. an.) – Generation of Animals
    1.1 715a   142
    1.2 716a   137, 144
    1.17 721b   137
    1.18 724a   137
    2.1 732a   145
    2.1 734a   143
    2.1 734b   145
    2.4 738b   144
    2.4 739b   144
    2.4 740b   145
    4.1 765b   144
    4.1 766b   145
    4.3 767b   145
De partibus animalium (Part. an.) – Parts of Animals
    1.1 639b   143
    2.1 735a   143
Physica (Phys.) – Physics
    2.3 194b   142
Problemata (Probl.) – Problems
    927a35   14

Demosthenes
De falsa legatione (Fals. leg.) – False Embassy 82 = *Oratio*
    19.82   150
In Midiam (Mid.) – Against Meidias 153 = *Oratio*
    21.153   149

Dio Cassius
Roman History
    53.27.2   76

Diogenes Laertius
Vitae philosophorum (Vitae phil.)
    5.32   150
    8.1.35   5

Euripides
Bacchae (Bacch.) -- Baccanals
    305   150

Medea (Med.)
    325   14

Galenus
    10.401   14

Lucian
De morte Peregrini (Peregr.) – The Passing of Peregrinus
    13   137

Pausanias
Graeciae description (Descr.) – Description of Greece
    10.16.3   76

Plato
Respublica (Resp.) – Republic
    4 432b   150

Pliny (the Elder)
Naturalis historia (Nat.) – Natural History
    31.34   8
    31.45   5

Plutarch
De cupiditate divitiarum (Cupid. divit.) 1 = Moralia (Mor.)
    523d   149

Suetonius
Nero
    34   62

www.ingramcontent.com/pod-product-compliance
Lightning Source LLC
Chambersburg PA
CBHW022148180426
43200CB00028BA/299